THE REPORT OF THE

NATIONAL CONFIDENTIAL

ENQUIRY

INTO

PERIOPERATIVE DEATHS

1993/1994

(1 April 1993 to 31 March 1994)

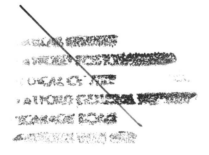

Published 27 November 1996

by the National Confidential Enquiry into Perioperative Deaths

35-43 Lincoln's Inn Fields
London
WC2A 3PN

Tel: 0171 831 6430

Requests for further information should be addressed to the Chief Executive.

ISBN 0 9522069 2 7

The National Confidential Enquiry into Perioperative Deaths is a company
limited by guarantee. Company number 3019382

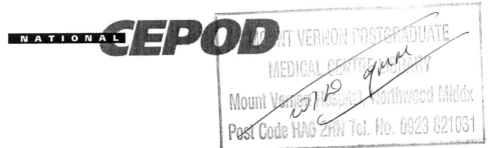

ROYAL COLLEGE OF ANAESTHETISTS

✦

ROYAL COLLEGE OF OBSTETRICIANS AND GYNAECOLOGISTS

✦

ROYAL COLLEGE OF OPHTHALMOLOGISTS

✦

ROYAL COLLEGE OF PATHOLOGISTS

✦

ROYAL COLLEGE OF PHYSICIANS OF LONDON

✦

ROYAL COLLEGE OF RADIOLOGISTS

✦

ROYAL COLLEGE OF SURGEONS OF ENGLAND

✦

FACULTY OF DENTAL SURGERY OF THE ROYAL COLLEGE OF SURGEONS
OF ENGLAND

✦

FACULTY OF PUBLIC HEALTH MEDICINE OF THE ROYAL COLLEGES OF
PHYSICIANS OF THE UK

✦

ASSOCIATION OF ANAESTHETISTS OF GREAT BRITAIN & IRELAND

✦

ASSOCIATION OF SURGEONS OF GREAT BRITAIN & IRELAND

3

Contents

Surgery

Pathology

References

Appendices

A   Abbreviations
B   Glossary
C   Anaesthetic questionnaire
D   Surgical questionnaire
E   Pathology proforma
F   Participants - anaesthetists
G   Participants - surgeons and gynaecologists
H   Local reporters

Foreword

Modern surgery and anaesthesia are so safe that when an operation is followed by death, the reason is nearly always because the underlying condition is fatal. The purpose of the National Confidential Enquiry into Perioperative Deaths is to identify remediable factors in anaesthesia and surgery, such as the provision of better facilities or different skills. The enquiry calls for the active cooperation and effort of busy surgeons, anaesthetists and gynaecologists.

No clinician in NCEPOD knows the identity of any of the hospitals or doctors referred to in this report. It is not a witch hunt and NCEPOD does not provide league tables to compare the risk of operation in one hospital or one region versus another: we do not know how many operations of each kind are done in each hospital let alone details of how old and sick were the patients. The purpose of the report is to see how the service may be still further improved in the future.

We are encouraged to see that in this report some of the deficiencies identified in our previous reports have been corrected: consultants were involved in more of the operations, infants were treated in specialised units and few trainee surgeons operated without senior assistance. But there is no room for complacency.

Once again we have to note the lack of high dependency and intensive care beds in the years covered by this report - although it is encouraging to know that this problem has been addressed by the Department of Health. Once again we note the lack of daytime emergency operating theatres. In vascular surgery nowadays it is considered that emergencies should be referred to specialist units with access to interventional radiology. In anaesthesia there is still the anomaly of locums who are 'trainees' but not in any recognised training programme. The use of audit is still patchy. There are still too few postmortem examinations, and there continues to be poor communication between clinicians, pathologists and Coroners.

Finally there is a surprising group of common disorders where even the best modern management is far from adequate and requires further research: these range from epistaxis, serious postoperative sepsis and thromboembolism to the increasing numbers of elderly patients with a fractured neck of femur.

J P Blandy CBE FRCS
Chairman
The National Confidential Enquiry into Perioperative Deaths
November 1996

Acknowledgements

We are indebted to the local reporters and administrative and clinical audit staff who provide the initial data on perioperative deaths.

The participation of consultant and junior clinical staff is essential to the success of National CEPOD, and we thank them for their valuable contribution. The information in this report represents many hours of work in completion of questionnaires.

We are very grateful to the advisors, named at the beginning of the relevant section, who have carefully reviewed questionnaires and data over many months. The report has been compiled by NCEPOD clinical coordinators;

Anaesthesia:	Dr J N Lunn
Surgery:	Mr H B Devlin
	Mr R W Hoile

and assistant clinical coordinators;

Anaesthesia:	Dr M C Derrington
	Dr G S Ingram
Surgery:	Mr M A Leonard
	Mr F E Loeffler

The data collection and analysis were managed by Mr S Gallimore (Project Manager) , overseen by Ms E A Campling (Chief Executive). The organization of the Enquiry would be impossible without the hard work and good humour of the NCEPOD staff; Peter Allison, Fatima Chowdhury, Paul Coote, Jennifer Drummond, Dolores Jarman, Monica Stubbings and Donna Wallace.

Data collection and review

The Enquiry reviews clinical practice and identifies potentially remediable factors in the practice of anaesthesia and surgery. We consider the *quality* of the delivery of care and do not study specifically causation of death. The commentary in this report is based on peer review of the data, questionnaires and notes submitted to us: it is not a research study based on differences against a control population. It cannot and does not attempt to produce any kind of comparison, let alone a league table.

NCEPOD does not provide clinical data to any person or organization outside the NCEPOD staff, coordinators and Steering Group. All questionnaires, reporting forms and other paper records relating to 1993/94 and earlier reports have been shredded, and the data have been removed from the computer database.

Scope

All National Health Service and Defence Medical Services hospitals in England, Wales and Northern Ireland, and public hospitals in Guernsey, Jersey and the Isle of Man are included in the Enquiry, as well as hospitals managed by BUPA Hospitals Limited, General Healthcare Group PLC, Nuffield Hospitals, St Martins Hospitals Limited, the Wellington Hospital and Benenden Hospital.

Reporting of deaths

The Enquiry depends on local reporters (see Appendix H) to provide data on deaths in their hospital(s). Although consultant clinicians still form the core of public sector local reporters, many have now delegated the data collection to administrative staff. Increasingly this work is being taken on by information and clinical audit departments who are often able to provide the data from hospital information systems. In the independent sector, hospital or nursing managers provide the data. When incomplete information is received, the NCEPOD staff contact the appropriate medical records or information officer or secretarial or clinical audit staff.

Deaths of patients *in hospital* within 30 days of a surgical procedure (excluding maternal deaths) are included. If local reporters are aware of postoperative deaths at home, they report them to us. A surgical procedure is defined by NCEPOD as;

> *"any procedure carried out by a surgeon or gynaecologist, with or without an anaesthetist, involving local, regional or general anaesthesia or sedation"*.

Reporters provide the following information:

> Name of authority/trust
> Name/sex/hospital number of patient
> Name of hospital in which the death occurred (and hospital where surgery took place, if different)
> Dates of birth, final operation and death
> Surgical procedure performed
> Name of consultant surgeon
> Name of anaesthetist

Sample for detailed review

The data collection year runs from 1 April to 31 March. Each year, a sample of the reported deaths is reviewed in more detail. The sample selection varies for each data collection year, and is determined by the Steering Group. The detailed sample for 1993/94 was based around the first perioperative death reported for each consultant surgeon or gynaecologist. Each consultant surgeon or gynaecologist thus received a maximum of one questionnaire. Certain procedures (as they were decribed on the local report forms) were excluded, e.g. purely diagnostic endoscopic procedures, in which case the next perioperative death (if any) for that surgeon or gynaecologist was chosen. The sample for this year comprised 2546 cases.

For each sample case, questionnaires (see Appendices C and D) were sent to the consultant surgeon or gynaecologist and consultant anaesthetist. These questionnaires were identified only by a number, allocated in the NCEPOD office. Copies of operation notes, anaesthetic records and fluid balance charts and postmortem reports were also requested. Surgical questionnaires were sent directly to the consultant surgeon or gynaecologist under whose care the patient was at the time of the final operation before death. When the local reporter had been able to identify the relevant consultant anaesthetist, the anaesthetic questionnaire was sent directly to him or her. However, in many cases this was not possible, and the local tutor of the Royal College of Anaesthetists was asked to name a consultant to whom the questionnaire should be sent. We did not restrict the number of questionnaires sent to each consultant anaesthetist.

Consultants

We hold a database, regularly updated, of all consultant anaesthetists, gynaecologist and surgeons in England, Wales and Northern Ireland. Appendices F and G list the consultants who returned a 1993/94 questionnaire to NCEPOD.

Data analysis

All questionnaires were examined by the NCEPOD administrative staff to identify any inconsistencies in the information provided and to prepare the data for entry to the computer database. The data were aggregated to produce the tables and information in this report. Overall data were aggregated to regional or national level only so that individual trusts and hospitals could not be identified.

Advisory groups

The completed questionnaires and the aggregated data were reviewed by the advisory groups for anaesthesia and surgery, together with the NCEPOD clinical coordinators. These groups were nominated by the relevant Colleges and specialist societies. They were drawn from a variety of hospitals in England, Wales and Northern Ireland. The advisory group in pathology reviewed postmortem data from the surgical questionnaires as well as copies of postmortem reports. All copies of medical notes were rendered anonymous on receipt so that the groups were unable to identify the source of the questionnaires.

Production of the report

The advisory groups commented on the overall quality of care within their specialty and on any individual cases which merited particular attention. These comments formed the basis for the sections on anaesthesia and surgery, and all advisory groups contributed to the draft for their specialty, prepared by the coordinators. The draft report for pathology was prepared by the chairman of the group and was based on a proforma used by the group (see Appendix E). All the anaesthetic, surgical and pathology drafts were then reviewed and amended by the coordinators and at least twice by the NCEPOD Steering Group.

General Recommendations 1993/94

- Consultation, collaboration and teamwork between anaesthetists, surgeons and physicians should be encouraged and should be the usual practice.

- Surgical management should be planned and should include all those provisions that are required for good outcomes.

- The availability of staffed (medical, nursing and ancillary) emergency operating theatres on a 24-hour basis is essential; Trusts admitting urgent and emergency cases must ensure that they are provided.

- The elderly and unfit constitute a large proportion of the workload; improved perioperative management is required to ensure that their care is appropriate.

- Protocols for the treatment of common conditions should be applied more widely to both elective and emergency admissions, and should be subject to audit.

- Continuity of care after operations is essential; local arrangements must ensure that it occurs.

- The roles and responsibilities of all doctors need to be more clearly defined nationally, and implemented locally.

- Clinicians and Coroners should make strenuous efforts to improve their local working relationships.

- Systems should be implemented by Trusts to improve the retention and availability of all notes and records of clinical activity.

- Trusts need to encourage more participation in clinical audit.

- More research is required on thromboembolism prophylaxis.

NCEPOD 1994 to 1997

1994/95

Deaths on the day of the surgical procedure or within three days of it were selected for review from the data for 1994/95. One questionnaire only was sent to each consultant surgeon or gynaecologist.

1995/96

Between 1 April 1995 and 31 March 1996 NCEPOD carried out a widespread review of the starting times of surgical procedures. NHS and independent hospitals participated. The method of the review is briefly described below.

1   From 1 April 1995, the initial questionnaire was completed by the hospital's local contact for all surgical procedures performed during a 24-hour period specified by NCEPOD. Each participating hospital provided data on seven different days of the week during the year. These days fell in different months. NCEPOD informed the contact of the relevant day two weeks in advance of each date.

2   Data from the completed questionnaires were entered into the NCEPOD database.

3   For all "out-of-hours" surgery (18.01 to 07.59 on weekdays plus weekends and bank holidays) a letter was sent to the consultant surgeon to ask for further information on why the operation was performed at this time.

4   The local contact was asked to inform NCEPOD of any patients included in (1) who died within 30 days of this procedure.

5   Detailed questionnaires were sent to the consultant surgeon and consultant anaesthetist about patients identified under (4).

1996/97

The sample for detailed review comprises all deaths following a specific set of surgical procedures. No more than five questionnaires will be sent to any individual consultant surgeon or gynaecologist.

Management of the Enquiry

Corporate structure

The National Confidential Enquiry into Perioperative Deaths (NCEPOD) is an independent body to which a corporate commitment has been made by the Associations, Colleges and Faculties related to its areas of activity. Each of these bodies nominates members of the Steering Group.

Steering Group

Chairman
Professor J P Blandy CBE

Vice-Chairman
Professor V R Tindall CBE   (Royal College of Obstetricians and Gynaecologists)

Secretary
Mr H B Devlin CBE   (Royal College of Surgeons of England)

Treasurer
Dr J N Lunn   (Royal College of Anaesthetists)

Mrs M Beck   (Royal College of Ophthalmologists)

Mr K G Callum   (Association of Surgeons of Great Britain and Ireland)

Professor D Cumberland   (Royal College of Radiologists)

Dr M Goldacre   (Faculty of Public Health Medicine)

Dr H H Gray   (Royal College of Physicians of London)

Mr R W Hoile   (NCEPOD Clinical Coordinator)

Dr J Lumley   (Royal College of Anaesthetists)

Professor V Lund   (Royal College of Surgeons of England)

Dr M Morgan   (Association of Anaesthetists of Great Britain and Ireland)

Dr P Simpson   (Royal College of Anaesthetists)

Mr M F Sullivan   (Royal College of Surgeons of England)

Professor P G Toner   (Royal College of Pathologists)

Mr J Ll Williams   (Faculty of Dental Surgery, Royal College of Surgeons of England)

Co-opted members;

Mr M J C Burgess   (Coroners' Society of England and Wales)
Dr P Dean

Mr T Matthews   (Institute of Health Services Management)

Dr M McGovern   (Department of Health - England)

Coordinators

Anaesthesia	Dr J N Lunn
Surgery	Mr H B Devlin
	Mr R W Hoile
Chief Executive	Ms E A Campling

Assistant Coordinators

Anaesthesia	Dr M C Derrington (until June 1996)
	Dr G S Ingram
Surgery	Mr M A C Leonard (until September 1996)
	Mr F E Loeffler (until October 1996)

Funding

The total annual cost of NCEPOD is approximately £520,000 (1995/96). We are pleased to acknowledge the continued support of;

Department of Health (England)
Welsh Office
Health and Social Services Executive (Northern Ireland)
States of Guernsey Board of Health
Jersey Group of Hospitals
Department of Health and Social Security, Isle of Man Government
BUPA Hospitals Limited
General Healthcare Group plc
Benenden Hospital
Nuffield Hospitals
St Martins Hospitals Limited
The Wellington Hospital

This funding covers the *total* cost of the Enquiry, including administrative salaries and payments for clinical coordinators, assistant clinical coordinators, office accommodation charges, computer and other equipment as well as travelling and other expenses for the coordinators, Steering Group and advisory groups.

General data 1993/94

Points

> - Non-availability of medical notes continues to be a major problem.
> - Some reporters were unable to provide data to NCEPOD in time for their hospitals to be included in the detailed sample.
> - There were wide regional variations in return rates of questionnaires.

Local reporters (see Appendix H) provided data to NCEPOD about patients who died in hospital between 1 April 1993 and 31 March 1994 within 30 days of a surgical procedure. We were also informed of a few deaths which occurred at home within the 30-day period, but most reporters are unable to provide this information.

Reporters have established their own methods of data collection; many are assisted by departments of clinical audit or information services. If an essential data item was omitted on the reporting form, the NCEPOD staff contacted the medical records officer or secretarial staff in the relevant hospital. We are grateful for the help given to us by the staff in these departments.

Tables G1 to G4 refer to the total number of 20442 reported deaths. This total does not include 13 reports where the data were incomplete, 132 reports received too late for inclusion in the analysis, and 524 inappropriate reports (see table G5). The totals of reports for previous years are shown in table G1 but we are not able to explain the fluctuations, which are more likely to be caused by local (hospital) problems with data collection rather than clinical factors.

Table G1
Deaths reported to NCEPOD

| | 1993/94 | Previous years | | | |
		1992/93	1991/92	1990	1989
England					
Northern	790	993	1141	1069	1089
Yorkshire	1847	1678	1126	1395	1596
Trent	2342	2036	2014	1722	1849
East Anglia	743	1054	739	768	722
North West Thames	787	803	771	1019	1026
North East Thames	1593	1422	1278	1427	1436
South East Thames	1337	1324	1262	1443	1599
South West Thames	1194	1121	1203	1014	1241
Wessex	1346	1299	874	913	1028
Oxford	834	808	817	599	649
South Western	1215	1194	973	1084	1278
West Midlands	1578	1565	1578	1826	1902
Mersey	1066	878	699	799	845
North Western	1570	1500	1810	1937	2019
Special Health Authorities	323	290	78	108	147
Wales	1078	1072	1079	1102	1162
Northern Ireland	529	474	375	316	380
Other authorities					
Guernsey	33	26	18	39	32
Jersey	27	32	25	22	26
Isle of Man	25	41	25	25	7
Defence Medical Services	36	40	75	60	94
Independent sector	149	166	172	130	120
Total	**20442**	19816	18132	18817	20247

Table G2
Calendar days from operation to death
(i.e. not 24 hour periods)

		%	%
0	2166	*10.6*	
1	2554	*12.5*	
2	1743	*8.5*	
3	1301	*6.4*	*37.8*
4	1056	*5.2*	
5	1054	*5.2*	
6	966	*4.7*	
7	832	*4.1*	
8	763	*3.7*	*19.2*
9	693	*3.4*	
10	667	*3.3*	
11	595	*2.9*	
12	598	*2.9*	
13	518	*2.5*	*12.9*
14	503	*2.5*	
15	428	*2.1*	
16 to 20	1814	*8.9*	
21 to 25	1275	*6.2*	*19.6*
26 to 30	916	*4.5*	
Total	**20442**		

Figure G1 (see table G2)
Calendar days from operation to death
(i.e. not 24 hour periods)

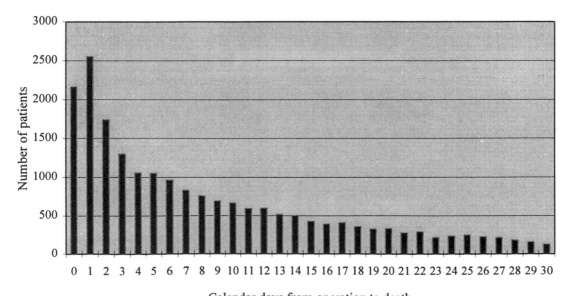

Table G3
Age/sex distribution of reported deaths

Age in years			Male	Female	Total
0	to	*4	137	102	239
5	to	9	14	13	27
10	to	14	16	15	31
15	to	19	37	25	62
20	to	24	68	27	95
25	to	29	69	44	113
30	to	34	80	55	135
35	to	39	100	61	161
40	to	44	134	106	240
45	to	49	218	188	406
50	to	54	338	234	572
55	to	59	545	315	860
60	to	64	945	594	1539
65	to	69	1412	930	2342
70	to	74	2007	1294	3301
75	to	79	1784	1500	3284
80	to	84	1502	1864	3366
85	to	89	848	1547	2395
90	to	94	264	666	930
95	to	99	73	215	288
100	+		21	35	56
Total			**10612**	**9830**	**20442**

* i.e. day of birth to the day preceding the fifth birthday

Table G4
Calendar days between death and receipt of report by NCEPOD
(i.e. not 24 hour periods)

1	to	29	6685
30	to	59	3858
60	to	89	2585
90	to	119	1688
120	to	149	1063
150	to	179	776
180	or	more	3787
Total			**20442**

It is disappointing that only 33% of the deaths were reported to us within one month, compared with 40% in 1992/93. It had been hoped that because more hospitals were able to provide data from computer systems, reporting would be easier and quicker. However, this has not proved to be the case.

Table G5
Inappropriate reports received and not included

318	More than 30 days (day of operation to day of death)
124	Procedure not performed by a surgeon
67	No surgical procedure performed or inappropriate procedure (according to NCEPOD criteria)
9	Maternal deaths
4	Duplicate report
2	Patient still alive (death wrongly reported)
524	**Total**

Sample for detailed review

Using the criteria detailed on page 10, the sample for more detailed study comprised 2546 (12.5%) cases.

Surgical questionnaires

Questionnaires were sent to consultant surgeons for further information on all of these cases, and 1950 completed questionnaires were returned to NCEPOD. The overall return rate (see table G6) was therefore 76.6% (1950/2546).

After excluding 31 questionnaires which were returned incomplete, or related to the wrong operation or patient, and six questionnaires which were returned too late to be included, 1913 questionnaires were analysed.

Anaesthetic questionnaires

Questionnaires were sent to consultant anaesthetists for further information on 2341 of the 2546 sample cases. No questionnaire was sent for the remaining 205 cases for the following reasons:

154   Name of appropriate consultant anaesthetist unobtainable or notified too late to send questionnaire
51   No anaesthetist involved *(local anaesthesia or sedation administered solely by the surgeon)*

The name of the anaesthetist is requested as a data item on the form completed by local reporters when informing us of a death. However, it is often not possible for the reporter to obtain this information because it is frequently omitted from computerised patient administration systems. For the 1993/94 sample, it was agreed that NCEPOD would continue the practice adopted in 1992/93 in that we would send all questionnaires directly to a consultant anaesthetist. Tutors of the Royal College of Anaesthetists were again extremely helpful in providing the name of the most appropriate consultant, if the name of a consultant was not provided on the local reporting form. Some tutors agreed to distribute questionnaires locally. The rate of return of questionnaires (78%) maintained the increase that had resulted from adopting this practice for the 1992/93 sample year.

After excluding 21 questionnaires which were returned incomplete or related to the wrong operation or patient, and three questionnaires which were returned too late to be included, 1802 questionnaires were analysed.

Table G6
Distribution and return of questionnaires by NHS region

SQ = Surgical Questionnaire
AQ = Anaesthetic Questionnaire

	No. of Qs distributed		No. of Qs returned		% Return rate		No. of Qs analysed		No. hospitals represented	
	SQ	AQ	SQ	AQ	SQ	AQ	SQ	AQ	SQ	AQ
England										
Northern	139	134	117	120	*84.2*	*89.6*	116	120	19	19
Yorkshire	195	177	152	148	*77.9*	*83.6*	151	145	23	22
Trent	238	223	184	165	*77.3*	*74.0*	179	163	21	20
East Anglia	94	88	71	72	*75.5*	*81.8*	70	71	11	10
N W Thames	123	111	95	81	*77.2*	*73.0*	95	80	19	18
N E Thames	174	153	122	99	*70.1*	*64.7*	119	97	22	21
S E Thames	165	139	120	100	*72.7*	*71.9*	117	98	23	19
S W Thames	155	131	127	106	*81.9*	*80.9*	124	106	19	19
Wessex	133	125	107	105	*80.5*	*84.0*	106	103	20	18
Oxford	113	107	82	81	*72.6*	*75.7*	82	80	14	16
South Western	143	139	116	129	*81.1*	*92.8*	113	129	15	15
West Midlands	222	213	147	157	*66.2*	*73.7*	144	156	30	27
Mersey	132	113	105	86	*79.5*	*76.1*	103	85	16	15
North Western	178	167	138	131	*77.5*	*78.4*	133	128	23	23
Special Health Authorities	26	25	21	18	*80.8*	*72.0*	20	17	5	5
Wales	154	143	106	98	*68.8*	*68.5*	105	97	20	21
Northern Ireland	92	83	81	75	*88.0*	*90.4*	81	72	17	17
Other authorities										
Guernsey	5	5	4	4	*80.0*	*80.0*	4	4	1	1
Jersey	4	4	4	4	*100.0*	*100.0*	4	4	1	1
Isle of Man	3	3	2	2	*66.7*	*66.7*	2	2	1	1
Defence Medical Services	15	15	15	14	*100.0*	*93.3*	14	14	4	4
Independent sector	43	43	34	31	*79.1*	*72.1*	31	31	12	14
Total	**2546**	**2341**	**1950**	**1826**	*76.6*	*78.0*	**1913**	**1802**	**336**	**326**

It is pleasing to note that several regions/authorities achieved return rates of 80% or higher; there is considerable room for improvement in the other regions.

Table G7
Distribution and return of surgical questionnaires by specialty

	Number of cases in sample	Number of questionnaires returned	% questionnaires returned	Number of questionnaires analysed
Cardiothoracic	143	95	66.4	92
Colorectal	296	240	81.1	238
General	515	375	72.8	369
Gynaecology	138	122	88.4	119
Neurosurgery	102	62	60.8	60
Ophthalmic	40	27	67.5	25
Oral/Maxillofacial	21	17	81.0	16
Orthopaedic	716	551	77.0	543
Otorhinolaryngological	56	48	85.7	47
Plastic	36	29	80.6	29
Urology	202	171	84.7	166
Vascular	281	213	75.8	209
Total	**2546**	**1950**	**76.6**	**1913**

NB: Laparotomies were included in "General" where the surgical questionnaire was not returned

Table G8
Reasons for the non-return of questionnaires

Surgical Questionnaires	Anaesthetic Questionnaires	
369	280	No reason given
159	190	Medical notes lost or unavailable
42	30	Surgeon no longer working at the hospital or on sick-leave
7	5	Did not wish to participate
19	10	Other
596	**515**	**Total**

The frequency of "lost notes" has been noted previously by NCEPOD.[3, 4, 5] Non-availability of notes was the stated reason for inability to return 27% (159/596) of the missing surgical questionnaires and 37% (190/515) of the missing anaesthetic questionnaires. These problems need the urgent attention of clinicians and managers. One consultant commented:

> "I very much regret that I have as yet been unable to complete the CEPOD questionnaire on this patient. This is because medical records for deceased patients are not stored in this hospital but in a central repository off-site. Unfortunately this is not the first time that patient records have been lost between the two sites and the Medical Records Department have so far been unable to trace these notes for me... I am very aware that the response rate for CEPOD is not as high as it ought to be and I am equally aware that this is not the first time I have been unable to help you because of lost notes."

In several cases, a relevant factor was lack of access to microfilmed notes, or the illegibility of notes in this format.

> "I am afraid that the patient's hospital notes have been microfilmed, and apparently the machine to print out the microfilmed pages is not working properly. In addition apparently no-one in the Medical Records Department knows when the machine will be repaired!"

Notes were also unavailable for a variety of other reasons: some were held by a Coroner, some were temporarily unavailable because of hospital relocation, and some were stored in a condemned building which was unsafe to enter.

There was no reply at all to any of the three letters (one initial request, two reminders) sent by NCEPOD for 369 surgical questionnaires and 280 anaesthetic questionnaires. This remains a particularly frustrating aspect of the Enquiry; if clinicians are unable to return questionnaires, we would at least like to be aware of the reason(s).

Table G9
Calendar days between death and receipt by NCEPOD of initial report (sample cases only)

	Surgical questionnaires sent	Surgical questionnaires returned	%	Anaesthetic questionnaires sent	Anaesthetic questionnaires returned	%
1 to 29	1151	893	77.5	1068	860	80.5
30 to 59	487	375	77.0	452	329	72.8
60 to 89	336	253	75.2	307	237	77.2
90 to 119	207	159	76.8	194	151	77.8
120 to 149	115	85	73.9	99	77	77.8
150 to 179	98	81	82.7	80	68	85.0
180 to 365*	152	104	68.4	141	104	73.8
Total	**2546**	**1950**	**76.6**	**2341**	**1826**	**78.0**

* Reports of deaths received more than one year after the death, and all reports received after 31 August 1994 were excluded from the sample

Delay in reporting of deaths causes an inevitable time lapse between the death and sending of questionnaires about sample cases. For the anaesthetic questionnaires, the time taken in obtaining the name of the most appropriate anaesthetist to whom a questionnaire should be sent often extended the gap even further between the patient's death and the distribution of the questionnaire.

Delays in receiving initial reports of deaths should only affect the return rate of surgical or anaesthetic questionnaires where the surgeon or anaesthetist is no longer working at the same hospital, or has retired by the time the questionnaire is sent (see table G8); most of the data requested in the questionnaires should be available from the notes.

However, in those cases where the surgeon could not return a questionnaire because of a problem with the notes (see table G8), further analysis showed that 13% (21/159) had been reported to NCEPOD more than six months after the patient's death, compared with 6% (109/1950) of returned questionnaires.

Anaesthesia

Anaesthesia

Advisors

We are very grateful to the following consultant anaesthetist advisors who gave their time unstintingly to the consideration of anaesthetic questionnaires and guided the anaesthetist coordinators at 17 meetings over two years.

Dr D L Coppel	(Northern Ireland)
Dr S G Cruickshank	(Northern and Yorkshire)
Dr D Fell	(Trent)
Dr J Lytle	(South and West)
Dr F J Pickford	(Wales)
Dr K M Sherry	(Trent)

Points

- Surgical operations should not be started in hospitals without appropriate critical care services.
- Serious sepsis is a frequent factor in perioperative deaths.
- Anaesthetists must have appropriately skilled and dedicated non-medical assistants.
- Consultation between surgeons and other specialists, including anaesthetists, needs to be more frequent in order to promote a team approach.
- A team approach with direction from consultants would facilitate optimal management in vulnerable patients.
- The roles and responsibilities suitable for staff grade anaesthetists need to be defined and implemented.
- Two thirds of locum 'trainees' were not in a recognised training programme.
- The use of protocols in the management of certain clinical conditions needs to be increased.

Method

Questionnaires about anaesthesia were completed for 1802 cases. The detailed sample was based on the first perioperative death reported for each consultant surgeon. This is assumed to represent the practice of one surgical team and thus, on this basis, the sample has some credibility as representative of common practice.

The method of scrutiny of anaesthetic questionnaires was very similar to that of earlier reports: a mixture of electronic selection on defined criteria,* individual inspection by the clinical coordinators who used implicit criteria, and random selection. The advisors had therefore to review 1002 questionnaires. Their opinions on these form the basis of the comments in the report. The compilers nevertheless accept responsibility for the actual contents.

The data retrieved from all the returned questionnaires are presented in the tables with a commentary. Attention is drawn particularly to the subject of **locum anaesthetists** which has, in earlier reports, been emphasised but on this occasion is analysed more deeply.

* grade/qualifications of anaesthetist, level of advice sought, location of preoperative assessment of patient, ASA grade and age of patient, history of drug reaction, classification of operation, time of start of anaesthesia, transferred cases, monitoring, availability of non-medical trained assistants, occurrence of a critical event, ability to transfer patient to an ICU/HDU, early postoperative death.

Subsets of data from the questionnaires about two clinical conditions, aortic aneurysm and fractured neck of femur, have received special attention, see pages 66-82. These are common conditions and, although we still do not know their precise incidence, appear frequently in NCEPOD reports. Both make considerable demands on resources: operating time and critical care services. It is hoped that a detailed review of their management might be useful.

Material indented is taken directly and summarized from questionnaires which are completed by practising clinicians. This information has not been altered. These vignettes are examples and serve to illustrate relevant points.

Detailed study of the anaesthetic questionnaires by the coordinators and their advisors revealed much practice of which we, as anaesthetists, may justly be proud and these are indicated by ◆.

Anaesthesia - Section I

Proxy anaesthetists

Table A1 (q1)
If you were not involved in any way with this anaesthetic and have filled out this questionnaire on behalf of someone else, please indicate your position.

Chairman of Division	30
College tutor	98
Duty consultant	197
Other consultant	118

Other:	
Registrar	10
Clinical director	2
ICU director	2
Senior house officer (SHO)	13
Senior registrar	5
Associate specialist	1
Clinical assistant	1
Hospital practitioner	1
Senior lecturer	1
Other (not specified)	2
Not answered	1321
Total	**1802**

Seventy-three percent (1321/1802) questionnaires were completed by an anaesthetist concerned with the patient.

The completion of NCEPOD forms by anyone other than the anaesthetist responsible for the case is not ideal, but to a degree is inevitable. A form completed by a duty consultant may be useful as a monitor of the work done by a trainee. In this respect it is reassuring that of the 13 forms completed by SHOs, 11 were confirmed as having been seen and agreed by a consultant (in the other two cases, question 88 was left blank). The completion of forms by Divisional Chairmen, College tutors and other consultants constitutes a chore. We are however grateful to them for their assistance in ensuring the completeness of the data.

Hospital

Table A2 (q2)
In what type of hospital did the anaesthetic take place?

District General hospital (DGH) or equivalent	1310
University/teaching hospital	393
Surgical specialty hospital	44
Other acute/partly acute hospital	9
Defence Medical Services hospital	15
Independent hospital	31
Total	**1802**

There are 316 separate hospitals represented in the above table. The differences between a university/teaching hospital, a DGH or even a specialist hospital are largely arbitrary and based on traditional terminology. NCEPOD uses them because there is no other classification. These terms had an historical basis, but have we now reached a stage within Trusts that they should be abandoned? A more comprehensive description might be more useful.

The anaesthetists

Table A3 (q3, derived)
Grade of most senior anaesthetist present at the start of this anaesthetic

		RCA Census	Proportions
Senior house officer	254	821	0.31
Registrar	223	738	0.30
Senior registrar	173	366	0.47
Consultant	991		
Staff grade	66	96	0.69
Associate specialist	42	122	0.34
Clinical assistant	45		
General practitioner	2		
Hospital practitioner	1		
Other ("Fellow")	2		
No anaesthetist present at start of operation	1		
Not answered	2		
Total	**1802**		

The Royal College of Anaesthetists carried out a national census in September 1992. This revealed details of all anaesthetists by grade in the UK. Data from this, which relate to the geographical areas covered by NCEPOD, are given above. The response rate to the census was excellent and the accuracy of the data greatly superior to that available from any other source. In combining these data the Royal College of Anaesthetists' figures are based on September 1992, whereas the NCEPOD data were collected between April 1993 and March 1994.

There were 96 staff grade anaesthetists at that time but this number has certainly increased since. Consultant numbers also cause difficulty in any comparison since either absolute numbers or whole time equivalents can be considered; so no inferences can be drawn.

For SHOs, registrars, senior registrars, staff grades and associate specialists a comparison is made between the cases done by the grades in this report, set against the absolute number at this grade from the census. This is expressed as a ratio (right hand column table A3). This ratio (deaths:grade) is much higher for staff grade anaesthetists than any other grade. It implies clearly that some of the more seriously ill patients were anaesthetised by them.

Figure A1

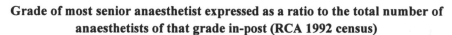

Grade of most senior anaesthetist expressed as a ratio to the total number of anaesthetists of that grade in-post (RCA 1992 census)

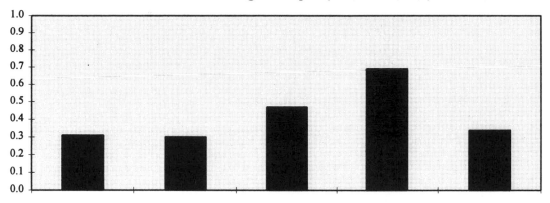

The 66 cases reported to NCEPOD as having been anaesthetised by a staff grade doctor related to 45 different hospitals with a broad geographical spread. The questionnaires show that the doctor held the FRCA in 30 cases, the DA in 33 and no qualification in three.

The validity of this approach may be questioned, but it does appear to assist in analysing the data. **Given the continuing uncertainty with regard to the role of staff grade doctors, should these data be a cause for concern?**

Table A4 (q5)
Which higher diploma in anaesthesia was held?

None	144
Fellowship	1280
DA (or Part 1 FCAnaes)	322
Other:	
MD (overseas)	9
Specialist anaesthetist	8
MD (Anaes)	6
DA (overseas)	3
MD (UK)	2
MSc (Anaes)	2
not answered	36
not known / not recorded	2
not specified	1
Total	**1802**

The possession of the Fellowship or, currently at a lesser level, the DA, demonstrates a defined educational standard. The relationship between this and clinical competence can be debated but it cannot be ignored. There has therefore to be a much tighter control over the clinical responsibilities of those anaesthetists who do not have the FRCA, than those who do. An SHO or registrar with long clinical experience but without the FRCA cannot be regarded as acceptable for complex clinical situations, particularly at isolated sites. The lack of appropriate qualification demonstrates that there is a fundamental deficiency in the process of their education.

Table A5 (q6, q3)
Was the most senior anaesthetist employed in a locum capacity?

		(possessing FRCA (or equivalent)
No	1650	
Locum senior house officer	20	
Locum registrar	32	
Locum senior registrar	18	(16)
Locum consultant	41	(32)
Locum staff grade	8	(3)
Locum associate specialist	3	(-)
Locum clinical assistant	6	(-)
Locum (grade not given)	1	(-)
Not answered	23	
Total	**1802**	

In 1992/1993 there were 5.5% locums;[5] this table shows that there were 7.1% (129 answers/1802). Those questionnaires completed by the actual anaesthetists indicate that eight out of nine consultant locums, three out of five staff grades, and four out of six clinical assistants, did not possess the FRCA. (The remaining questionnaires were completed by proxy anaesthetists and this may be the explanation for the apparent absence of higher qualifications of locums indicated here).

Previous reports have recognised that the term 'locum' can be all-embracing, encompassing from one extreme recently retired consultants continuing with responsibilities they have had over many years, to itinerant SHOs and registrars of varying competence, employed by agencies and covering the occasional on-call night or weekend. These are very different. **An ideal service should rarely need locums**. It is to be hoped that the increased numbers, noted here, are not the start of a new trend. The period covered was one during which some Trusts were beginning to expand. Were more locums needed to cover this sudden expansion or perhaps for waiting list initiatives?

Table A6 (q7, q3)
Is this locum post part of a recognised training programme?

	Yes	No	Not answered	Not known/not recorded	Total
Locum senior house officer*	7	12	1	-	20
Locum registrar*	11	20	1	-	32
Locum senior registrar*	11	5	1	1	18
Locum consultant	1	37	3	-	41
Locum staff grade	2	6	-	-	8
Locum associate specialist	-	3	-	-	3
Locum clinical assistant	1	3	2	-	6
Locum (grade not given)	-	-	1	-	1
Total	**33**	**86**	**9**	**1**	**129**

This question was asked (but it may be ambiguous) in order to try to define within training programmes where trainees (see *, table A6) were acting as locums in acceptable circumstances, e.g. acting up to a higher grade perhaps whilst an appointment was being made to a vacancy. The numbers are small but the replies are not reassuring. Only seven of 20 SHOs and eleven of 32 registrars working as locums were part of a recognised training programme. The remainder, it has to be assumed, **were occupying posts primarily for the needs of service rather than for training.**

Table A7 (q8, q3, derived)
How long had this locum anaesthetist been in this post at the time of this operation?

	< 1 month	1 to 6 months	> 6 months to 1 year	> 1 year	Not answered	Total
Locum senior house officer	7	10	-	-	3	20
Locum registrar	6	14	1	5	6	32
Locum senior registrar	3	9	6	-	-	18
Locum consultant	3	16	9	4	9	41
Locum staff grade	2	-	2	3	1	8
Locum associate specialist	-	1	1	1	-	3
Locum clinical assistant	-	1	4	-	1	6
Locum (grade not given)	-	-	-	-	1	1
Total	**21**	**51**	**23**	**13**	**21**	**129**

The duration of a locum appointment is another factor which must be considered. Long term sickness or maternity leave for the substantive employee may lead to durations of locums which are otherwise undesirable. Should these instances be more closely examined?

There were 36 questionnaires from long-term (more than six months) locums of whom 13 were consultants.

Table A8 (q9, q3, derived)
Is this locum post an exchange one with another country?

	Yes	No	Not answered	Total
Locum senior house officer	3	16	1	20
Locum registrar	2	30	-	32
Locum senior registrar	1	17	-	18
Locum consultant	3	34	4	41
Locum staff grade	-	8	-	8
Locum associate specialist	-	3	-	3
Locum clinical assistant	-	6	-	6
Locum (grade not given)	-	-	1	1
Total	**9**	**114**	**6**	**129**

The information presented in the two previous tables is difficult to interpret. It does nevertheless appear that there were a number of registrars spending long periods in locum posts in 1993/94.

Table A9 (qs 10 and 3, derived)
Is this locum anaesthetist accredited by the Royal College of Anaesthetists?

	Yes	No	Not answered*	Not known/not recorded†	Total
Locum senior house officer	5	13	2	-	20
Locum registrar	4	23	3	2	32
Locum senior registrar	6	12	-	-	18
Locum consultant	13	24	4	-	41
Locum staff grade	-	8	-	-	8
Locum associate specialist	-	3	-	-	3
Locum clinical assistant	-	4	2	-	6
Locum (grade not given)	-	-	1	-	1
Total	**28**	**87**	**12**	**2**	**129**

* i.e. box in questionnaire empty;
† statement that the answer is not known to respondent or not recorded in notes.

This question is inappropriate as far as trainees are concerned. It is our understanding that official policy is that locum appointees should have the same qualifications, skills and experience as those required for a substantive appointment. **The 24 consultant locums who were not accredited are unlikely to meet this criterion.**

Table A10 (q12)
Did the anaesthetist (of whatever grade) seek advice at any time from another anaesthetist (not mentioned in question 3)?

Yes	312
No	1444
Not answered	26
Not known/not recorded	20

If yes, grade of most senior anaesthetist from whom advice sought:

Senior house officer	4
Registrar	37
Senior registrar	35
Consultant	229
Staff grade	2
Associate specialist	3
Grade not specified	2
Total	**1802**

The pattern of response to this question is encouraging; it would seem that the line of command is being used appropriately in seeking advice. Previous NCEPOD reports[5] have advocated the use of protocols to define local arrangements. These might define, for trainees, when advice should be sought but consultants might need to be reminded of their responsibilities.

Table A11 (q13)
Did any colleague(s) (not mentioned in question 3) come to help at any time?

Yes	171
No	1529
Not answered	95
Not known/not recorded	7

If yes, grade of most senior anaesthetist who came to help

Senior house officer	22
Registrar	35
Senior registrar	25
Consultant	76
Staff grade	5
Associate specialist	3
Clinical assistant	2
Grade not specified	3
Total	**1802**

Table A12 (qs 12 and 3, derived)
Grade of most senior anaesthetist and whether advice sought

	All	Advice sought		Advice not sought	Not known/not answered
Senior house officer	254	96	38%	145	13
Registrar	223	76	34%	138	9
Senior registrar	173	55	32%	112	6
Consultant	991	50		925	16
Staff grade	66	17	26%	49	-
Associate specialist	42	6		35	1
Clinical assistant	45	9		36	-
General practitioner	2	1		1	-
Hospital practitioner	1	-		1	-
Other/not specified	5	2		2	1
Total	**1802**	**312**		**1444**	**46**

It seems self evident that the more junior the individual the more frequently advice should be sought. This is not demonstrated convincingly here. How can the culture be changed?

The patient

Table A13 (q15)
Age of patient at time of operation

0 to 10	20
11 to 20	13
21 to 30	20
31 to 40	25
41 to 50	60
51 to 60	112
61 to 70	330
71 to 80	566
81 to 90	525
91 to 100	130
101 +	1
Total	**1802**

Figure A2
Age of patient at time of operation

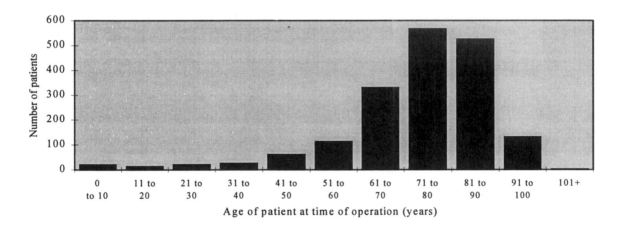

Table A14 (qs 18 and 19, derived)
Number of calendar days between operation and death
(i.e. not 24 hour periods)

Same day	203
Next day	221
2 days	167
3 days	107
4 days	111
5 days	77
6 to 10 days	348
11 to 15 days	257
More than 15 days	311
Total	**1802**

Figure A3
Number of calendar days between operation and death
(i.e. not 24 hour periods)

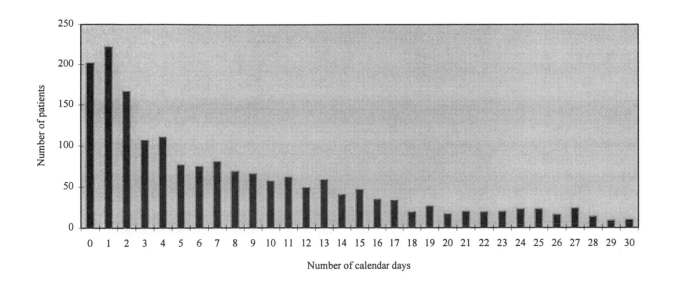

Number of calendar days

This pattern is similar to all previous NCEPOD enquiries. The first day will inevitably cover a period of less than 24 hours, giving an apparently lower figure for day 0.

Figure A4 (qs 17 and 18)
Number of calendar days between admission and operation
(i.e. not 24 hour periods)

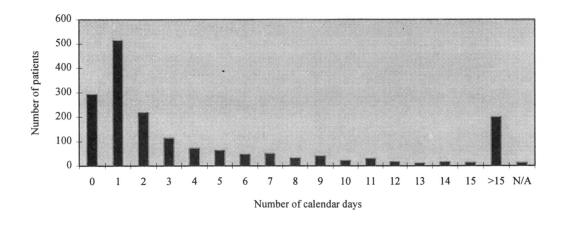

Number of calendar days

Table A15 (q20)
Was the patient transferred from another hospital?

Yes	201
No	1594
Not answered	7
Total	**1802**

Table A16 (q21)
If yes, had the patient's condition apparently deteriorated during transfer?

Yes	17
No	137
Not answered	44
Not known/not recorded	3
Total	**201**

The problems relating to the transfer of acutely ill patients were highlighted in previous reports.[5] The information requested for the present series was intentionally limited. Seventeen patients deteriorated during transfer.

The operation

Table A17 (q22)
Specialty of the procedure

Cardiothoracic	78
Colorectal	213
General	361
Gynaecology	104
Neurosurgery	67
Ophthalmic	22
Oral/maxillofacial	13
Orthopaedic	532
Otorhinolaryngology	36
Plastic	25
Urology	146
Vascular	205
Total	**1802**

This table shows the distribution of cases by surgical specialty based on the information given in the anaesthetic questionnaire. There is inevitably a greater number of cases for large specialties dealing with acute, old and very sick patients. Many were destined to die soon.

Table A18 (q26)
Classification of operation (last before death)

Emergency	276
Urgent	748
Scheduled	546
Elective	212
Not answered	20
Total	**1802**

Figure A5 (see table A18)
Classification of operation

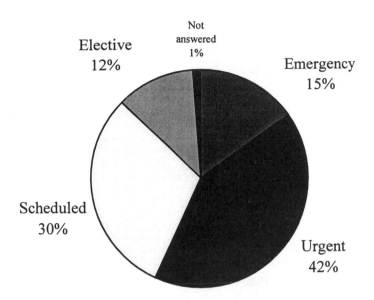

Table A19 (qs 3 and 26)
Classification of operation by grade of most senior anaesthetist present at the start of anaesthesia

	Emergency	Urgent	Scheduled	Elective	Not answered	Total
Senior house officer	19	172	49	12	2	**254**
Registrar	28	127	48	18	2	**223**
Senior registrar	55	78	33	7	-	**173**
Consultant	162	296	364	155	14	**991**
Staff grade	4	32	21	9	-	**66**
Associate specialist	6	17	11	7	1	**42**
Clinical assistant	2	22	17	3	1	**45**
General practitioner	-	-	2	-	-	**2**
Hospital practitioner	-	-	1	-	-	**1**
Other	-	2	-	-	-	**2**
None present	-	1	-	-	-	**1**
Not answered	-	1	-	1	-	**2**
Total	**276**	**748**	**546**	**212**	**20**	**1802**

See also page 43 table A30.

Preoperative assessment, diagnoses and treatment

Table A20 (q27)
Was a record of the patient's weight available?

Yes	714
No	1075
Not answered	11
Not known/not recorded	2
Total	**1802**

Table A21 (q28)
Was a record of the patient's height available?

Yes	162
No	1617
Not answered	20
Not known/not recorded	3
Total	**1802**

The advisors were in agreement that for a routine operation they would find it useful to have both the weight and the height of the patient recorded. Most patients nowadays know their own weight and height, and can be asked. The apparent failure to obtain and to record this information in the relevant records is surprising.

Table A22 (q29)
Was an anaesthetist consulted by the surgeon (as distinct from informed) before the operation?

Yes	896
No	839
Not answered	37
Not known/not recorded	30
Total	**1802**

◆ There is evidence from the questionnaires returned that some surgeons and anaesthetists consult each other regularly preoperatively and this is encouraging. There are instances where medical, surgical and anaesthetic consultation has resulted in a balanced decision to operate but these are relatively rare in this enquiry. It is possible that consultation occurs in that group of patients who do not have operations.

There is a case for departmental or hospital protocols to encourage surgeons and anaesthetists to consult widely with colleagues.

Table A23 (q30)
Where did the anaesthetist assess the patient before the operation?

Ward	1467
Outpatient department	11
Theatre suite	94
Accident and Emergency Department	54
ICU/HDU	124

Other:

CT scanning unit	3
Burns unit	2
Special care baby unit	2
Adjacent hospital	2
Radiology	1
Recovery ward	1
Coronary care unit	1
Admissions unit	1
Angiography suite	1
Not assessed	*8
Not answered	14
Not known/not recorded	16
Total	**1802**

* There were good clinical reasons to account for the absence of a formal assessment in these cases.

◆ Ninety-two percent (1670/1802) of the questionnaires indicate that assessment before anaesthesia by anaesthetists did happen before the patient came to the operating theatre. This is a good quality of care.

Table A24 (q30b)
Was this anaesthetist present at the start of the operation?

Yes	1666
No	114
Not answered	11
Not known/not recorded	3
Not assessed (see table A23)	8
Total	**1802**

◆ These figures are very encouraging. Ninety-four percent (1666/1764) of those who assessed patients were present at the start of the anaesthetic. Ideally all patients should be seen and assessed by their own anaesthetist preoperatively, but it is understandable that on rare occasions this is just not possible.

Table A25 (q31)

Were any investigations done before the operation ? (Including tests carried out in the referral hospital and available before the operation.)

Yes	1770
No	23
Not answered	6
Not known/not recorded	3

If yes, which of the following?

Haemoglobin		1739
Packed cell volume (haematocrit)		1327
White cell count		1659
Sickle cell test (e.g. Sickledex)		27
Coagulation screen		503
Plasma electrolytes	Na	1677
	K	1661
	Cl	552
	HCO_3	800
Blood urea		1617
Creatinine		1456
Serum albumin		789
Bilirubin (total)		695
Glucose		896
Amylase		230
Urinalysis (ward or lab)		667
Blood gas analysis		312
Chest X-ray		1281
Electrocardiography		1486
Respiratory function tests		88
Special cardiac investigation (e.g. cardiac catheterization)		104
Special neurological investigation (e.g. imaging)		57
Investigations not specified		5
Details of investigations not known/not recorded		1

Other:

Abdominal X-ray/ultrasound	16
Blood group/cross match/group & save	27
Miscellaneous	124
Total cases *(answers may be multiple)*	**1802**

Six-hundred-and-sixty-seven patients had urinalysis; this is a low proportion of these cases. The level of justification for tests which are cheap, easy and non-invasive need not be high. It is known that the diagnosis of diabetes is often first made after urinalysis in hospital has suggested a problem, and it is sad to note the decline in the numbers of patients who received this simple test routinely. The justification of this view is exemplified in the patient of a general surgeon whose urinalysis was not available until laparotomy for a non-existent ruptured aortic aneurysm was started. The patient had hitherto unrecognized diabetes mellitus.

Table A26 (q32)
Coexisting medical diagnoses:

None	172
Respiratory	568
Cardiac	990
Neurological	393
Endocrine	226
Alimentary	327
Renal	246
Musculoskeletal	244
Haematological	152
Genetic abnormality	5
Obesity	119
Other :	
Malignancy	67
Cachexia	42
Ophthalmic	26
Hepatic	30
Vascular	38
Sepsis	26
Other (miscellaneous)	10
Not answered	50
Not known/not recorded	7
Total *(answers may be multiple)*	**1802**

The large proportion of patients with respiratory and/or cardiac disease together with the preponderance of patients over 70 years of age, reinforces the fact that this is a high risk group in relation to anaesthesia.

Examination of the questionnaires confirms that there were many more cases of sepsis than the 26 reported here and that this condition was often unrecognised before operation.

Table A27 (q34)
Was there any history of a drug reaction?

Yes	145
No	1638
Not answered	15
Not known/not recorded	4
Total	**1802**

None of these reactions appeared to be significant to the current anaesthetic.

Table A28 (q35)
ASA grade

ASA 1	38
ASA 2	343
ASA 3	647
ASA 4	472
ASA 5	200
Not answered	102
Total	**1802**

Figure A6 (see table A28)
ASA grade

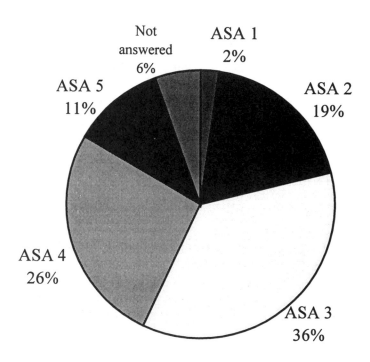

Table A29 (qs 35 and 26)
ASA grade by classification of operation

	ASA 1	ASA 2	ASA 3	ASA 4	ASA 5	Not answered	Total
Emergency	*1	14	28	68	148	17	**276**
Urgent	6	121	295	246	46	34	**748**
Scheduled	10	132	228	134	3	39	**546**
Elective	20	75	86	20	-	11	**212**
Not answered	1	1	10	4	3	1	**20**
Total	**38**	**343**	**647**	**472**	**200**	**102**	**1802**

* This patient had a head injury and was graded inappropriately.

Table A30 (qs 3 and 35)
ASA grade by grade of most senior anaesthetist present at the start of anaesthesia

	ASA 1	ASA 2	ASA 3	ASA 4	ASA 5	Not answered	**Total**
Senior house officer	3	62	130	44	8	7	**254**
Registrar	4	45	69	74	19	12	**223**
Senior registrar	-	16	48	58	43	8	**173**
Consultant	27	187	335	267	119	56	**991**
Staff grade	-	14	28	12	6	6	**66**
Associate specialist	1	9	20	5	2	5	**42**
Clinical assistant	3	10	16	8	2	6	**45**
General practitioner	-	-	-	1	-	1	**2**
Hospital practitioner	-	-	-	1	-	-	**1**
Other	-	-	-	2	-	-	**2**
None present	-	-	-	-	-	1	**1**
Not answered	-	-	1	-	1	-	**2**
Total	**38**	**343**	**647**	**472**	**200**	**102**	**1802**

The ASA system is a crude summary[6] but is widely used. It appears from this review that sometimes the categorisation is somewhat arbitrary. Difficulties arise with fit patients who suddenly develop a life-threatening condition: a patient with multiple injuries, for example, is often graded as ASA 1 rather than, correctly, as 4 or 5.

Thirty-eight patients were stated to be ASA 1, but died; some cases were incorrectly graded, but the majority were unexpected late deaths from thromboembolism.

It is alarming, in the light of our earlier recommendations, that 21% (52/247) of the patients anaesthetised by SHOs (to say nothing of 44% [93/211] by registrars) were ASA 4 or 5.

Eight of the patients anaesthetised by SHOs were ASA 5. This grading appeared appropriate. The SHO usually asked for advice and received help from an appropriate colleague. This arrangement failed on one occasion.

> An SHO without qualifications in, and less than one year's experience of, anaesthesia gave an intravenous regional anaesthetic to a 61-year-old man with a small palmar abscess. The patient was extremely ill beforehand in cardiac, renal and hepatic failure. He was clearly dying and did so on the next day from septicaemia. No advice or help was sought.

Should trainee doctors be allowed to manage patients as ill as this?

Table A31 (q36)
When was the last fluid given by mouth?

more than 6 hours before operation	1331
between 4-6 hours before operation	170
less than 4 hours before operation	46
not answered	245
not known/not recorded	10
Total	**1802**

Table A32 (q38)
Did the patient receive intravenous fluid therapy in the 12 hours before induction?

Yes	1001
No	783
Not answered	12
Not known/not recorded	6
Total	**1802**

Table A33 (q39)
Were measures taken to improve or protect the cardiorespiratory system before induction of anaesthesia?

Yes	709
No	1067
Not answered	21
Not known/not recorded	5

If yes, please indicate which measure(s)

Antibiotic therapy	373
Inotropes or vasoactive drugs	235
Chest physiotherapy	227
Bronchodilators	158
Airway management (*e.g. oral airway, tracheostomy*)	110
Steroids	55

Other:

Ventilation (IPPV/PEEP)	21
Pleural aspiration	6
Cardiac resuscitation	3
Pacemaker	2
Alfentanil	2
Prostaglandin	1
Miscellaneous	2
Not stated	8

Table A34 (q40)
Were premedicant drugs prescribed?

Yes	562
No	1231
Not answered	6
Not known/not recorded	3

If yes, please specify drug(s) prescribed

Atropine	32
Diazepam (e.g. Valium)	54
Droperidol	16
Fentanyl	7
Glycopyrronium (Robinul)	11
Hyoscine (Scopolamine)	27
Lorazepam (e.g. Ativan)	36
Ketamine	1
Metoclopramide	140
Midazolam (Hypnovel)	9
Morphine	62
Papaveretum (Omnopon)	40
Pethidine	65
Prochlorperazine (e.g. Stemetil)	33
Temazepam	266
Promethazine (e.g. Phenergan)	33
Trimeprazine (Vallergan)	1
Drug(s) not specified	4

Other:

Other analgesics	12
Miscellaneous	21
Total cases (answers may be nultiple)	**1802**

Table A35 (q41)
Was non-invasive monitoring established just before the induction of anaesthesia?

Yes	1680
No	78
Not answered	14
Not known/not recorded	30

If yes, please specify

ECG	1463
BP	1308
Pulse oximetry	1556

Other:

Capnography	49
Inspired O_2	16
Pulse	6
Temperature	12
Miscellaneous	8
Not answered	6
Total cases (answers may be multiple)	**1802**

Table A36 (q42)
Was invasive monitoring established before induction of anaesthesia e.g. CVP, arterial line?

Yes	368
No	1397
Not answered	31
Not known/not recorded	6

If yes, please indicate

CVP	289
Arterial line	281

Other:

Pulmonary arterial line	55
Intracranial pressure monitoring	1
Other (unspecified)	2
Total cases (answers may be multiple)	**1802**

The data in this table are alarming since we know that 672 patients were reported as ASA 4 or 5 (table A28). See also table A43.

Table A37 (q43)
Were any measures taken (before, during or after operation) to prevent venous thrombosis?

Yes	1073
No	696
Not answered	15
Not known/not recorded	18
Total	**1802**

	Before or during	After
Any measure	**928**	**732**
Aspirin	98	42
Heparin	475	482
Dextran infusion	29	12
Leg stockings	303	260
Calf compression	176	28
Electrical stimulation of calves	15	5
Warfarin	19	18
Heel supports	233	64
Other:		
Ripple mattress	68	45
Spinal/epidural/regional anaesthetic	12	5
Plaquenil	2	2
Positioning of legs	1	-
Persantin	1	-
Early mobilisation	-	3
Praxilene	2	-
Foot pump	2	1

See previous reports[2-5] for all the comments that may be made on this subject.

The operation

Table A38 (qs 44 and 46, derived)
Duration of procedure from time of start of anaesthetic to transfer out of operating room

0-29 mins	58
30-59 mins	336
1 hr to 1 hr 59mins	738
2 hrs to 3 hrs 59 mins	453
4 hrs or more	139
Not answered	78
Total	**1802**

Table A39 (q47)
What was the grade of the most senior surgeon in the operating room?

House officer	*1
Senior house officer	56
Registrar	385
Senior registrar	223
Associate specialist	66
Clinical assistant	9
Staff grade	45
Consultant	993
Other:	
Research fellow	1
Research registrar	1
Lecturer	1
Not answered	15
Not known/not recorded	6
Total	**1802**

* The operation which was reported in the anaesthetic questionnaire as having been performed by a house officer, was reported on the surgical one as having been performed by a senior registrar. The operation was the debridement of a sacral abscess, the anaesthetic was uneventful and the patient died on the 24th day after operation. NCEPOD has no way of determining which questionnaire is correct.

Comparing the information in the above table with table A3, (the grade of the most senior anaesthetist present at the start of the anaesthetic), the cases done by consultants, associate specialists and staff grades are very similar. For trainees there is, however, a significant difference in the distribution between the two specialties.

Figure A7 (see tables A3 and A39)
Most senior trainee anaesthetist/most senior trainee surgeon

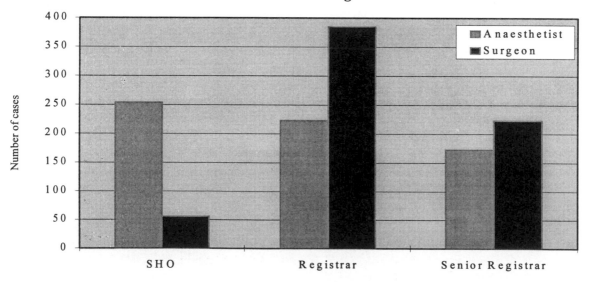

Specialist surgical trainees at SHO grade will often have already completed a period of basic general surgical training. The apparent differences between the disciplines of surgery and anaesthesia disappear when SHOs and registrars are considered together.

We were concerned that so many SHOs (presumably early in their training in anaesthesia) were taking responsibility for patients who died within 30 days of their operations. This should also concern others.

Table A40 (q48)
Was there a trained anaesthetist's assistant (i.e. ODA, SODA, anaesthetic nurse) present for this case?

Yes	1763
No	29
Not answered	8
Not known/not recorded	2
Total	**1802**

NCEPOD has emphasised the importance of non-medical help and the last report[5] suggested that this should be standard.

In analysing data, NCEPOD does not identify individual Trusts and hospitals, but anonymous data are examined by region when appropriate.

Figure A7 (see table A40)
Distribution by NHS regions (coded) of those cases where no trained anaesthetist's assistant was present

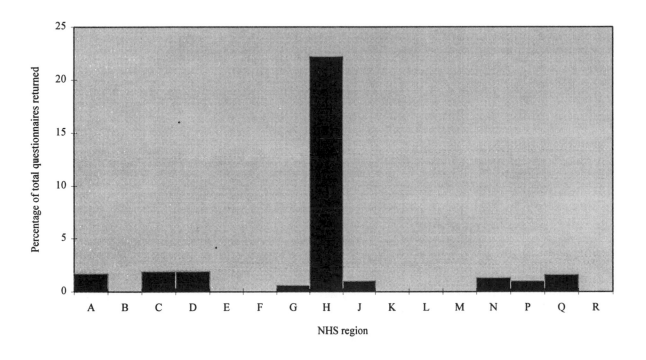

The regions here designated A to R represent a total of 291 different hospitals.

It seems that in one region there is not full acceptance by management of the need for trained assistance for the anaesthetist. No doubt the anaesthetists who work there are fully aware of the reasons for this, but the provision there is very different from national norms. Is this reasonable?

All published guidelines and standards condemn the absence of non-medical help for anaesthetists.[7, 8, 9, 10]

Table A41 (q49)
Is there an anaesthetic record for this operation in the notes?

Yes	1764
No	36
Not answered	2
Total	**1802**

The advisors thought that there should be a far wider use of printouts of the data from monitors. This provision is essential for the emergency cases such as multiple injuries and ruptured aortic aneurysms. Printouts do not, however, replace the need for an anaesthetic record. The Royal College of Anaesthetists has now (1996) advised on this matter.[11]

Table A42 (q51)
Did the patient receive intravenous fluids during the operation?

Yes	1668
No	102
Not answered	12
Not known/not recorded	20

Crystalloid - if yes please indicate which

Dextrose 5%	97
Dextrose 4% saline 0.18%	165
Dextrose 10%	18
Saline 0.9%	470
Hartmann's *(compound sodium lactate)*	1087
Other	26
Not specified	16

Colloid - if yes please indicate which

Modified gelatin *(Gelofusine, Haemaccel)*	800
Human albumin solution	98
Starch *(HES)*	97
Dextran	30
Mannitol	83
Other	5
Not specified	14

Blood - if yes please indicate which

Whole blood	222
Red cell component	335
Other component	171
Not specified	13
Total cases *(answers may be multiple)*	**1802**

Table A43 (q52)
Were monitoring devices used during the management of this anaesthetic?

Yes   1798
Not known/not recorded   4

If yes please indicate which monitors were used

	Anaesthetic Room	Operating Room†
ECG	1158	1791
Pulse oximeter	1249	1789
Indirect BP	1049	1666
Pulse meter	206	353
Oesophageal or precordial (chest wall) stethoscope	15	29
Fresh gas O_2 analyser	256	944
Inspired gas O_2 analyser	216	1171
Anaesthetic vapour analyser	97	696
Expired CO_2 analyser	233	1451
Airway pressure gauge	203	1240
Ventilation volume	122	917
Ventilation disconnect device	172	1225
Peripheral nerve stimulator	34	362
Temperature	14	187
Urine output	131	719
CVP	111	553
Direct arterial BP (invasive)	98	430
Pulmonary arterial pressure	15	75
Intracranial pressure	-	5
EEG /evoked responses/CFAM	-	4
Other	*2	*21
Not answered	106	1
Not known/not recorded	16	-
Anaesthetic room not used	434	n/a
Operating room not used	n/a	**1
Total cases (answers may be multiple)		**1802**

† Including operations performed in the anaesthetic room or an ICU.

* This figure includes atrial pressure monitoring (five) and a number of esoteric measurements.

** Patient died in the anaesthetic room during induction of anaesthesia.

There were nine patients who were not monitored with pulse oximeters, although monitors were used. All except two died more than one day after operation. One exception was a patient who had a mitral valve replacement and died on the table.

When examining the figures for the use of the ECG, pulse oximeter and indirect BP in the anaesthetic room, it should be noted that the anaesthetic room was not used in 434 cases and in a further 106 this part was not answered. This was sometimes because the transfer to the operating room was direct from an ICU.

◆ Allowing for this, when the anaesthetic room was used, pulse oximeters were on 99% of patients, ECGs on 92% and indirect BP on 83%.

The measurement of pulmonary artery pressure was used in 27% of cardiac cases and 6% of vascular cases. Pulmonary artery pressure monitoring might have been used more often in these patients, since they all died within 30 days of operation and some had complex procedures as well as serious medical disease.

Table A44 (q53)
Was there any malfunction of monitoring equipment?

Yes	22
No	1758
Not answered	12
Not known/not recorded	10

If yes

Pulse oximeter	7
Blood pressure	4
Miscellaneous	5
Not specified	6
Total cases (answers may be multiple)	**1802**

There were no deaths directly attributed to the failure of equipment. Failures were usually the result of vasoconstriction which caused most problems with pulse oximetry.

Table A45 (q54)
Did anything hinder full monitoring?

Yes	65
No	1705
Not answered	22
Not known/not recorded	10

If yes

Non-availability of monitors	17
Problems with CVP line	12
Problems with pulse oximeter	5
Miscellaneous	28
Not stated	3
Total cases (answers may be multiple)	**1802**

It is regrettable that anaesthetists still reported that all the instruments for monitoring which they wanted were not available.

Table A46 (q55)
What was the position of the patient during surgery?

Supine	1433
Lateral	153
Prone	19
Sitting	5
Knee-elbow	1
Lithotomy *(inc. Lloyd Davies)*	140
Head down	12
Head up	6
Not answered	21
Not known/not recorded	12
Total	**1802**

Table A47 (q56)
What type of anaesthetic was used?

		(93/94) %	(92/93) %
General alone	1308		
Local infiltration alone	2		
Regional alone	109	*6.0*	*1.7*
General and regional	196	*10.9*	*9.2*
General and local infiltration	48		
Sedation alone	4		
Sedation and local infiltration	15		
Sedation and regional	117	*6.5*	*1.4*
No anaesthetic given	1		
Not known/not recorded	2		
Total	**1802**		

There were 1552 patients who received general anaesthesia, as part or all, of their anaesthetic.
The comparison of percentages for regional techniques in this group with the previous report might suggest a significant increase in their popularity. But this sample has resulted in a very large number of orthopaedic cases; this may be the true explanation for this apparent increase.

General anaesthesia

Table A48 (q57)
Did you take precautions at induction to minimise pulmonary aspiration?

Yes	811
No	717
Not answered	12
Not known/not recorded	12

If yes, please indicate which:

Cricoid pressure	538
Postural changes - head up	18
Postural changes - head down	7
Postural changes - lateral	2
Preoxygenation without inflation of the lungs	595
Aspiration of nasogastric tube	195
Trachea already intubated on arrival in theatre	128
Other	9
Not answered	4
Total cases *(answers may be multiple)*	**1552**

Table A49 (q58)
How was the airway established during general anaesthesia?

Face mask *(with or without oral airway)*	53
Laryngeal mask	150
Orotracheal intubation	1192
Nasotracheal intubation	16
Endobronchial	30
Tracheostomy	3
Patient already intubated prior to arrival in theatre suite	128
Other	4
Not answered	4
Not known/not recorded	4
Total cases *(answers may be multiple)*	**1552**

Table A50 (q59)
If the trachea was intubated, how was the position of the tube confirmed?

Tube seen passing through cords	1111
Chest movement with inflation	1075
Ausculation	822
Expired CO_2 monitoring	948
Oesophageal detector device	2
Other	30
Not answered	231
Not known/not recorded	43
Total	**1552**

Table A51 (q60)
What was the mode of ventilation during the operation?

Spontaneous	186
Controlled	1368
Not answered	6
Not known/not recorded	1
Total cases *(answers may be multiple)*	**1552**

Table A52 (q61)
Were muscle relaxants used during the anaesthetic?

Yes	1376
No	170
Not answered	5
Not known/not recorded	1

If yes, please indicate which

Depolarising	583
Non-depolarising	1283
Not answered	9
Total cases *(answers may be multiple)*	**1552**

Table A53 (q62)
Were there any problems with airway maintenance or ventilation?

Yes	52
No	1471
Not answered	24
Not known/not recorded	5
Total	**1552**

Respondents interpreted this question (q62) broadly. The three vignettes below were taken from the positive answers to this question.

> Increased end-tidal CO_2, low oxygen saturation, high inflation pressures and the requirement for a higher than anticipated inspired oxygen concentration alerted a consultant and registrar anaesthetist during a craniotomy for cerebral aneurysm in a 32-year-old man. Two hours later in the ICU a chest X-ray revealed a collapsed right lung. The anaesthetic questionnaire (but not the anaesthetic record) reveals that limitation of access to the airway because of the surgical field prevented them from any manipulation of the tracheal tube. The patient died four days later from cerebral oedema. However, the surgical questionnaire and note of the operation state emphatically that the problems with oxygenation started in the anaesthetic room where in addition a pyrexia was noted. The operation was foreshortened because of brain swelling and oozing.

NCEPOD has no means of determining why there was this discrepancy in the records. Should there have been more attention before the operation began and less enthusiasm to start? Why bother to attach monitors if the coherent information they reveal is to be ignored until it is too late?

> An EEC national, qualified in 1988 and with the DA, was working alone as an SHO after two years' training in anaesthesia. A 78-year-old woman had sustained multiple injuries and a head injury in a road traffic accident the previous evening. Bilateral internal fixations of fractured tibiae (later changed to unilateral) and debridement of some wounds were planned. The consultant anaesthetist was told about this patient whose haemoglobin was now 7.3gm/100ml and who had had a triple vessel bypass graft four years earlier. Exemplary completion of the anaesthetic questionnaire and the anaesthetic record reveals that the patient was desaturated during and after the procedure: oxygen saturation could only be kept acceptable with 50-60% inspired oxygen.

The Coroner did not release the postmortem report and no questionnaire was received from the surgeon. Pulmonary aspiration or fat embolism syndrome may have been responsible at first for respiratory failure, but she died 11 days later with multiple organ failure and there is no more information about the diagnosis. The postmortem examination might not have helped understanding, but surely the report should have been released. The SHO's management (technique, drugs, fluids, monitoring, records) could not be faulted, but why did he have to work without senior medical assistance in this far-from-straightforward case on a Sunday evening?

> A senior registrar and a registrar anaesthetised a 68-year-old man who had a ruptured aortic aneurysm. The patient was having treatment (isosorbide and atenolol) for ischaemic heart disease and hypertension and had previously had a cerebrovascular accident. Asbestosis was also present. His trachea was difficult to intubate: three doses of suxamethonium were required and a bougie was used during the application of cricoid pressure. Massive fluid replacement through three large bore cannulae was insufficient to maintain cardiac output when bradycardia developed; finally cardiac arrest supervened after heroic efforts at resuscitation.

◆ The advisors reviewed this questionnaire because the anaesthetist reported a difficult airway. The patient was going to die whatever was attempted. The management was exemplary.

Table A54 (q63)
How was general anaesthesia maintained?

Nitrous oxide	1378
Volatile agent	1412
Narcotic agent	1185
Intravenous infusions	114
Not answered	12
Not known/not recorded	1
None	*1
Total cases (answers may be multiple)	**1552**

* This patient, with a ruptured aortic aneurysm, died before induction of anaesthesia.

Regional anaesthesia

There were 422 patients who received regional anaesthesia as part, or all, of their anaesthetic.

Table A55 (q64)
If the anaesthetic included a regional technique, which method was used?

Epidural - caudal	16
Epidural - lumbar	73
Epidural - thoracic	43
Interpleural	1
Intravenous regional	2
Peripheral nerve block e.g. paravertebral, sciatic, intercostal	42
Plexus block *(e.g. brachial, 3-in-1 block)*	34
Subarachnoid *(spinal)*	221
Not answered	3
Total cases *(answers may be multiple)*	**422**

Table A56 (q65)
Which agent was used?

Local	406
Narcotic	77
Other	16
Not answered	5
Total cases *(answers may be multiple)*	**422**

Sedation

There were 136 patients who received sedation as part, or all, of their anaesthetic.

Table A57 (q66)
Which sedative drugs were given for this procedure (excluding premedication)?

Benzodiazepine	94
Sub-anaesthetic doses of IV anaesthetic drugs	53
Narcotic analgesic	23
Inhalant	5
Other	4
Not answered	3
Total	**136**

Table A58 (q67)
Was oxygen given?
(relevant only for patients who received sedation and/or regional anaesthesia only)

Yes	214
No	17
Not answered	13
Not known/not recorded	1

If yes, for what reason?

Routine	173
Otherwise indicated	43
Not answered	7
Total cases (answers may be multiple)	**245**

Postoperative care

Table A59 (q68)
Which special care areas exist in the hospital in which the operation took place?

Recovery area/room	1715
High dependency unit	439
Intensive care unit	1420

Other:

Special respiratory unit	1
Trauma unit	1
None	2
Not answered	22
Total	**1802**

Table A60 (q69)
Where did the patient go on leaving theatre?

Recovery area/room	1210
Intensive care unit	356
High dependency unit	28
Specialised ICU	71
Ward	41
Another hospital	3
Corridor outside theatre	2
Special baby care unit	1
Not answered	2
Not known/not recorded	2
Died in theatre	86
Total	**1802**

The 41 questionnaires which stated that the patient went straight to the ward from the operating theatre were examined more closely. In 21 cases it was clear that the patient had spent some time in the recovery room before being returned to the ward and that the question had been misinterpreted. There were other instances where the questionnaires were not filled in clearly and it was not possible to tell where the patient had gone from the operating room.

Table A61 (q70)
Was that an optimal location for this patient?

Yes	1523
No	72
Not answered	120
Not known/not recorded	1
Not applicable - died in theatre	86
Total	**1802**

Table A62 (q71)
Would this destination represent your normal practice?

Yes	1565
No	91
Not answered	59
Not known/not recorded	1
Not applicable - died in theatre	86
Total	**1802**

◆ One patient with methicillin-resistant staphylococcal infection was returned immediately postoperatively to a well-staffed and equipped side room on the ward. A small number of patients were made comfortable in theatre and sent straight back to the ward: laparotomy had revealed inoperable intra-abdominal pathology, further treatment was considered to be inappropriate and this course of action was in the patients' best interest.

Three patients went straight to the ward after surgery for cataract, and this was stated to be the regular sequence of events. They all received local anaesthesia without sedation. One patient (aged 96 years) was given oxygen to breathe during the procedure. He was one of the three patients who had saturations and pulse rates charted during the procedure. Monitoring devices were said to have been used in the other two patients but there was no evidence of an attempt to record their readings.

On several occasions the recovery room was not used because it was closed in the evenings. **Critical care services should be available to support anaesthesia and surgery at all times.** On one occasion the anaesthetist stated that this did not affect the outcome, although the patient (aged 47 years), described as ASA 1, arrested and died on the ward on the day of surgery. On another occasion the anaesthetist monitored the patient for 25 minutes before sending him back to the ward. Other circumstances were not so clear-cut.

Three patients went straight to the ward from theatre following neurosurgery, presumably to a high dependency area. Two were patients in their forties having had cerebral aneurysms clipped. In both instances the location was described as optimal.

Table A63 (q72)
Were you unable at any time to transfer the patient into an ICU or HDU?

Yes	79
No	1535
Not answered	90
Not known/not recorded	12
Not applicable - died in theatre	86

If yes, why?

Understaffing	16
Lack of beds	46
No ICU or HDU in hospital	30
Other	2
Not answered	7
Total (answers may be multiple)	**1802**

Table A64 (q73)
Were monitoring devices used during the management of this patient in the recovery room?

Yes	1158
No	2
Not answered	41
Not known/not recorded	8
Not applicable - recovery room not used	593

If yes, please indicate which monitors were used

Indirect BP	1114
Pulse oximeter	1076
Urine output	190
ECG	608
Pulse meter	151
Temperature	114
CVP	84
Direct arterial BP (invasive)	28
Expired CO_2 analyser	10
Airway pressure gauge	9
Ventilator disconnect device	8
Inspired gas O_2 analyser	7
Ventilation volume	7
Peripheral nerve stimulator	5
Oesophageal or precordial (chest wall) stethoscope	2
Other	3
Not answered	1
Not known/not recorded	1
Total (answers may be multiple)	**1802**

◆ The fact that 94% of these patients had pulse oximeters attached to them during recovery must benefit them. This figure is an improvement on the previous reports[5] but surely it should be 100%?

Table A65 (q75)
Where did this patient go next (i.e. after the recovery room)?

Not applicable - recovery room not used	593
Ward	1074
High dependency unit	36
Intensive care unit	38
Specialised ICU	11
Home	1
Another hospital	4
Died in recovery area	19
Other	1
Not answered	25
Total	**1802**

Table A66 (q76)
Was controlled ventilation used postoperatively?

Yes	422
No	1254
Not answered	39
Not known/not recorded	1
Not applicable - died in theatre	86

If yes, why?

Routine management	195
Respiratory inadequacy	177
Control of intracranial pressure or other neurosurgical indications	39
Part of the management of pain	56

Other:

Poor condition of patient	14
Sepsis	18
Cardiac problems	41
Correction of temperature	9
Other reasons	43
Not answered	7
Total	**1802**

Table A67 (q77)

Did any of the following events, which required specific treatment, occur during anaesthesia or immediate recovery (i.e. the first few hours after the end of the operation)?

Yes	595
No	1160
Not answered	43
Not known/not recorded	4

If yes, please specify

Air embolus	2
Airway obstruction	12
Anaphylaxis	2
Arrhythmia	83
Bradycardia *(to or less than 50% of resting)*	73
Bronchospasm	25
Cardiac arrest (unexpected)	112
Convulsions	1
Disconnection of breathing system	1
Hyperpyrexia *(greater than 40°C or very rapid increase in temperature)*	1
Hypertension *(increase of more than 50% resting systolic)*	24
Hypotension *(decrease of more than 50% resting systolic)*	335
Hypoxaemia	86
Misplaced tracheal tube	1
Pneumothorax	10
Pulmonary aspiration	9
Pulmonary oedema	31
Respiratory arrest *(unintended)*	11
Tachycardia *(increase of 50% or more)*	48
Unintentional delayed recovery of consciousness	28
Ventilatory inadequacy	60
Wrong dose or overdose of drug	3

Other:

Haemorrhage	10
Death in theatre	9
ST depression	6
Hypothermia	3
Anuria	2
Miscellaneous	18
Total	**1802**

Table A68 (q78)
Was there any mechanical failure of equipment during anaesthesia or recovery (excluding that for monitoring)?

Yes	3
No	1775
Not answered	18
Not known/not recorded	6

If yes, please specify

Equipment for IPPV	2
Not specified	1
Total	**1802**

Table A69 (q79)
Were there early (i.e. up to seven days) complications or events after this operation?

Yes	1257
No	361
Not answered	94
Not known/not recorded	4
Not applicable - died in theatre	86

If yes, please specify

Ventilatory problems	557
Cardiac problems	649
Hepatic failure	46
Septicaemia	223
Renal failure	357
Central nervous system failure	183

Other:

Progress of surgical condition/failure of operation	21
Haematological disorder/coagulopathy/DIC	12
Electrolyte imbalance	8
Diabetic, hypo-/hyperglycaemia	4
Vomiting, ileus	2
Other (unspecified)	84
Total	**1802**

Table A70 (q80)
Were narcotic analgesic drugs given in the first 48 hours after operation?

Yes	1296
No	352
Not answered	55
Not known/not recorded	13
Not applicable - died in theatre	86
Total	**1802**

Table A71 (q81)
Did complications occur as a result of these analgesic methods?

Yes	48
No	1223
Not answered	19
Not known/not recorded	6
Total	**1296**

Table A72 (q82)
Were other sedative/hypnotic or other analgesic (non-narcotic) drugs given?

Yes	739
No	860
Not answered	108
Not known/not recorded	9
Not applicable - died in theatre	86
Total	**1802**

Death

Table A73 (q85)
Place of death

Theatre	90
Recovery area	20
Intensive care unit	451
High dependency unit	30
Ward	1116
Home	27
Another hospital	33

Other:

Coronary care unit	7
Accident and emergency	2
X-ray department	2
Hospice	2
Nursing home	1
Special baby care unit	1
Special respiratory unit	1
Burns unit	1
Other (unspecified)	2
Not answered	13
Not known/not recorded	3
Total	**1802**

Audit

Table A74 (q87)
Do you have morbidity/mortality review meetings in your department?

Yes	1680
No	101
Not answered	20
Not known/not recorded	1
Total	**1802**

If yes, will this case be, or has it been, discussed at your departmental meeting?

Yes	529
No	1112
Not answered	29
Not known/not recorded	10
Total	**1680**

The fact that 101 deaths could not be discussed at meetings in 69 hospitals is of concern since the Royal Colleges stipulate that such meetings shall take place. The absence of discussion about 1112 cases is less surprising but both these answers reveal missed opportunities for continuing medical education.

Table A75 (q88)
Has a consultant anaesthetist seen and agreed this form?

Yes	1617
No	57
Not answered	128
Total	**1802**

Anaesthesia - Section II

Aortic aneurysms

◆ Once again the advisors were very impressed with the high standard of anaesthesia provided for this group of patients.[5]

There were 109 questionnaires returned by anaesthetists. Nine were designated elective operations, 10 scheduled, five urgent and 85 emergency. Ninety were reviewed by the advisors.

Comorbidity

It is sometimes necessary to refuse a patient an elective operation for abdominal aortic aneurysm on account of severe medical disease although this is probably now rare. It is unlikely that, in the event of rupture, the same patient would survive an emergency operation.

> This 72-year-old man died on the same day of operation after a surgically successful repair of a leaking abdominal aortic aneurysm. He had a long history of ischaemic heart disease and had been treated four weeks earlier by physicians for a further subendocardial infarct. An asymptomatic aneurysm was found at that time. The consultant surgeon thought surgery was inadvisable then and referred him for consideration by cardiologists for coronary angioplasty. A CT scan, during another medical admission for severe back pain, showed no leak but 24 hours later he became hypotensive and was taken to theatre.

Is it possible to construct some plan for the individual patient which would avoid this undesirable sequence of events?

The presence of intercurrent medical diseases makes the occurrence of rapid changes in physiological variables during anaesthesia and surgery almost inevitable. Admission to ICU is appropriate after operation because multi-organ failure often supervenes.

It is essential that senior staff determine the clinical management strategy so that this remains logical. It is useful sometimes to recognise early when further treatment is likely to achieve nothing.

> A 78-year-old blind man was sent by a general practitioner to hospital with a diagnosis of abdominal aortic aneurysm. He previously had had a cerebrovascular incident and a myocardial infarction; he was receiving warfarin. The casualty officer diagnosed renal colic and admitted him to a medical ward. Twenty-four hours later the rupture of his aneurysm was diagnosed; he did well during and immediately after the operation but died one day later of multi-organ failure.

Would earlier and more senior opinion have resulted in a different, perhaps more measured, management?

Emergency abdominal aortic aneurysm

Table A76 (qs 3 and 44)
Most senior <u>anaesthetist</u> present at start of anaesthetic by time of start of anaesthesia

	00.01 to 07.59	08.00 to 17.59	18.00 to 24.00	Not stated	Total
Senior house officer	-	1	-	-	1
Registrar	-	1	1	-	2
Senior registrar	3	6	3	1	13
Consultant	6	46	14	1	67
Staff grade	-	-	-	-	-
Associate specialist	2	-	-	-	2
Total	**11**	**54**	**18**	**2**	**85**

Table A77 (qs 44 and 47)
Most senior <u>surgeon</u> present in the operating room by time of start of anaesthesia

	00.01 to 07.59	08.00 to 17.59	18.00 to 24.00	Not stated	Total
Registrar	-	-	1	-	1
Senior registrar	2	8	3	-	13
Consultant	9	45	13	2	69
Clinical assistant	-	1	-	-	1
Not answered	-	-	1	-	1
Total	**11**	**54**	**18**	**2**	**85**

◆ It is gratifying that 94% of the anaesthetics for emergency operations on abdominal aortic aneurysms were managed by senior registrars or consultant anaesthetists. It is doubtful if this proportion can realistically be expected to increase any further.

> One patient was 66 years old and sustained a rupture of an aortic graft which had been inserted four years earlier. Clotting was seriously deranged before, during and after the procedure. The anaesthetic was started, on a Sunday afternoon, by two senior house officers who were joined by a consultant. The incision itself was made two minutes after the patient arrived in the operating room and full invasive monitoring was established after this. The operation appeared to take a long time, almost five hours, but this was the result of serious organisational difficulties in obtaining platelets from the regional transfusion service. The patient died six days later in the intensive care unit. No surgical questionnaire was received.

◆ This case was reviewed by the coordinators because of the staff involved (trainee staff alone at the start of anaesthetic). It provides an example of excellent management by the team of anaesthetists who were not however helped by the poor service provided by the haematologists. Earlier cooperation might not have altered the outcome.

Table A78 (q 68)
Which special care areas exist in the hospital in which the operation took place?

Recovery area/room	74
Intensive care unit	78
High dependency unit	21
None of the above	1
Not answered	4
Total cases (*answers may be multiple*)	**85**

The need for critical care services is well known and their apparent absence has been noted in previous reports.[2-5]

> A 78-year-old man was transferred from a hospital without a vascular service for operation on a ruptured abdominal aortic aneurysm. The operation was done by a consultant surgeon and started at 16.00 hours. The recovery room was not staffed after 17.00 hours and, although both HDU and ICU existed in the hospital, there were no vacant beds. The patient required adrenaline and dobutamine after the operation to treat hypotension, and a pneumothorax developed during this time. Two hours later he was transferred back to the referring hospital, where he died.

Was the lack of an ICU bed known to the referring surgeon? Can transfer under these circumstances ever be justified?

Table A79 (q 52)
Monitoring devices used

	Anaesthetic room	Operating room
ECG	18	85
Pulse oximeter	18	85
Indirect BP	19	82
Expired CO_2 analyser	3	82
CVP	4	79
Direct arterial BP	2	68
Pulmonary arterial pressure	0	6
Total cases (*answers may be multiple*)	***19**	**85**

* Anaesthetic room not used or section not completed for 66/85 cases.

The role of invasive monitoring is undisputed; central venous and arterial pressures are recognised to be valuable aids to safe management of patients during and after these operations. Many anaesthetists consider that these lines should be in place before general anaesthesia is induced. Some anaesthetists consider that pulmonary artery catheterisation is desirable. Insertion of lines should however be expeditious and, where this is not possible, repeated attempts should not cause delay in the application of a clamp across the aorta. Once the latter is achieved, temporary cessation of surgery may allow time for the lines to be placed, and suitable resuscitation completed.

A registrar, associate specialist and a consultant anaesthetised a 73-year-old man with a leaking abdominal aortic aneurysm, in the operating room. Major deterioration occurred during preparation for operation and this caused difficulties in the insertion of lines so that monitoring was incomplete before surgery. The records are not clear, but it appears that about one hour was spent after induction and before the incision. [A Seldinger wire floated freely into the internal jugular vein and had to be retrieved surgically: there were no sequelae to this.] The graft was inserted by a consultant surgeon and appeared to function well. Inotropic support, together with state-of-the-art intensive therapy and monitoring, were to no avail and he died two days later. There was no evidence of re-bleeding and the precise cause of death was not established.

Was there a significant delay before the operation was started and the clamp applied, and did this contribute to his death?

Problems with blood transfusion

A 71-year-old man died five days after the surgically successful repair of a ruptured abdominal aortic aneurysm. Seventeen units of group-specific uncrossmatched blood were used together with six litres of crystalloids, three litres of gelatin, cryoprecipitate and fresh frozen plasma. Hypotension persisted and he eventually died of multisystem failure, but no explanation of the haematological failure to cross-match blood was recorded. This probably contributed to the renal failure which started during the operation.

It was surprising that compatible blood transfusion was not always possible; the use of group-specific blood is not always satisfactory.

A 76-year-old man with ischaemic heart disease had a ruptured abdominal aortic aneurysm. He had a two-and-half hour operation and required seven-and-half litres of blood, 800 ml fresh frozen plasma and six litres of colloid. He died on the table when the clamps were released. The consultant anaesthetist, who was accompanied by a senior house officer, stated that he had an overwhelming coagulopathy.

The use of massive transfusions without supplements is often ineffective. Is there a case for closer and earlier involvement of expert haematologists to guide clinicians?

Anaesthetic records

The importance of anaesthetic records has been emphasised before; the near impossibility of completion of the traditional record at the same time as the safe conduct of the anaesthetic is well understood. There may be a role for automated records for emergency cases in the future, but at least a written record of physiological variables should be retained.

A consultant anaesthetist worked without medical assistance, but with an ODA, during a successful procedure for aortic aneurysm. The blood pressure chart is blank apart from the times of the application and release of the aortic clamp.

If anaesthetists are obliged to work single-handed, surely they should have automatic recorders provided to help them.

Table A80 (qs 18 and 19)
Calendar days between operation and death
(i.e. not 24 hour periods)

Same day	37
Next day	12
2 days	8
3 days	1
4 days	4
5 days	3
6 to 10 days	10
11 to 15 days	5
More than 15 days	5
Total	**85**

It is hardly surprising that 57% of this group of patients who were going to die did so on the same day or the next after operation, in contrast to 21% (table A14) in the remainder of the sample.

Local protocols (see glossary)

These might be useful in this condition particularly in relation to the decision to operate, staff requirements, critical care services, and blood products. It is crucial to avoid futile operations and selection must be scrupulous; once the decision is made, priorities concerning invasive monitoring and early clamping need to be determined.

Anaesthesia - Section III

Fractured neck of femur

Four-hundred-and-two (23%) anaesthetic questionnaires concerned deaths after operations for fixation of fractured necks of femur. The coordinators decided that these deserved special attention, because it was recognised that they constituted a large inpatient case load and made a considerable demand on hospital resources. Each case reflected the practice of a different consultant surgeon. There were many similarities but some cases were associated with remediable factors.

◆ It must be understood that many of the questionnaires described care that was of a high standard.

One-hundred-and-eighty-seven questionnaires were examined in detail by the group of anaesthetist advisors (see Method, page 25). Noteworthy factors in the conduct of the anaesthetic and surgical care and the resources available were identified.

Decision to operate

There is an unwritten, possibly unsubstantiated, doctrine that <u>every</u> patient should be operated upon to achieve pain relief and ease nursing care. **This deserves to be reconsidered in the light of modern methods of pain relief**. There needs to be a recognised way of making a decision (joint if necessary) about optimal treatment.

Fifty-four (13%) of these patients had died by the end of the first postoperative day.

The advisors doubted the wisdom of the decision to operate in the following **ten** instances.

> A man with kyphoscoliosis, fibrosing alveolitis and emphysema (pO_2 5.4, pCO_2 3.6 kPa) was classed as ASA 4. He was 94 years old. He was anaesthetised the day after admission at 8.00pm by an SHO and a senior registrar who had discussed the case with a consultant. He was given a spinal anaesthetic and a total of 36mg ephedrine was used to maintain his blood pressure intraoperatively. There was no bed available in HDU or ICU. He sustained an unexplained cardiac arrest at 2.30am the following morning, six hours after leaving the operating room.

> An 89-year-old woman with rheumatic heart disease was described preoperatively as cyanosed and breathless (ASA 4) with consolidation of her lungs on chest X-ray. Having had general and epidural anaesthesia administered by a registrar, she arrived in the recovery room unconscious and cyanosed, and died there.

> An 84-year-old woman (ASA 3) was given 10mg morphine two days previously after which she required resuscitation. She was still deeply sedated when anaesthetised for her operation by a staff grade anaesthetist. She died of bronchopneumonia six days later.

> A woman with disseminated carcinoma of the breast underwent a bilateral operation for fractured neck of femur. She was 77 years of age and was classed as ASA 3. Bilateral intramedullary screws were inserted as prophylaxis against further pathological fractures. The anaesthetist was an SHO of less than one year's experience. Her temperature was $34^{o}C$ in the recovery room after operation where she became hypotensive. Nothing further was done in view of her underlying disease.

Would it be better to make this type of decision on the ward before operation?

Richards' screws were inserted for fractured neck of femur in a 99-year-old woman (ASA 4) who was deaf and confused having suffered three cerebrovascular accidents. She had an increased serum urea and creatinine. She was anaesthetised by a staff grade anaesthetist who obtained advice from a consultant. She was said to die of cardiac failure and a possible chronic subdural haematoma by the anaesthetists and of "general lack of will to live" by the surgeons.

The surgeons had acquiesced to pressure from her son to operate.

An 84-year-old woman who was wheelchair-bound and breathing oxygen continuously was classed as ASA 4. She was in hospital for 20 days before surgery. She had spinal anaesthesia, administered by an SHO, but no further analgesia after operation and was found dead in bed two days later.

A 74-year-old man with terminal lung cancer was operated on by a registrar and anaesthetised by an SHO. He was described as ASA 4 and was on oral morphine for his cancer pain. He died three days later of carcinomatosis.

A 79-year-old woman had a dynamic hip screw inserted. She was anaesthetised by an SHO who had been qualified since 1968. The patient had myeloma, carcinomatosis and ascites and was classed as ASA 4. She was given a combination of general and spinal anaesthesia and her blood pressure varied between extremes of 205/118 and 82/40 mmHg during operation. She died four days later.

A 73-year-old woman died 24 hours after uneventful anaesthesia and surgery for fractured neck of femur. A consultant anaesthetist looked after her. She had carcinoma of the breast, hepatomegaly, cardiac disease and cancer of the stomach. She was described as ASA 4. She was hypoxic on admission and in liver failure. She had bilateral pleural effusions. Cause of death was stated to be haematemesis and carcinomatosis.

A 67-year-old patient with chronic obstructive airways disease, ischaemic heart disease, congestive cardiac failure and non-insulin dependent diabetes had also sustained a cerebrovascular accident. The patient was in a teaching hospital for five days preoperatively during which time there was full work-up and a preoperative consultation. She was described as ASA 4 by a consultant anaesthetist. The decision was made to proceed with a Thompson's hemiarthroplasty during which there were two cardiac arrests in theatre. Death occurred the same day as the operation.

Clearly all these patients were very sick. Even in the best hands death was almost inevitable; all except one could have been admitted to HDU or ICU, but were not. Nevertheless the surgical and anaesthetic team have a commitment to individual patients and appropriate critical care services must be available for postoperative care.

Preoperative assessment

Table A81 (qs 3 and 35)
ASA grade and most senior anaesthetist - fractured neck of femur

	ASA 1	ASA 2	ASA 3	ASA 4	ASA 5	Not answered	Total
Senior house officer	-	33	66	20	1	4	124
Registrar	-	15	32	15	-	5	67
Senior registrar	-	3	9	6	-	1	19
Consultant	1	21	51	44	-	6	123
Staff grade	-	7	17	4	1	1	30
Associate specialist	-	-	11	3	-	3	17
Clinical assistant	1	3	11	4	-	3	22
Other							
Total	**2**	**82**	**197**	**96**	**2**	**23**	**402**

The fact that there were more patients classed as ASA 2 and 3 in the group anaesthetised by SHOs may be an indication that some of the sicker patients were referred to the consultants. But it may be that inexperienced SHO anaesthetists were assessing these patients too optimistically.

Table A82 (qs 3, 16 and 18)
Calendar days from admission to operation - cases anaesthetised by consultant or by SHO

	Consultant	SHO	Total
Same day	11	16	27
Next day	43	56	99
2 days	22	28	50
3 days or more	46	24	70
Not stated	1	-	1
Total	**123**	**124**	**247**

There is a suggestion from this table that some cases were being left for consultants. Whilst this may be in some ways commendable it does create delay. Is not the solution to have more trauma lists with consultant cover?

Consultant involvement and continuity of care for patients whose operations are cancelled or postponed are important factors in the provision of optimum management. Local protocols about this could stipulate a minimum grade of anaesthetist for a postponement decision. The reasons should be fully documented; the identity of the senior person consulted and a predetermined time for follow-up by anaesthetists would clarify the situation. An action plan or pathway for care for improvement before surgery is an essential prerequisite, and nurses should be involved.

Time of day

Table A81 (qs 3 and 44)
Most senior <u>anaesthetist</u> present at start of anaesthesia by time of start of anaesthesia

	00.01 to 07.59	08.00 to 17.59	18.00 to 24.00	Not stated	Total
Senior house officer	1	100	21	2	124
Registrar	1	54	9	3	67
Senior registar	-	16	3	-	19
Consultant	1	118	-	4	123
Staff grade	-	29	-	1	30
Associate specialist	-	13	1	3	17
Clinical assistant	-	19	3	-	22
Total	***3**	**349**	**37**	**13**	**402**

Table A82 (qs 44 and 47)
Most senior <u>surgeon</u> present at start of anaesthesia by time of start of anaesthesia

	00.01 to 07.59	08.00 to 17.59	18.00 to 24.00	Not stated	Total
Senior house officer	1	28	4	2	35
Registrar	1	142	20	3	166
Senior registrar	-	36	6	3	45
Consultant	1	77	1	1	80
Staff grade	-	20	3	1	24
Associate specialist	-	38	1	2	41
Clinical assistant	-	4	-	-	4
Not answered	-	4	2	1	7
Total	***3**	**349**	**37**	**13**	**402**

(NB all these data came from anaesthetic questionnaires)

◆ The majority of these cases were operated on between 08.00 hours and 17.59 hours. It must be rare for there to be a medical reason to operate on patients with fractured hips during the night.

* One of these was at 07.30; the other two operations were done in the early hours for no apparent medical reason.

Day of the week

Table A83 (qs 3 and 18)
Most senior anaesthetist present at the start of anaesthesia

	Total		SHO	Registrar	Senior registrar	Consultant	Staff grade	Associate specialist	Clinical assistant
Monday	**59**	)							
Tuesday	**53**	)							
Wednesday	**62**	)	83	47	15	111	27	13	15
Thursday	**58**	)							
Friday	**79**	)							
Saturday	**50**		23	11	3	5	2	3	3
Sunday	**41**		18	9	1	7	1	1	4

Consultants (36%) were more frequently involved than SHOs (27%) during the week but at the weekend 13% patients were anaesthetised by consultants and 45% by SHOs.

Sixty-five percent of SHOs did not ask for advice during the day (0800 to 1759).

There could have been more supervision on some occasions. More consultant sessions for urgent cases during the day on weekdays would allow better supervision and training. The allocation of staff to operations during the day is a direct responsibility of clinical directors.

> A patient aged 91 years with pernicious anaemia and senile dementia was described as ASA 2. An SHO with no qualifications in anaesthesia looked after her during a stormy general anaesthetic with hypoxia, bradycardia, tachyarrhythmias and hypotension. These were variously treated with methoxamine, adrenaline, 1.5 litres of gelofusine, ephedrine, atropine, glycopyrronium, amiodarone and frusemide. A senior registrar came to help and the patient died less than 24 hours later after controlled ventilation of her lungs in the recovery ward. Severe coronary atheroma was demonstrated at the postmortem examination.

Would earlier supervision have averted this outcome?

Table A84 (qs3 and 47)
Grade of most senior anaesthetist and surgeon present in the operating room

	Anaesthetist %	Surgeon %
Senior house officer	31	9
Registrar	17	42
Senior registrar	5	11
Consultant	31	20
Staff grade	7	6
Associate specialist	4	10
Clinical assistant	5	1

There is room for both disciplines to increase the proportion of operations under the direct supervision of more senior staff.

Hypotension

Hypotensive episodes during anaesthesia were common irrespective of the technique of anaesthesia. There may be remediable causes; for example, inadequate preoperative resuscitation with fluids or inappropriate management of frail sick patients. NCEPOD has no information about hypotension amongst those who survived. Common experience is that hypotension is frequent.

It seems reasonable that hypotension should be treated expeditiously: in this group of patients delay is not well tolerated.

> A three-and-a-half-hour operation was performed by a surgical registrar in an 84-year-old patient classed as ASA 2. An SHO anaesthetist with no qualifications in anaesthesia discussed the case with a consultant but had no help in theatre. There was hypotension after induction which persisted for one and a half hours and was treated with fluids (3.5 litres), calcium and then adrenaline. The patient went to ICU postoperatively and death occurred two days later from cardiac failure.

> A clinical assistant with the DA anaesthetised a patient described as ASA 4 by the senior registrar anaesthetist who assessed her preoperatively. It was stated that there were no contraindications to surgery despite diabetes mellitus, angina, a previous myocardial infarction and antihypertensive therapy. A registrar surgeon performed the operation which took three and a half hours. The blood pressure was below 80 mmHg for long periods of time and below 100 mmHg for almost the entire operation without adequate treatment. The patient had a cardiac arrest on the table and could not be resuscitated.

> A consultant (qualified 1976) anaesthetised an 86-year-old woman classed as ASA 4. She suffered from insulin-dependent diabetes, asthma and chronic obstructive airways disease. She was given pethidine and promethazine premedication and allowed to breathe isoflurane spontaneously through the Bain system. Her blood pressure was very low during the 23-minute operation (Austin Moore prosthesis inserted by a consultant surgeon) despite treatment with ephedrine and fluids and the oxygen saturation varied between 88 and 91%. She was sent from recovery to the ward where she died of a respiratory arrest within 12 hours.

Inappropriate technique

Management of anaesthesia was, in general, of a high standard but there were exceptions. Some of the problems were as a result of a lack of experience on the part of anaesthetists.

> An SHO anaesthetist with no qualifications was to anaesthetise a 97-year-old patient for a dynamic hip screw. A registrar anaesthetist came to help. The patient was described as ASA 3, was in atrial fibrillation and suffered from hypertension and angina which were treated with enalapril and digoxin. 65mg atracurium *(sic)* was administered as part of a general anaesthetic. Then 2mg vecuronium was given because the former relaxant did not work. The patient failed to breathe postoperatively. Ventilation of the lungs was maintained using a bag and mask while neostigmine and glycopyrronium, doxapram and then naloxone were administered. One hour later bradycardia occurred, the trachea was intubated, cardiac arrest followed soon after and then cardiac output returned. The patient was admitted to the intensive care unit, remained unstable and died 18 hours later.

Inappropriate anaesthesia was not only provided by trainees but also occasionally by consultants.

> A senior registrar and a consultant together anaesthetised a patient for insertion of an Austin Moore prosthesis. The patient was described as ASA 3, had sustained a myocardial infarction in the past and suffered from angina, epilepsy and Parkinson's disease. She was 80 years old. Medication included propranolol and GTN. Anaesthesia was induced with thiopentone 300mg, fentanyl 100 micrograms and vecuronium. The printed record from the automatic blood pressure machine was attached to the anaesthetic record. The first blood pressure reading after induction was 93/60 mmHg. The blood pressure then decreased to 35/20 for five minutes and was less than 70 mmHg for a further five minutes. The heart rate was 40/min and 70/min after administration of 600 micrograms atropine. The highest blood pressure recorded during the operation was 100/55 mmHg which was achieved 25 minutes after induction. The blood pressure then decreased to 90 until the end of the operation. No vasopressors were given and intravenous fluids consisted of Hartmanns solution (1 litre) and haemaccel (500ml). Death occurred on the third day after operation from left ventricular failure and myocardial infarction.

The notes made at the time were very poor but there was no evidence of preinduction or induction monitoring sent to NCEPOD. The patient's weight was not recorded but drug doses appeared to be generous. This group of patients has a high morbidity and some mortality is inevitable. Were these senior anaesthetists sufficiently vigilant? Was the moment-to-moment responsibility for this patient clearly defined?

Cement

There were six questionnaires about deaths which were thought to be directly due to the use of cement. Surgeons noted on the questionnaires of two such cases that they did try to avoid the use of cement in elderly or frail patients.

> A 90-year-old woman fell one Saturday evening. She was found by a care assistant the following morning having spent the night on the floor. On admission to A&E she was drowsy and dehydrated and was given intravenous fluids. Concurrent medical problems included mild chronic obstructive airways disease, and ischaemic heart disease. She had had two myocardial infarctions in the past and she had atrial fibrillation. The operation was planned for the Sunday evening and she was anaesthetised by a long term locum clinical assistant. She became severely hypotensive and bradycardic immediately after insertion of the cement. This was treated with atropine and rapid infusion of fluids but she remained hypotensive. The trachea was extubated and she was transferred to the intensive care unit at the end of surgery. Soon after arrival in intensive care she deteriorated, her trachea was reintubated and her lungs ventilated but she died four hours later after cardiac arrest and intractable arrhythmias.

The consultant surgeon stated that it was their policy to use cement in this group of patients. He wrote that although there is some risk from cardiovascular collapse all their surgical colleagues agreed that this is outweighed by the relative freedom from other complications, rapidity of mobilisation and lack of discomfort.

Risk factors with insertion of cement are quoted as osteoporosis, advanced age, long-stem femoral component, previously undisturbed intramedullary canal and underlying malignant disease. It is suggested that advanced age may play a role in the quantity of material that escapes to the lungs or in the ability of the patient to withstand the physiological insult. It is advised that in at-risk patients inspired oxygen should be 100%, there should be adequate volume replacement, invasive haemodynamic monitoring and ready mixed vasopressor solutions.[12]

Postoperative care

Anaesthetists do have some continuing responsibility for postoperative care. This must be limited for organisational reasons. These patients reported here with fractured neck of femur often deteriorated postoperatively and the medical skills required for their optimal care were beyond those of the orthopaedic team.

> A 78-year-old woman was operated on the day after admission. She had severe rheumatoid arthritis and was on long term steroid therapy and mildly anaemic (Hb 10.9gm/100ml before operation); she also had a chest infection. A spinal anaesthetic was given by an SHO and registrar. Two days later she became extremely anaemic (Hb 5.3gm/100ml), developed progressive congestive cardiac failure, suffered a cerebrovascular accident and died ten days later on the ward.

Would a more experienced team have foreseen and attempted to treat this anaemia?

> A 72-year-old woman had ischaemic heart disease, epilepsy, non-insulin-dependent diabetes, chronic renal failure and multiple myeloma. She had a history of a cerebrovascular accident and she was blind. Her urea was 30mmol/litre, serum creatinine 509mmol/litre and she was classed as ASA 4. She was admitted at midnight and operated on next day under spinal anaesthesia alone administered by a consultant anaesthetist. She was well for three days and then she had a fit and was started on a chlormethiazole (320mg/hr) infusion. She was also started on insulin at this stage. She died nine days later; the cause of death was given as acute-on-chronic renal failure. No medical consultation was mentioned in the nine days during which she deteriorated and died.

Appropriate consultation by the orthopaedic surgeons with anaesthetists before operations are planned is essential.

The management of these elderly patients' medical problems might be improved if it were conducted by physicians for the elderly. In some hospitals physicians specialising in the care of the elderly help in the management of patients with fractured neck of femur throughout their hospital stay.[13, 14, 15] The best time for surgery, if indeed operation is indicated, should be discussed between surgeon, anaesthetist and physician so that any medical diseases are managed optimally.

Some surgical postoperative problems were ignored.

> A woman aged 90 years underwent unremarkable anaesthesia and surgery. The SHO anaesthetist noted on the chart that the patient's abdomen was distended and that a nasogastric tube was passed with 600ml fluid removed. The orthopaedic surgeon wrote in the notes that the patient would be referred to the general surgeons. Fluid charts show the patient receiving oral fluids postoperatively and then, within three days of operation, pulmonary aspiration and cardiac arrest occurred. The postmortem report states aspiration and paralytic ileus as causes of death.

> An 85-year-old woman complained of abdominal pain four days after her Thompson's hemiarthroplasty. Nothing was done and postmortem examination revealed a perforated gall bladder and peritonitis.

> A 73-year-old woman died from a perforated viscus with no surgical intervention four days after surgery for fractured neck of femur.

Would proper management by other specialists have averted these deaths?

Resources

Resources did not always seem to be available for these patients. Many anaesthetists would not even consider the use of invasive monitoring such as a pulmonary artery catheter or elective admission to ICU or HDU because of a general lack of resources. NCEPOD does not claim to know the 'correct' answer to the implied question but considers that it needs to be asked. What are the 'appropriate' resources for the management of this condition?

		%
CVP line	8	2.0
Arterial line	5	1.2
Pulmonary artery catheter	-	
ICU admission	18	4.5
HDU admission	6	1.5

It is of course possible that some of these resources were used in the patients who survived for more than 30 days after operation for fractured neck of femur; NCEPOD does not know, but it is unlikely. The widespread use of CVP lines and pulmonary artery catheters would represent a huge expense and workload. Nevertheless there were cases where their insertion would have provided a valuable guide to treatment but no guarantee of a change in outcome.

A 64-year-old man had sustained the fracture **four months** before operation. He had been advised against surgery by his general practitioner because the risk was too high. He weighed 14 stone and was 6ft 3ins tall. He suffered from a cardiomyopathy and was in congestive cardiac failure. He had had a pacemaker inserted in the past. His drug therapy included frusemide, slow K, digoxin, phenytoin, enalapril, warfarin and mucodyne and he was described as ASA 4. He was admitted 11 days before his operation and there was much discussion between doctors and family about his condition and risk of surgery. He had serious pain and a decision was reached to attempt a hemiarthroplasty. A consultant anaesthetist (FRCA, 1984) discussed the anaesthetic management of this patient with another consultant. The patient was monitored with direct arterial pressure line, ECG and oximetry and he was given spinal anaesthetic with ketamine sedation. He became hypotensive postoperatively in spite of dopamine and dobutamine. He went to ICU and died on the first postoperative day.

These cases are not common but are very difficult to manage. Both central venous pressure and pulmonary artery pressure monitoring would be essential for the optimal management of a patient with this degree of compromise; he received neither. Appropriate experts would be prepared to help.

A 78-year-old woman was described as ASA 3 by the consultant anaesthetist who looked after her. She suffered with congestive cardiac failure and had a raised serum creatinine. Neither ECG nor blood pressure were monitored before induction but she was given 200mg thiopentone after which her blood pressure was 70 mmHg and it remained less than 100 mmHg throughout the operation. The anaesthetists discussed her further management with the orthopaedic SHO and it was decided that insertion of a CVP line was "inappropriate". She was sent to the ward from recovery five minutes after her systolic blood pressure had measured 75 mmHg. Three units of blood were administered later on the ward. Her fluid chart showed that she was in a positive balance of 700ml the first postoperative day, 2,850ml the second and 1,650ml on the third. She died on the fourth day after operation and postmortem examination showed left ventricular failure, atheroma and chronic cirrhosis.

Do anaesthetists in Britain need to consider a more active approach, at least in some patients?

It would seem that it is possible that at the present time the intensive care unit is not considered a suitable place for elderly patients after surgery for fractured neck of femur.

A 92-year-old woman was anaesthetised by an SHO for operation on her fractured neck of femur. She had pernicious anaemia (Hb 12.7gm/100ml) and had had a cerebrovascular accident in the past. She was classed as ASA 2. At the end of the procedure which was performed under spinal anaesthesia with midazolam given intravenously for sedation, she became hypotensive. In recovery she was hypothermic (35°C) and hypotensive (90/40 mmHg). She was sent back to the ward with a dobutamine infusion. The ward staff were instructed to maintain systolic blood pressure over 120 mmHg and pulse rate less than 110 beats per minute. The anaesthetist wrote in the questionnaire that the ward staff were "left to cope" and that there was no HDU in the hospital and "ICU (was) not available for 92-year-old femur fracture".

Intensive care admissions

In order to determine whether the admission to intensive care of the patients after surgery for fractured neck of femur was planned as part of the overall management of the case or followed unexpected events in theatre, each questionnaire was examined. A brief summary of the 18 intensive care admissions follows. The grade of anaesthetist, at what stage the patient was admitted to the intensive care unit and the reason for admission are summarised.

Age	Grade	Reason
64yrs	Consultant	planned admission - pre-existing medical disease
80yrs	Consultant	planned admission - pre-existing medical disease
71yrs	Consultant	planned admission - pre-existing medical disease
82yrs	Consultant	planned admission - pre-existing medical disease
78yrs	Consultant	ICU from theatre - hypotension (died seven mins after arrival)
90yrs	Consultant	ICU from theatre - bleeding
77yrs	Consultant	aspiration via LMA when turned in theatre
45yrs	Consultant	ICU 10 days postop - no relation to anaesthesia
81yrs	Associate Specialist	cardiac arrest on ward two days postop
89yrs	Senior Registrar + SHO	ICU from theatre - bleeding
90yrs	Clinical assistant	Cardiovascular collapse after cement insertion
82yrs	Registrar	ICU from ward 16 days postop no anaesthetic problems
82yrs	Registrar	slow to wake, doxapram, naloxone then cardiac arrest in recovery
88yrs	Registrar +SHO	ICU from theatre - hypotension at the end of the procedure
85yrs	Staff grade	arrhythmia in recovery
89yrs	Staff grade + SHO	cardiac arrest on ward one day postop
84yrs	SHO	ICU from theatre - hypotension
97yrs	SHO	cardiac arrest in recovery

Intensive care was not often part of the medical plan. When it was, consultant anaesthetists were involved.

High dependency unit

Four patients went to the high dependency unit from theatre or recovery after their operation.

> A 99-year-old woman described as ASA 4 had well-planned anaesthetic management with preoperative assessment by a consultant anaesthetist. The problems were discussed with the SHO, registrar and senior registrar who anaesthetised her as a team. She was blind and demented with a pre-existing respiratory tract infection to which she succumbed 48 hours later. This was in spite of her planned admission to the high dependency unit with attempts at early mobilisation and chest physiotherapy.

What appears to be state-of-the-art care may not result in survival.

Nothing is known about similar patients who survived their operation for fractured neck of femur but it does seem that these critical care facilities are often not considered for this group of patients.

> A 94-year-old woman with cardiac failure and hypothyroidism treated with frusemide and thyroxine had an operation in the middle of the day on a Saturday. The SHO anaesthetist gave a general anaesthetic and noted that in recovery she had ventilatory inadequacy with hypoxaemia, bradycardia and hypotension. Her trachea was reintubated and her lungs ventilated with 100% oxygen. Naloxone was given, and the absence of residual paralysis was checked with a nerve stimulator; full blood count, serum electrolytes and arterial blood gases were stated to be normal. Consciousness never returned and adequate spontaneous ventilation never recovered. She was disconnected from the ventilator after four hours. It was suggested by the anaesthetist that the respiratory failure may have been secondary to pulmonary aspiration of stomach contents before she reached the anaesthetic room.

Should this operation have been done? Was the decision after the operation right? Whether or not this decision was correct, a consultant anaesthetist and intensivist should have been involved.

Discussion

Previous NCEPOD reports have contained information about anaesthesia for operations for fixation for fractured neck of femur. Successive reports have commented that this condition is almost a mode of death in the elderly. Nevertheless these operations are quite common. The clinical coordinators therefore chose in this report to concentrate on this procedure with the aim of amalgamating many views.

There are three specific matters for consideration.

- The case for **conservative management** may need to be considered more frequently. Active intervention remains the mainstay of treatment. Sometimes, and this may be quite rarely, repeated nerve blocks or intravenous analgesia might alleviate pain in terminally ill patients more humanely than a surgical operation.

- Everyone must consider the **use of resources** in the health service but, in particular, hospital managers and clinicians should address the problem of defining them for elderly patients with fractured neck of femur which will be an increasing problem. There is a question of priorities which must be answered.[16, 17] This particular group of patients requires the consideration of the appropriate anaesthetists, appropriate critical care facilities, and the place of invasive monitoring. These decisions should probably then be part of a local protocol particularly for trainee staff who should not make decisions in isolation.

- A **team approach** with direction from senior physicians, anaesthetists and surgeons would facilitate optimal management. This would involve changes so that more consultant anaesthetists had sessional commitments. This would allow for preoperative assessment and review of all patients with fractured neck of femur. Supervision and teaching of trainee anaesthetists could then be properly arranged.

Surgery

Surgery

Contents

Introduction

Although we have commented on many perioperative deaths in this report, we must emphasise that the overwhelming majority of these deaths are inevitable and that the cases are just a small part of the vast panorama of modern surgery in England, Wales and Northern Ireland, the Isle of Man and the Channel Islands. Many of the patients who die are elderly with severe associated surgical and medical disorders.

The sample reviewed for the year 1993/94 was one perioperative death for each consultant surgeon/gynaecologist team. This mechanism of sampling gave NCEPOD a sample of 2456 deaths from the total of 20,442 reported. From this, surgeons returned 76.6% of their questionnaires (compared with an anaesthetic return rate of 78.0%). It is satisfying to note the very high return rate of surgical questionnaires from some regions, where the return rate was over 80% (e.g. Northern Ireland, Northern) We remain concerned however at the low return rate from those regions where a return rate of less than 70% was recorded (see table G6, page 20 for complete list). There was also considerable variation in return rates between surgical specialties (see table G7, page 21), ranging from the best (gynaecology - 88.4%) to the worst (neurosurgery - 60.8%).

An important and encouraging change in surgeons' behaviour has been the impact of local clinical audit, which now fills a very real role in modern 'reflective' surgical practice. NCEPOD has, over the years, always asked the question in its questionnaires "was this death considered at a local audit meeting?". Whilst the overall figure (77%) is encouraging, the figures for individual specialties varied widely, and were particularly low for gynaecology (35% of cases), which to some extent was a result of the nature of the cases.

Why were many of the deaths (across all specialties) not discussed? Managers have a crucial role in facilitating local audit; Chief Executives should review their provision for and encouragement of clinical audit, and consultants should remember that it is now part of their contracts.

In previous reports we have highlighted problems with critical care facilities. These have been highlighted again in this report and we again draw attention to these shortcomings. Many of these problems are organisational and managers, nurses and doctors need to collaborate to resolve them.

Over 3 million surgical operations are carried out each year; we are unable to quote the exact number because of difficulties with routine data systems. Yet again, the frustration imposed by inadequate data systems in both the NHS and the independent sector mean that we still do not have complete information about the population who undergo surgical operations. Without these data surgeons are unable to really monitor their work and its outcome. Both the NHS and independent sector should publish good epidemiological data about what they do.

This year we draw attention to difficulties consultant surgeons are having with a minority of Coroners and we ask "are these local difficulties with Coroners necessary?" Both consultant surgeons and Coroners are there to serve the public interest. Could they not always cooperate more effectively? Surgeons and anaesthetists have a duty to always ask for copies of postmortem reports; Coroners need to supply them. While 76% of Coroners' postmortem reports were returned to surgeons, and NCEPOD is grateful to them for this, we find that a minority of Coroners still do not help NCEPOD as much as they could, and refuse to divulge details of postmortem examinations to the relevant clinician. The section on pathology in this report needs to be read carefully by clinicians, pathologists and Coroners. Surgeons should not hesitate to refer to the Coroner if:

- The cause of death appears to be unknown.
- There is any element of suspicious circumstances or a history of violence.
- The death may be linked to an unnatural event.
- The death may be due to industrial disease or related in some way to the deceased's occupation.
- The death is linked with an abortion.
- The death occurred during an operation or before full recovery from the effects of anaesthesia, or was in some way related to the anaesthesia.
- The death was related to a medical procedure or treatment.
- The actions of the deceased may have contributed to his or her own death, for example by suicide, self-neglect or drug abuse.
- The death occurred in police or prison custody.

Not statutory but desirable:

- The deceased was detained on a criminal charge under the Mental Health Act.
- The death occurred within 24 hours of admission to hospital.

Lastly, readers should remember that this report deals with the situation prior to the implementation of the specialist registrar grade (the Calman reforms) and the mandatory reduction of junior doctors' hours. NCEPOD will seek to monitor the effect of the implementation of these reforms on patient care.

Cardiothoracic Surgery

The advisors in cardiothoracic surgery were:

Mr R Bonser	(West Midlands)
Mr M Elliott	(North Thames)
Mr K McManus	(Northern Ireland)
Professor T Treasure	(South Thames)

NCEPOD is very grateful to these advisors for their help and advice.

Points

- At least 98% of operations were carried out by a senior surgeon.
- The principle of continuity of care in dealing with postoperative complications needs re-emphasis.

Sample

The 1993/94 NCEPOD survey was based on questionnaires concerning the first perioperative death reported for individual consultant surgeons. Thus no consultant surgeon received more than one questionnaire (see page 10). In cardiothoracic surgery 143 cases were selected for the sample, of which 92 questionnaires from 41 hospitals were returned and analysed. A further three questionnaires were returned but for various reasons not included in the analysis. The overall return rate was therefore 66%.

Audit

Seventy-seven (84%) patients were considered at a local audit meeting. Postmortem examinations were performed in 48 (52%) cases; 38 were done at the request of the Coroner and ten carried out by the hospital pathologist. There appeared to be good communication between pathologists and clinicians.

List of procedures

These may be multiple for individual patients. Cases of trauma and revisional surgery have not been identified separately.

Table S1 (q47)
Final operation performed

Cardiac/vascular procedures

Coronary artery bypass graft (any number of vessels)	40
Aortic valve replacement	16
Mitral valve replacement	12
Correction of congenital cardiac anomalies	4
Replacement of thoracic aorta (aneurysm, dissection or tear)	3
Repair of VSD (post infarct)	2
Ventricular aneurysmectomy	1
Evacuation of tamponade	1
Pulmonary embolectomy	1
Repair thoracoabdominal aortic aneurysm	1

Pulmonary/pleural procedures

Pulmonary resection	11
Exploratory thoracotomy	6
Bronchoscopy	5
Pleurodesis	1

Oesophageal procedures

Oesophagogastrectomy	1
Oesophagogastroscopy (+/- dilatation)	1

Miscellaneous	15
Total cases *(answers may be multiple)*	**92**

In some cases the procedures performed may have been inappropriate.

> A 17-year-old man was admitted for complex mitral valve repair. He was known to have subacute bacterial endocarditis with mitral regurgitation; he was also known to have aortic valve disease. Following a complex mitral valve procedure the patient was well for two weeks, but suddenly developed severe mitral regurgitation and the mitral valve was replaced. During surgery he became acidotic, unresponsive and died. At postmortem examination, aortic stenosis was noted to be very severe.

Aortic stenosis was a significant factor in this case and aortic valve surgery should also have been undertaken.

> A 71-year-old man was treated for an adenocarcinoma of the gastro-oesophageal junction by total gastrectomy with oesophago-jejunal anastomosis. His condition slowly deteriorated postoperatively. He developed an anastomotic leak associated with severe bronchopneumonia and adult respiratory distress syndrome. A re-exploration operation was undertaken at five days and an attempt made to oversew the leaking anastomosis. The patient died one week later. The surgeon himself commented that the anastomosis should have been completely redone at the second procedure.

Patient profile

Table S2 (qs3 and 4)
Age of patient at final operation

Years		Male	Female
0 to 10	8	5	3
11 to 20	4	3	1
21 to 30	-	-	-
31 to 40	2	1	1
41 to 50	4	4	-
51 to 60	12	8	4
61 to 70	34	17	17
71 to 80	22	13	9
81 to 90	5	2	3
91 to 100	1	1	-
Total	**92**	**54**	**38**

Admission details

Table S3 (q1)
Type of hospital in which the final operation took place

University/teaching hospital	46
Surgical specialty hospital	22
Independent hospital	12
District General hospital	11
Other acute/partly acute hospital	1
Total	**92**

In one case the patient was admitted to an inappropriate hospital with postoperative complications.

> A 74-year-old man presenting with progressive dysphagia and weight loss was found to have an oesophageal tumour. An oesophagogastrectomy was performed and initially he made a good recovery. He was discharged home ten days after surgery, but readmitted the following day to another hospital with dyspnoea. He had an isotope lung scan, for the purpose of demonstrating ventilation and perfusion mismatches, which suggested a diagnosis of pulmonary embolus. He had a respiratory arrest four days later.

Patients requiring re-admission within 30 days of major surgery, with what is potentially a complication of that surgery, should be re-admitted to the unit where that surgery was performed.

Table S4 (q12)
Admission category

Elective	55
Urgent	15
Emergency	21
Not answered	1
Total	**92**

Table S5 (q29)
Co-existing problems at time of final surgery

None	18
Respiratory	30
Cardiac	25
Vascular	16
Renal	13
Haematological	9
Gastrointestinal	8
Neurological	8
Musculoskeletal	7
Sepsis	6
Endocrine *(including diabetes mellitus)*	6
Psychiatric	4
Drug addiction	1
Other	18
Not answered	4
Total cases *(answers may be multiple)*	**92**

Table S6 (q28)
ASA Class

ASA Class 1	4
ASA Class 2	16
ASA Class 3	25
ASA Class 4	31
ASA Class 5	11
Not answered	5
Total	**92**

The nature of the overall problems in cardiothoracic surgery is highlighted by the fact that 73% of the patients were in ASA grades 3 to 5.

Table S7 (q35)
Anticipated risk of death related to the proposed operation

Not expected	2
Small but significant risk	24
Definite risk	58
Expected	8
Total	**92**

Two patients were not expected to die; the surgeons may have misinterpreted the question.

A 66-year-old man was admitted with a recent history of haemoptysis and was shown to have a bronchial carcinoma. He underwent a left upper lobectomy in an uneventful operation. Postoperatively he developed a persistent empyema and in spite of antiobiotics, physiotherapy and tracheostomy he developed a secondary pulmonary haemorrhage and died nineteen days after surgery.

A 75-year-old woman was admitted for treatment of aortic stenosis. She was graded ASA 3 and needed considerable preoperative preparation. She had an aortic valve replacement and one coronary artery bypass graft. It proved impossible to wean the patient from bypass, and she died in the ICU.

In both cases a small but significant risk must have existed in relation to the known pathology and proposed surgery.

Preparation for surgery

Table S8 (q30)
Preoperative precautions or therapeutic manoeuvres to improve the patient's preoperative condition

None	9
Antibiotics (pre- or intra-operative)	50
Cardiac support drugs or anti-arrhythmic agents	41
Chest physiotherapy	38
Oxygen therapy	32
Intravenous fluids	26
Diuretics	26
Urinary catheterisation	22
Tracheal intubation	16
Mechanical ventilation	15
Correction of hypovolaemia	12
Anticoagulants	9
Gastric aspiration	7
Blood transfusion	6
Nutritional support	6
Vitamin K	5
Airway protection (e.g. in unconscious patients)	4
Bowel preparation	1
Others	9
Not answered	2
Total cases (answers may be multiple)	**92**

There were several instances in which preoperative precautions and therapeutic manoeuvres may have been inadequate.

The surgical team

Table S9 (q22)
Specialty of consultant surgeon in charge at time of final operation

Cardiac - adult	38
Thoracic	21
Cardiac - mixed	16
Cardiothoracic	9
Cardiac - paediatric	5
Cardiac/transplantation	1
Cardiothoracic/transplantation	1
General with an interest in gastroenterology and breast surgery	1
Total	**92**

Table S10 (qs 43 and 46)
Grade of most senior operating surgeon

		(locums)	Supervision?
Consultant	80	(4)	n/a
Associate specialist	1		1
Senior registrar	9	(3)	7
Clinical assistant	1		1
Not answered	1		
Total	**92**		

In all cases a consultant surgeon made the final decision to operate. Eighty-seven per cent of all operations were carried out by a consultant and 10% were carried out by a senior registrar (the consultant being immediately available in seven out of nine cases).

Time of surgery

Table S11 (q37)
Classification of the final operation

Emergency	14
Urgent	22
Scheduled	39
Elective	17
Total	**92**

Table S12 (q40)
Day of operation

Monday	17
Tuesday	20
Wednesday	17
Thursday	16
Friday	14
Saturday	5
Sunday	3
Total	**92**

Unanticipated intra-operative problems

In 34 cases there were unanticipated intra-operative problems. The majority of these problems related to cardiac failure, difficulties in withdrawal of cardiopulmonary bypass and haemodynamic instability.

Postoperative complications

Table S13 (q56)
Specific postoperative complications:

Low cardiac output	41
Cardiac arrest	27
Renal failure	24
Haemorrhage/postoperative bleeding requiring transfusion	22
Respiratory distress	21
Generalised sepsis	10
Stroke or other neurological problems	10
Persistent coma	5
Nutritional problems	4
Hepatic failure	2
Other organ failure	2
Peripheral ischaemia	2
Wound infection	1
Wound dehiscence	1
Anastomotic failure	1
DVT and/or pulmonary embolus	1
Pressure sores	1
Other	8
Not answered	2
Total cases* *(answers may be multiple)*	**74**

* (Excluding death in theatre - 18 cases)

The majority of problems were associated with low cardiac output, cardiac arrest and respiratory distress. Bleeding and low cardiac output are intrinsically related. They are important postoperative complications of cardiac surgery and emphasise the need for immediate postoperative intensive care. If uncorrected they would lead to early postoperative deaths.

Availability of facilities

Table S14 (q2)
Availability of facilities

	Available in the hospital
Theatre recovery area	85
Adult ICU	90
Adult HDU	63
Paediatric ICU/HDU	45
Emergency theatre	81
Total cases (answers may be multiple)	**92**

Appropriate adult ICU facilities were available in all of the hospitals. However, two of the paediatric patients (ages 6 and 9) were treated in hospitals without paediatric ICU facilities.

Table S15 (q51)
Was the patient admitted immediately to an ICU or HDU postoperatively?

ICU	56
HDU	10
Neither of the above	8
Total*	**74**

* (Excluding death in theatre - 18 cases)

Table S16 (q51a)
If neither, was the patient admitted to an ICU/HDU after an initial period on a routine postoperative ward?

Yes	3
No	5
Total	**8**

Only five patients were not admitted to an ICU/HDU at some time as part of their postoperative management.

Table S17 (q53)
Discharge from ICU/HDU was due to:

Death	47
Elective transfer to ward	14
Pressure on beds	1
Other	6
Not answered	1
Total	**69**

Table S18 (qs 39 and 58)
Calendar days between operation and death
(i.e. not 24 hour periods)

Same day	23
Next day	18
2 days	11
3 days	5
4 days	5
5 days	1
6 to 10 days	12
11 to 15 days	7
16 to 20 days	6
21 to 30 days	4
Total	**92**

Table S19 (q60)
Place of death

Theatre	*21
Recovery room	1
Ward	12
ICU/HDU	56
Home	1
Another hospital	1
Total	**92**

* *(Initially 18, plus 3 cases where patient taken back to theatre and then died)*

—————— o o o o ——————

Colorectal Surgery

The advisors in colorectal surgery were:

Mr A R Berry	(Anglia and Oxford)
Mr P A Farrands	(South Thames)
Mr M J Kelly	(Trent)
Miss C A Makin	(North West)
Mr W Stebbings	(Anglia and Oxford)

NCEPOD is very grateful to these advisors for their help and advice.

Points

- Right hemicolectomy is a more dangerous operation than is widely perceived.
- There was inadequate provision of high dependency services for patients after colorectal surgery.
- Mechanisms should be in place to ensure that routinely used protocols for thromboembolic prophylaxis are also applied to urgent and emergency admissions.
- Postmortem examination reports (both hospital and Coroners') must always be available to clinicians.

Sample

The 1993/94 NCEPOD survey was based on questionnaires concerning the first perioperative death reported for individual consultant surgeons. Thus, no consultant surgeon received more than one questionnaire (see page 10). In colorectal surgery, 296 cases were selected for the sample, of which 238 questionnaires from 191 hospitals were returned and analysed. A further two questionnaires were returned but for various reasons (see page 19), not analysed. The overall return rate was therefore 81%.

Audit

Two-hundred-and-eleven (89%) patients were considered at a local audit meeting. Postmortem examinations were done in 91 (38%) cases. Twenty-one of these were hospital postmortems and 70 were done at a Coroner's request. A copy of the report was received by the surgical team in 19/21 (90%) of the hospital postmortems and 56/70 (80%) of the Coroners' postmortems. The quality of postmortem examinations varied and did not always help to explain the cause of death (see Pathology section, page 201). It is recommended that surgeons liaise with their local Coroner to ensure that information from postmortem examinations can be obtained with the minimum of effort and delay.

List of procedures

Table S20 (q47)
Final operation performed

Right hemicolectomy	55
Hartmann's procedure	45
Defunctioning colostomy	26
Sigmoid colectomy	18
"Open and close" laparotomy	10
Total colectomy and ileostomy	9
Abdomino-perineal resection of rectum	9
Defunctioning ileostomy	9
Drainage of abscess (any site)	8
Anterior resection of rectum	7
Closure of colonic perforation (with/without defunctioning colostomy)	6
Laparotomy and biopsy of mass	6
Left hemicolectomy	6
Small bowel resection	6
Splenectomy	5
Ileocolic bypass	4
Refashioning of colostomy	3
Laparotomy for haemorrhage	2
Ileorectal anastomosis	2
Division of adhesions	2
Laparoscopic procedures (right hemicolectomy and rectopexy)	2
Miscellaneous (one each of: laparostomy, refashioning of ileostomy, colonoscopy, repair iliac artery, tracheostomy, reversal of Hartmann's, Thiersch wire, hysterectomy, partial gastrectomy, appendicectomy, transverse colectomy, closure of ileostomy, cholecystectomy, insertion of Denver shunt, repair of urinary bladder, ovarian cystectomy, oversewing of perforated duodenal ulcer, repair of incisional hernia)	19
Total cases *(answers may be multiple)*	**238**

Thirteen operations were considered to be inappropriate.

Of the 26 defunctioning colostomies, 22 were transverse loop colostomies and four were sigmoid colostomies. Most were done to defunction perforated diverticular disease or to bypass nonresectable malignant obstruction. Two colostomies were fashioned to defunction distal anastomoses. In modern practice, a defunctioning colostomy for a distal anastomosis is often life-saving. On the other hand, a simple diverting colostomy without resection, or exteriorisation of a distal perforation, inflammatory mass or obstructing cancer, is no longer appropriate. There were six instances where colonic perforations were closed without exteriorisation or resection. Only two of these were covered by a defunctioning colostomy.

Four out of five splenectomies were done because of surgical damage to the spleen. One splenectomy was done because of the proximity of a tumour to the spleen.

Table S21 (q1)
Type of hospital in which the final operation took place

District General hospital	183
University/teaching hospital	50
Defence Medical Services hospital	2
Independent hospital	2
Other acute/partly acute hospital	1
Total	**238**

Table S22 (q2)
Availability of facilities

	Available in the hospital	Available 24hrs per day, 7 days per week
Theatre recovery area	236	180
Adult ICU	224	207
Adult HDU	71	60
Emergency theatre	189	122
Total cases *(answers may be multiple)*	**238**	

A distressing feature of these data is the apparent lack of emergency theatre and HDU provision for these patients. All these services should be available 24 hours a day, seven days a week.

Table S23 (qs 3 and 4)
Age of patient at final operation

Years		Male	Female
21 to 30	2	2	-
31 to 40	1	1	-
41 to 50	8	2	6
51 to 60	16	7	9
61 to 70	57	32	25
71 to 80	86	37	49
81 to 90	58	15	43
91 to 100	10	3	7
Total	**238**	99	139

Table S24 (q7)
Source of referral

General Medical Practitioner	168
A&E department	30
Transfer from another hospital	21
Other*	19
Total cases	**238**

* Physicians (8), Outpatients (3), Surgeons (3), Miscellaneous (5)

Table S25 (q12)
Admission category

		%
Elective	58	*25*
Urgent	32	*13*
Emergency	148	*62*
Total	**238**	

Seventy-five percent of admissions for colorectal surgery were either emergencies or urgent.

Table S26 (q13)
Type of area to which patient first admitted

Surgical ward	177
Medical ward	22
A&E holding area *(or other emergency admission ward)*	19
Geriatric ward	8
Gynaecological/obstetric ward	5
Mixed medical/surgical ward	2
ICU	2
Admission ward	1
Direct to theatre	1
Renal unit	1
Total	**238**

Table S27 (q22)
Specialty of consultant surgeon in charge at time of final operation

General surgery (no stated specialist interest)	48 — 20%
Paediatric surgery	2
Cardiac surgery	1
Vascular surgery	1
Vascular surgery/transplantation	1
General surgery with a stated interest in :	
gastroenterology	92 —
vascular surgery	34
endocrine/breast surgery	18
urology	17
coloproctology/colorectal surgery	15 – 45
transplantation	5
surgical oncology	3
trauma	1
Total	**238**

Overall, 155 (65%) patients were treated by general surgeons without a stated specialist interest or with a stated interest in colorectal surgery or gastroenterology. Surgeons should not hesitate to refer patients to the appropriate specialist. Such arrangements are especially important for emergency admissions and, with increasing specialism, will become more important in the future.

Table S28 (qs 24 and 34)
The most senior surgeon involved in decision-making prior to surgery

		(locums)
Consultant	217	(13)
Associate specialist	3	-
Senior registrar	13	(1)
Registrar	4	(1)
Staff grade	1	-
Total	**238**	

233

Table S29 (q28)
ASA Class

ASA Class 1	4
ASA Class 2	63
ASA Class 3	76
ASA Class 4	71
ASA Class 5	18
Not answered	6
Total	**238**

Table S30 (q29)
Co-existing problems at time of final operation

None	20
Cardiac	112
Respiratory	77
Sepsis	45
Renal	36
Gastrointestinal	31
Musculoskeletal	31
Haematological	30
Neurological	21
Endocrine *(including diabetes mellitus)*	21
Vascular	15
Psychiatric	13
Alcohol-related problems	5
Drug addiction	2
Other	39
Not answered	7
Total cases *(answers may be multiple)*	**238**

Table S31 (q30)
Preoperative precautions or therapeutic manoeuvres to improve the patient's preoperative condition

None	11
Intravenous fluids	176
Antibiotics (pre- or intra-operative)	172
Urinary catheterisation	144
Correction of hypovolaemia	118
Gastric aspiration	115
Oxygen therapy	62
Chest physiotherapy	50
Cardiac support drugs or anti-arrhythmic agents	49
Blood transfusion	48
Bowel preparation	47
Anticoagulants	45
Diuretics	40
Nutritional support	16
Tracheal intubation	13
Mechanical ventilation	10
Airway protection *(e.g. in unconscious patients)*	9
Vitamin K	8
Others	15
Not answered	1
Total cases *(answers may be multiple)*	**238**

Eleven patients were said to have had no specific preoperative preparation. It is of concern that these patients did not receive antibiotics or intravenous fluids. If the responses to this question are accurate then these patients were given inadequate preoperative care. The general use of antibiotics and anticoagulants for thromboembolic prophylaxis was low.

Table S32 (qs 31 and 37)
DVT prophylaxis

The data have been tabulated to show the difference between the use of thromboembolic prophylaxis in scheduled/elective cases compared to emergency/urgent cases.

Scheduled/Elective
(Total of 83 cases "had measures")

	Before/during only	After only	Both
Heparin	24	3	48
Leg stockings	16	10	25
Calf compression	19	-	2
Heel support	11	-	4
Ripple mattress	-	1	1
Warfarin	1	-	-
Electrical stimulation of calves	1	-	1
Other	1	-	2
None	2	26	5

Emergency/Urgent
(Total of 127 cases "had measures")

	Before/during only	After only	Both
Heparin	20	17	61
Leg stockings	22	6	49
Calf compression	25	-	3
Heel support	25	-	2
Ripple mattress	2	-	-
Warfarin	-	-	1
Electrical stimulation of calves	2	-	-
Other	-	-	1
None	6	31	22

In twenty-two of the emergency/urgent cases, <u>no</u> measures at all were taken (plus one questionnaire blank for this question). In the scheduled/elective cases, five patients had <u>no</u> measures.

Patients who are admitted and operated on as emergency or urgent cases are less likely to receive thromboembolic prophylaxis. This is borne out by other studies.[18] On admission, all patients should be assessed for risk factors, according to locally accepted protocols, and prophylaxis prescribed if appropriate.

Question 32
Did the patient's medication (excluding premedication) in any way contribute to the fatal outcome in this case?

This was answered "yes" in 15 cases. There were three patients who were receiving steroids; these patients may be prone to complications and require cautious management.

Table S33 (q35)
Anticipated risk of death related to the proposed operation

Not expected	21
Small but significant risk	55
Definite risk	150
Expected	11
Not answered	1
Total	**238**

Previous CEPOD and NCEPOD reports have made surgeons aware of the need to make decisions not to operate. It is acknowledged that these are difficult decisions and should be consultant-led. However, despite the best surgical advice against surgery, there are occasions when either the patient or the relatives are desperate to explore all avenues; the surgeon may then operate knowing that the outcome is likely to be fatal.

Table S34 (q37)
Classification of the final operation

Emergency	32
Urgent	118
Scheduled	70
Elective	18
Total	**238**

Question 38
Were there any delays (between admission and surgery) due to factors other than clinical?

There were 13 positive answers. Some delays occurred between admission to a medical ward and referral for surgery for various reasons such as slow recognition of the problem by admitting physicians and confusion in identifying the surgeon in charge of the case after referral. Other delays were caused by reluctance to operate; this was due to both patient-related factors and surgical hesitation. There were also instances where patients refused surgery or showed reluctance.

Table S35 (q40)
Day of operation

Monday	23
Tuesday	56
Wednesday	42
Thursday	42
Friday	33
Saturday	16
Sunday	26
Total	**238**

Out-of-hours operations

Fifty operations were done "out-of-hours" (see Glossary, Appendix B) during the week and a further 42 were done at weekends. No information about the time of surgery during a weekday was given for 21 cases. At best this means that 92/217 (42%) of operations were done out-of-hours; at worst this figure could be 113/238 (48%). NCEPOD has previously promoted the use of emergency theatres in order to reduce this out-of-hours workload. Efficient usage of such theatres must occur alongside a restructuring of the consultants' working day in order to allow for supervision and teaching.

Table S36 (qs 43 and 46)
Grade of most senior operating surgeon

		(locums)	Supervision?
Consultant	138	(12)	n/a
Associate specialist	4	-	1
Senior registrar	37	(5)	6
Registrar	52	(3)	13
Staff grade	3	-	-
Senior house officer	3	(1)	2
Not answered	1	-	-
Total	**238**		

Generally the level of involvement of senior surgeons (consultant, associate specialist and senior registrar) was good but three procedures were done by SHOs. Two were supervised and were appropriate procedures for a basic surgical trainee. The third case was a laparotomy for faecal peritonitis. The unsupervised trainee surgeon used a simple suture to close the perforation in the sigmoid colon and added a transverse colostomy. It is not acceptable for an SHO to be doing this type of surgery and the choice of procedure was incorrect. Senior help should have been available.

There were 39 instances where registrars operated without immediate senior supervision. The procedures are listed in table S37.

Table S37
Unsupervised registrar operations

	Total number in sample	Number done by unsupervised registrar
Hartmann's procedure	45	12
Right hemicolectomy	55	7
Total colectomy & ileostomy	9	5
Defunctioning colostomy	28	4
Ileocolic bypass	4	3
Sigmoid colectomy	18	2
Miscellaneous *(one each of: "open & close" laparotomy, refashioning of colostomy, loop ileostomy, drainage of abscess, closure of sigmoid perforation, left hemicolectomy)*		6

Question 49
Were there any unanticipated intra-operative problems?

There were 60 positive answers to this question. The advisors identified several common events which included difficulties with multiple adhesions, haemorrhage from sacral veins, pneumothoraces and haemothoraces related to the insertion of central venous lines and problems with unexpectedly large tumours. Surgeons should be aware of the problems associated with bulky colonic tumours and the fact that some patients have a short colonic mesentery which may pose problems when an anastomosis is attempted. Unexpected problems also included massive haemorrhage and iatrogenic damage to adjacent organs e.g. spleen and lung.

Table S38 (q51)
Was the patient admitted immediately to an ICU or HDU postoperatively?

ICU	85
HDU	20
Neither of the above	128
Total*	**233**

* *(Excluding death in theatre - five cases)*

Table S39 (q51a)
If neither, was the patient admitted to an ICU/HDU after an initial period on a routine postoperative ward?

Yes	20
No	103
Not answered	5
Total	**128**

Six patients were readmitted to an ICU after initial discharge from ICU to a general ward.

Table S40 (q52)
Indications for the admission to ICU or HDU

General monitoring	93
Ventilation	75
Specialist nursing	59
Presence of experienced intensivists	50
Metabolic monitoring	45
Coincident medical diseases	34
Routine for this surgical procedure	23
Surgical complications	12
Anaesthetic complications	6
Inadequate nursing on general wards	6
Transfer from hospital without facilities	2
Other	15
Not answered	2
Total cases *(answers may be multiple)*	**125**

The anaesthetic questionnaires for the same patients revealed a total of 87 patients for whom admission to ICU/HDU was felt to be needed (whether or not it happened) compared with 91 patients reported by surgeons as needing ICU/HDU. The discrepancy is probably explained by minor differences in the wording of questions in the questionnaires rather than differences of opinion concerning clinical management of sick patients.

Table S41 (q53)
Discharge from ICU/HDU due to:

Death	79
Elective transfer to ward	38
Pressure on beds	1
Other	4
Not answered	3
Total	**125**

Table S42 (q56)
Specific postoperative complications:

Low cardiac output	84
Respiratory distress	70
Generalised sepsis	66
Renal failure	59
Cardiac arrest	51
Anastomotic failure	18
Haemorrhage/postoperative bleeding requiring transfusion	17
Stroke or other neurological problems	14
DVT and/or pulmonary embolus	13
Nutritional problems	13
Hepatic failure	11
Wound infection	10
Other organ failure	8
Persistent coma	5
Peripheral ischaemia	5
Problems with analgesia	4
Urinary tract infection	4
Upper respiratory obstruction	3
Endocrine system failure	3
Urinary retention/catheter blockage	2
Ureteric injury/fistula	2
Other	44
Total cases* *(answers may be multiple)*	**233**

* *(Excluding death in theatre - five cases)*

Postoperative complications were related more to the patients' general condition than to technical problems. However, when anastomotic leakage occurred this was often missed initially. The continuity of postoperative care is a key clinical activity. Consultants should ensure that their junior staff are adequately trained and supervised in this area. It is unfortunate that one consultant blamed his junior staff for failing to notice an anastomotic leak and the postoperative deterioration of the patient.

Figure S1 (qs 39 and 58)
Calendar days between operation and death
(i.e. not 24 hour periods)

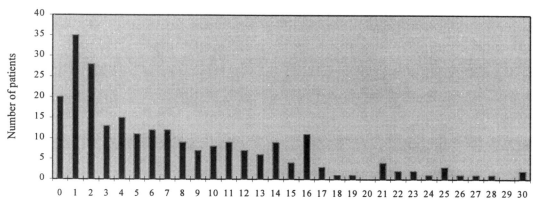

Calendar days between operation and death

Right hemicolectomy

There were 54 deaths following right hemicolectomy. This procedure is traditionally seen as an easy training operation with "friendly" anatomy and a low complication rate but it is a potentially dangerous operation.

Most of the patients in this group were elderly and none were in ASA class 1; most were admitted as urgent or emergency cases.

Table S43 (q37)
Classification of the final operation (right hemicolectomy)

Emergency	6
Urgent	29
Scheduled	17
Elective	2
Total	**54**

Twenty-two procedures were done out-of-hours (12 between 18.01 and 07.59 on weekdays, and 10 at weekends).

Table S44 (q22)
Specialty of consultant surgeon in charge at time of final operation (right hemicolectomy)

General surgery	6
General surgery with a stated interest in :	
gastroenterology	19
vascular surgery	12
endocrine/breast surgery	7
coloproctology/colorectal surgery	4
urology	4
transplantation	2
Total	**54**

Twenty-five patients were under the care of surgeons working in disciplines where there would be infrequent exposure to colorectal surgery.

Table S45 (qs 43 and 46)
Grade of most senior operating surgeon (right hemicolectomy)

		(locums)	Supervision?
Consultant	29	-	n/a
Associate specialist	2	-	-
Senior registrar	12	(2)	2
Registrar	11	(1)	4
Total	**54**		

Seven procedures were done by unsupervised registrars.

Table S46 (q56)
Postoperative complications (right hemicolectomy):

Cardiac problems	28
Respiratory problems	17
Renal failure	13
Generalised sepsis	11
Stroke or other neurological problems	8
Haemorrhage/postoperative bleeding requiring transfusion	4
Nutritional problems	4
DVT and/or pulmonary embolus	3
Problems with analgesia	3
Anastomotic failure	2
Endocrine system failure	2
Other organ failure	2
Urinary retention/catheter blockage	2
Urinary tract infection	2
Wound infection	2
Other	14
Not answered	2
Total cases* *(answers may be multiple)*	**53**

* *(Excluding death in theatre - one case)*

Where technical problems led to complications there was no difference between cases in which anastomoses were made with sutures or staples.

——————— o o o o ———————

General Surgery

The advisors in general surgery were:

Mr P Burgess	(South and West)
Mr R A Cobb	(West Midlands)
Mr P Finan	(Yorkshire)
Mr R A Kipping	(Anglia and Oxford)
Mr M Parker	(South Thames)

NCEPOD is very grateful to these advisors for their help and advice. Miss E Dykes (South Thames) assisted with the review of the paediatric cases.

Points

- There was a high level of senior involvement in the preoperative decision-making process, but collaborative care ought to have been developed further for high risk patients.
- Some patients should have been referred to more specialised surgeons, and to hospitals where ICU/HDU facilities were available.
- Many patients were in poor condition at the time of surgery as a result of their presenting disease, their age and co-existent diseases.
- Up to thirty-five percent of the operations were done out-of-hours.
- All infants under the age of six months in this sample were treated in a specialist unit.

Sample

The 1993/94 NCEPOD survey was based on questionnaires concerning the first perioperative death reported for individual consultant surgeons. Thus, no consultant surgeon received more than one questionnaire (see page 10). In general surgery, 515 cases were selected for the sample, of which 369 questionnaires from 206 hospitals, were returned and analysed. A further six questionnaires were returned but for various reasons (see page 19), not analysed. The overall return rate was therefore 73%.

Audit

Three-hundred-and-thirteen (85%) patients were considered at a local audit meeting. This is commendable and an improvement on the figure reported in previous years. Postmortem examinations were done in 141 (38%) cases. Thirty-five of these were hospital postmortems and 106 were done at a Coroner's request. A copy of the pathologist's report was received by the surgical team in 81 (76%) of the Coroners' and 31 (89%) of the hospital postmortem examinations.

List of procedures

These procedures may be multiple for any individual patient.

Table S47 (q47)
Final operation performed

Hernia surgery

Strangulated inguinal hernia repair	7
Uncomplicated unilateral inguinal hernia repair	5
Uncomplicated bilateral inguinal hernia repair	1
Recurrent inguinal hernia repair	1
Uncomplicated femoral hernia repair	1
Uncomplicated bilateral femoral hernia repair	1
Strangulated femoral hernia repair	1
Incisional hernia repair	4
Umbilical hernia repair	1
Resection of gangrenous small bowel	6
Laparoscopic repair bilateral hernias	1
Para-ileostomy hernia	1

Oesophageal surgery

Oesophagectomy (all approaches for malignant disease)	13
Endoscopic dilatation and intubation (carcinoma)	7
Diagnostic fibreoptic oesophagogastroduodenoscopy	4
Endoscopic sclerotherapy for oesophageal varices	3
Oversewing of oesophageal varices	2
Closure of oesophageal perforation	1

Gastroduodenal surgery

Closure of perforated duodenal ulcer	34
Partial gastrectomy (all causes)	17
Closure of perforated gastric ulcer	10
Palliative gastric bypass	9
Under-running of bleeding duodenal ulcer	5
Total gastrectomy (all causes)	5
Truncal vagotomy and pyloroplasty	5
Under-running of bleeding gastric ulcer	4
Repair of iatrogenic duodenal injury	3
Laparotomy and feeding gastrostomy	2
Repair hiatus hernia	1
Percutaneous gastrostomy	1

Hepatopancreaticobiliary surgery

Open cholecystectomy (includes conversion from laparoscopic procedure)	17
Bypass surgery for malignant obstructive jaundice	13
Splenectomy (all causes)	11
Laparoscopic cholecystectomy	6
Removal of abdominal packs	5
Pancreatic necrosectomy	3
Cholecystectomy and exploration of common bile duct	3
Pancreaticoduodenectomy	2
Liver transplant	2
Laparotomy for biliary fistula	2
ERCP (with/without insertion of stent)	2
Miscellaneous *(one each of: excision of pancreatic cyst, closure of duodenal fistula, insertion of peritoneo-venous fistula, hemihepatectomy for trauma)*	4

Abdominal surgery

"Open and shut" laparotomy for widespread malignancy	32
Small bowel resection (all causes)	28
Laparotomy for acute mesenteric ischaemia (with/without small bowel resection)	20
Laparotomy for adhesive obstruction (with/without small bowel resection)	17
Drainage of intra-abdominal abscess	12
Defunctioning ileostomy	9
Laparotomy for obstruction due to widespread malignancy with small bowel bypass or resection	8
Laparotomy for necrotising enterocolitis	7
Appendicectomy	5
Laparotomy for bleeding (trauma)	4
Resuture of abdominal wound dehiscence	3
Repair diaphragmatic hernia	3
Small bowel stricturoplasty	2
Right hemicolectomy	2
Refashioning of ileostomy	2
Transverse colostomy	1
Diagnostic laparoscopy	1
Feeding jejunostomy	1

Other

Drainage of soft tissue abscess	4
Tracheostomy	4
Debridement for necrotising fasciitis	3
Miscellaneous *(one each of: mastectomy, wide excision of breast lump, evacuation of mastectomy wound haematoma, insertion of chest drain, thyroid lobectomy, debridement of pressure sores, suturing of self-inflicted neck wound, renal transplant)*	8

Most of these procedures were appropriate but 36 were unwise;

- Laparotomy in the presence of advanced cancers and ascites where surgery offered no benefit.
- Complex biliary disease where intraoperative problems arose but trainees struggled on without senior help.
- Choice of an outmoded or inappropriate procedure.
- Failure to call upon specialist advice.
- Precipitous action when surgery should have been delayed until the results of preoperative investigations were available, and resuscitation completed.

If preoperative investigations are done this means that the results should be heeded and, if necessary, surgery should be delayed until the results are available. However, in true emergencies (see Glossary, Appendix B), it is necessary to control the haemodynamic state prior to the availability of the results of preoperative investigations.

Admission details

Table S48 (q12)
Admission category

Elective	81
Urgent	25
Emergency	261
Not answered	2
Total	**369**

There were a high number (286, 78%) of emergency and urgent admissions. This workload has implications for the organisation and provision of care within general surgery, because there has been a national rise in emergency admissions and this unpredictable workload tends to displace elective and scheduled work.

Table S49 (q7)
Source of referral

General Medical Practitioner	248
A&E department	48
Transfer from another hospital	40
Physicians	10
Self-referral by patient	3
Other	19
Not answered	1
Total	**369**

Of the 40 transferred patients, twenty-two needed specialist services e.g. cardiac, paediatric and hepatic surgery. Ten patients were transferred from departments caring for the elderly, two were referred from a purely "medical" hospital and two were transferred because of the lack of ICU/HDU beds. The remaining four patients were transferred for chemotherapy, for treatment of multiple injuries, for social reasons or the need for an emergency operation when no theatre was free at the referring hospital.

Table S50 (q8)
Type of referring hospital (transferred cases only)

District General hospital	19
University/teaching hospital	5
Community hospital	5
Other acute/partly acute hospital	4
Surgical specialty hospital	2
Independent hospital	1
Other	2
Overseas	1
Not answered	1
Total	**40**

Table S51 (q1)
Type of hospital in which the final operation took place

District General hospital	258
University/teaching hospital	94
Surgical specialty hospital	8
Defence Medical Services hospital	4
Independent	4
Other acute/partly acute hospital	1
Total	**369**

Table S52 (q2)
Availability of essential services

	Available in the hospital	Available 24hrs per day, 7 days per week
Theatre recovery area	367	284
Adult ICU	345	317
Adult HDU	107	89
Paediatric ICU/HDU	122	102
Emergency theatre	302	172
Total cases (*answers may be multiple*)	**369**	

Some hospitals were not providing (or were unable to provide) adequate recovery and ICU services on a 24-hour basis. The inadequate arrangements which were in place in some units were alarmingly unsuited to the type of case being admitted and treated (bearing in mind that these figures relate to patients who died after surgery). Based on the above figures, it appears that high dependency units were poorly provided in 1993-94. NCEPOD has commented on this deficiency before[5] and supports the expansion of this service as a means of offering proper and progressive care to patients who are not sufficiently ill to require the high-technology services offered by a fully equipped ICU but who are too ill to be managed on a general ward.

Patient profile

Table S53 (qs 3 and 4)
Age of patient at final operation

Years		%	Male	%	Female	%
0 to 10	*12	3.3	8	4.3	4	2.2
11 to 20	4	1.1	2	1.1	2	1.1
21 to 30	6	1.6	6	3.3	0	0.0
31 to 40	6	1.6	5	2.7	1	0.5
41 to 50	15	4.1	7	3.8	8	4.3
51 to 60	31	8.4	15	8.2	16	8.6
61 to 70	83	22.5	45	24.5	38	20.5
71 to 80	124	33.6	61	33.2	63	34.1
81 to 90	79	21.4	33	17.9	46	24.9
91 to 100	9	2.4	2	1.1	7	3.8
Total	**369**		**184**		**185**	

* All these patients were aged between three days and two months. A separate analysis of those patients who were under 10 years of age at the time of their death is given at the end of this chapter (page 121).

Table S54 (q28)
ASA Class

		%
ASA Class 1	10	2.7
ASA Class 2	88	23.8
ASA Class 3	116	31.4
ASA Class 4	114	30.9
ASA Class 5	37	10.0
Not answered	3	0.8
Not known/not recorded	1	0.3
Total	**369**	

Seventy-two percent of the patients were in ASA classes 3, 4 or 5 and there were many co-existing problems.

Table S55 (q29)
Co-existing problems at time of final operation

Cardiac	160
Respiratory	136
Gastrointestinal	84
Renal/urological	63
Sepsis	60
Haematological	45
Musculoskeletal	42
Endocrine *(including at least 13 cases of diabetes mellitus)*	39
Vascular	33
Neurological	33
Psychiatric	10
Alcohol-related problems	10
Drug addiction	1
Genetic abnormality	1
Other (see list below)	47
None	43
Not answered	7
Total cases *(answers may be multiple)*	**369**

Other:

Multiple metabolic problems *(including malnutrition, dehydration, inappropriate ADH secretion & deranged liver function)*	11
Malignancy	8
Obesity	5
Old age and frailty	4
Prematurity	3
Heavy smoker	2
Psoriasis	2
Self neglect	1
Depression and aspirin overdose	1
Cystic fibrosis	1
Immobility - wheelchair bound	1

These multiple co-existing problems illustrate the poor condition of many patients who present acutely to general surgeons. In the questionnaire surgeons were asked to assess the risk of death related to the operation. This assessment was made retrospectively, but the table below shows the awareness amongst surgeons of the risks.

Table S56 (q35)
Anticipated risk of death related to the proposed operation

Not expected	43
Small but significant risk	71
Definite risk	222
Expected	28
Not answered	5
Total	**369**

In 28 cases (listed below) the surgeon stated that death was expected following surgery. In some cases there was an outside chance of success and the surgeon felt that this chance could not be denied to the patient. On the other hand the surgery might have been inappropriate in the circumstances.

Disease process present

Mesenteric ischaemia	7
Carcinomatosis	5
Generalised peritonitis - perforation	5
Acute pancreatitis	3
Intra-abdominal abscess	2
Malignant intestinal obstruction	2
Perforated gall bladder	1
Ruptured abdominal aortic aneurysm (missed)	1
Bleeding gastric ulcer	1
Burst abdomen	1

Table S57 (q23)
Was care undertaken on a formal shared basis with another specialty (excluding anaesthesia)?

General & specialist medicine	57
Haematology	7
Intensive care staff	6
Neonatology/neonatal ICU	6
Another colleague in general surgery	5
Orthopaedic surgery	5
Cardiothoracic surgery	3
Geriatrics	3
Radiology	3
Urology	2
Gynaecology	2
ENT surgery	2
Radiotherapy	2
Paediatric medicine	1
Neurosurgery	1
Not specified	2
Total cases (answers may be multiple)	**97**

High risk patients with multiple pathologies need collaborative care. The table above shows that such collaboration did take place in the management of 97 (26%) patients. Given the influence of co-existing diseases on the likelihood of the successful outcome after surgery, collaborative care is an area of preoperative management which could be developed further for the benefit of the patients.

The surgical team

Table S58 (q22)
Specialty of consultant surgeon in charge at time of final operation

General surgery	74
General surgery with a stated special interest	271
Paediatric surgery	11
Transplantation	5
Urology	4
Thoracic surgery	2
Breast surgery	1
Not answered	1
Total	**369**

General surgeons, with or without a professed special interest, operated on 97% of the 357 patients over the age of 10 years. None of the specialties were inappropriate.

Table S59 (qs 24 and 34)
The most senior surgeon involved in decision-making prior to surgery

		(locums)
Consultant	325	(12)
Associate specialist	3	-
Senior registrar	22	-
Registrar	19	-
Total	**369**	

Senior surgeons were involved in the preoperative decision-making process in 95% of cases.

Table S60 (qs 43 and 46)
Grade of most senior operating surgeon and the availability of help

		(locums)	Supervision?
Consultant	191	(14)	n/a
Associate specialist	9	-	3
Senior registrar	68	(3)	15
Registrar	86	(8)	21
Staff grade	4	-	1
Senior house officer	7	-	5
Not answered	4	-	-
Total	**369**		

Senior surgeons operated on 73% of the patients. It is disappointing that more senior help was not immediately available to registrars for 65 of the procedures.

There were seven operations done by senior house officers. Five were supervised: there were two procedures for drainage of an abscess, two for closure of a perforated duodenal ulcer and one for debridement of pressure sores. There were only two operations done by unsupervised senior house officers. Basic surgical trainees should not operate unsupervised or without the knowledge of the responsible consultant or a senior surgeon. It is the responsibility of the trainee to seek advice and/or help from a senior colleague.

Preparation for surgery

Table S61 (q30)
Preoperative precautions or therapeutic manoeuvres to improve the patient's preoperative condition

Intravenous fluids	298
Antibiotics (pre- or intra-operative)	266
Correction of hypovolaemia	221
Urinary catheterisation	214
Gastric aspiration	199
Oxygen therapy	138
Blood transfusion	79
Chest physiotherapy	73
Cardiac support drugs or anti-arrhythmic agents	65
Diuretics	45
Anticoagulants	43
Tracheal intubation	42
Mechanical ventilation	42
Nutritional support	39
Vitamin K	31
Airway protection (e.g. in unconscious patients)	18
Bowel preparation	9
Others	45
None	16
Not answered	2
Total cases (answers may be multiple)	**369**

This table shows the various means used to prepare patients for their operations. The impression given is that most patients were well prepared for surgery.

Table S62 (q31)
Prophylaxis against venous thromboembolism

	Before/during	After
None	90	151
Leg stockings	181	154
Heparin	171	154
Heel support	62	12
Calf compression	52	7
Ripple mattress	15	12
Warfarin	5	1
Electrical stimulation of calves	3	1
Dextran infusion	2	-
Other	2	1
Total cases (answers may be multiple):	**369**	**360***

* (Excluding death in theatre - nine cases)

A third (123/369) of all patients who died received prophylaxis in the form of heparin both before and after surgery; slightly fewer patients (117/369) had graduated compression stockings. Seventy-eight patients were not offered prophylaxis throughout.

Thirteen pulmonary emboli were recorded as postoperative complications (table S65), but a total of 18 were confirmed at postmortem examination, half of whom had received heparin.

Time of surgery

Table S62 (q37)
Classification of the final operation

Emergency	107	70%
Urgent	150	
Scheduled	88	
Elective	22	
Not answered	2	
Total	**369**	

Table S63 (q40)
Day of operation

Monday	62
Tuesday	54
Wednesday	67
Thursday	73
Friday	59
Saturday	24
Sunday	30
Total	**369**

At least 81 (26%) of the weekday operations were performed out of hours (we have no information on the time of surgery for a further 28 patients who had surgery during the week). Thus it is possible that the weekday "out-of-hours" operating was as high as 35% (109/315). Were all these cases emergencies as defined by NCEPOD (see Glossary, Appendix B). If so, "out-of-hours" operating could be reduced by the proper use of emergency theatres.

Unanticipated intra-operative problems

Problems arose in seven operations performed by trainees. Most of these patients were high risk; surgery was difficult and prolonged. The trainees should have summoned help when difficulties were recognised.

Unsupervised senior registrars also encountered problems in eight instances. In a further 54 cases consultants were operating. None of these problems were associated with inappropriate surgery.

Use of local anaesthesia and/or sedation

Nine patients died after a procedure which was done solely under local anaesthesia or sedation administered by the surgeon. Three of these were *diagnostic* upper gastrointestinal endoscopies in patients who had presented with advanced malignancy; the deaths were not related to the procedures.

There were, in addition, four *therapeutic* endoscopies. In one patient there was an unsuccessful attempt to dilate a recurrent tumour at an oesophagogastric anastomosis. In the second case there was failure to stent a malignant bile duct stricture during an ERCP in a jaundiced patient. The third death followed a fibreoptic oesophagogastroscopy and successful injection sclerotherapy of oesophageal varices (death was due to deteriorating liver function). The fourth death occurred three weeks after the insertion of a PEG feeding gastrostomy in an elderly patient who was unable to swallow due to a cerebrovascular accident; death was a result of an extension of her stroke. The risks and dangers associated with endoscopic procedures should not be underestimated.[19]

One death occurred after the insertion of a chest drain for a malignant pleural effusion, and another after the percutaneous drainage of an abdominal abscess in an elderly woman with advanced breast cancer.

In none of these patients was the death related to the administration of local anaesthesia or sedation.

Table S64 (q51)
Was the patient admitted immediately to an ICU or HDU postoperatively?

ICU	148
HDU	21
Neither of the above	187
Not answered	4
Total*	**360**

* (Excluding death in theatre - nine cases)

There were 11 instances when the surgeon was unable to admit a patient into an ICU/HDU within the hospital in which surgery took place. The reasons given were:

No ICU/HDU available	5
No bed available	2
No explanation given	2
ICU at another site of split-site hospital	1
Inadequate staffing	1

Table S65 (q56)
Specific postoperative complications:

Complication	
Respiratory distress	130
Low cardiac output	118
Generalised sepsis	91
Renal failure	86
Cardiac arrest	80
Hepatic failure	31
Haemorrhage/postoperative bleeding requiring transfusion	31
Nutritional problems	20
Other organ failure	16
Anastomotic failure mn	16
Persistent coma	14
DVT and/or pulmonary embolus	13
Stroke or other neurological problems	13
Wound infection	9
Endocrine system failure	6
Peripheral ischaemia	4
Wound dehiscence	4
Problems with analgesia	4
Upper respiratory obstruction	3
Urinary tract infection	3
Urinary retention/catheter blockage	3
Pressure sores	1
Other	60
Not answered	33
Total cases* (answers may be multiple)	**360**

* (Excluding death in theatre - nine cases)

Figure S2
Calendar days between operation and death
(i.e. not 24 hour periods)

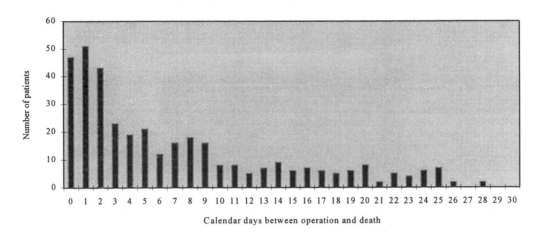

Calendar days between operation and death

Deaths of children

There were 12 deaths of children under 10 years of age. All of these children were aged between three days and two months. These children were reviewed separately by a paediatric surgeon.

The final procedures were as follows:

Procedure (indication)		Cause of death
Surgery for enterocolitis	8	Multi-organ failure
Repair right diaphragmatic hernia and insertion of peritoneal dialysis catheter	1	Haemorrhage
Revision of ileostomy (cystic fibrosis)	1	Coagulopathy
Repair congenital diaphragmatic hernia	1	Pulmonary hypoplasia
Laparotomy, gastrostomy, repair of duodenum (pyloric stenosis, missed perforation of duodenum)	1	Septicaemia, multiorgan failure

The conditions and procedures listed above demonstrate the serious condition of these young patients and the challenge they present to anaesthetists and surgeons.

All these children were emergency admissions and were gravely ill. Two were ASA Class 3, seven were ASA Class 4 and three were classed as ASA 5. They were all transferred from other hospitals and operated on in university/teaching hospitals (8) or specialist paediatric surgical units (4). All these units had theatre recovery areas and in nine out of 12 instances these were available 24 hours per day, 7 days per week. Paediatric ICU/HDU facilities were good and adequately staffed. Eleven children were nursed in ICU/HDU postoperatively (one child died in theatre).

Without exception the children were cared for by surgeons with a special interest in paediatric surgery and there was 100% involvement of consultants in decision-making. Similarly, senior surgeons operated; 10 consultants and two senior registrars (both of whom were immediately supervised by consultants).

Postmortem examinations were done on 7/12 of these children and all cases were considered at local audit meetings. These children received a good quality of care.

Gynaecology

The advisors in gynaecology were:

Mr P M Coats   (South Thames)
Mr M J Emens   (West Midlands)
Mr G J Jarvis   (Northern and Yorkshire)
Mr P A R Niven   (South and West)
Dr J H Price   (Northern Ireland)

NCEPOD is very grateful to these advisors for their help and advice.

Points

- The decision to perform surgery in patients with obvious gynaecological malignancy should be made on an individual patient basis, ideally by a gynaecological oncologist.
- The level of audit and the number of postmortem examinations need to be increased.
- The efficacy of prophylaxis against venous thrombosis and infection needs to be evaluated.

Sample

The 1993/94 NCEPOD survey was based on questionnaires concerning the first perioperative death reported for individual consultant surgeons. Thus no consultant gynaecologist received more than one questionnaire (see page 10). In gynaecology, 138 cases were selected for the sample, of which 119 questionnaires from 99 hospitals were returned and analysed. A further three questionnaires were returned but for various reasons (see page 19), not analysed. The overall return rate was therefore **88%**.

Audit

Forty-two (35%) of the deaths were considered at a local audit meeting. This low percentage probably reflects the high proportion of patients with advanced malignant disease in whom perioperative death was regarded as inevitable. But audit would help address the question of whether or not it was justifiable to subject such patients to surgery.

Postmortem examinations were done in 31 (26%) instances of which 27 were Coroners' postmortem examinations. These can also be used for retrospective audit.

Local audit systems do not mirror the apparent enthusiasm for audit which obstetricians and gynaecologists have demonstrated for many years by their ready participation in the Confidential Enquiry into Maternal Deaths.

List of procedures

Table S66 (q47)
Final operation performed

For benign disease:

Total abdominal hysterectomy	6
Repair pelvic floor/prolapse	5
Bilateral or unilateral salpingo-oophorectomy	4
Anterior/posterior repair	3
Dilatation and curettage/EUA	2
Vaginal hysterectomy	2
Laparotomy with/without biopsy	1
Sterilisation	1
Trans-cervical resection of endometrium	1
Miscellaneous	4
Total cases *(answers may be multiple)*	**20**

For malignant disease:

Laparotomy with/without biopsy	39
Total abdominal hysterectomy and bilateral salpingo-oophorectomy	18
Debulking carcinoma	17
Bilateral or unilateral salpingo-oophorectomy	8
Removal/incision of ovaries	7
Omentectomy	3
Laparoscopy	2
Sub-total abdominal hysterectomy	2
Radical vulvectomy	1
Miscellaneous	30
Total cases *(answers may be multiple)*	**99**

Total cases *(benign and malignant)*	**119**

Type of hospital and services

Table S67 (q1)
Type of hospital in which the final operation took place

District General hospital	96
University/teaching hospital	19
Surgical specialty hospital	1
Other acute/partly acute hospital	1
Independent hospital	1
Other	1
Total	**119**

Table S68 (q2)
Availability of services

	Available in the hospital	Available 24 hrs per day, 7 days per week
Theatre recovery area	119	92
Adult ICU	97	87
Adult HDU	43	31
Emergency theatre	96	74
Total cases (answers may be multiple)	**119**	

Age of patients at final operation

The age of patients at final operation is shown in table S69 and it can be seen that ten of the 22 patients without pelvic malignancy were aged less than 70 years. Table S70 lists the final operation, the cause of death and the possible avoidable factors in this small group of patients with no pelvic malignancy.

Table S69 (qs 3 and 4)
Age of patient at final operation

Years	No pelvic malignancy	Pelvic malignancy	Total
31 to 40	2	1	3
41 to 50	6	3	9
51 to 60	-	8	8
61 to 70	2	22	24
71 to 80	6	37	43
81 to 90	6	25	31
91 to 100	-	1	1
Total	**22**	**97**	**119**

Table S70

Final operations and cause of death in ten patients under the age of 70 who did not have pelvic malignancy

Age	Operation and indication	Cause of death	Questions
37	Laparoscopic Filshie clip sterilisation by experienced locum associate specialist in a woman with previous history of two caesarean sections, myomectomy and right ovarian cystectomy.	Collapsed day after operation. Faecal peritonitis due to bowel perforation.	Did the operator fully appreciate the dangers of laparoscopy and clip sterilisation in someone with distortion of pelvic anatomy from adhesions after four previous pelvic surgical procedures?
40	Removal of vulval warts.	SLE. On dialysis. Immunosuppressed. Death from septicaemia.	Was this an appropriate operation?
44*	Hysterectomy, bilateral salpingo-oophorectomy. Colposuspension. Oestrogen implant.	Massive pulmonary embolism within 48 hours of operation (confirmed at postmortem examination). Preoperative heparin given.	Were there any risk factors from venous thromboembolism for this patient? (The information available to NCEPOD is limited).
45	Hysterectomy for menorrhagia.	Respiratory arrest on arrival in recovery room	Was the significance of a previous history of slow recovery from anaesthesia appreciated?
45*	Hysterectomy, bilateral salpingo-oophorectomy for menorrhagia and endometriosis.	Obese patient. Discharged at six days. Readmitted with pulmonary embolism. Died 18 days after surgery. DVT prophylaxis including heparin given for first six postoperative days.	
45	Transcervical resection of endometrium.	Haemorrhage into unsuspected intracranial tumour (oligodendroglioma). Preoperative heparin given.	Did DVT prophylaxis precipitate the intracranial haemorrhage?
50	EUA. Hysteroscopy. D&C for menorrhagia.	SLE. On anticoagulants. Died of mesenteric thrombosis one month after operation.	
52*	Total abdominal hysterectomy. Bilateral salpingo-oophorectomy. Omentectomy and removal of para-aortic nodes for what turned out to be a benign serous cystadenoma.	Patient had sickle cell trait. Pulmonary embolism on day of operation despite heparin prophylaxis.	Were there any risk factors from venous thromboembolism for this patient? (The information available to NCEPOD is limited).
65	D&C and polypectomy and intravenous sedation.	Myocardial infarct while leaving hospital two days after operation.	
66†	D&C for postmenopausal bleeding.	Obese cirrhotic. Respiratory failure in recovery area. Reintubated. Died next day.	Were the SHO surgeon and the anaesthetist sufficiently experienced to cope with a patient who had serious medical problems?

† Not reported to Coroner
* It should be noted that this table lists three patients who died of pulmonary embolism despite the use of heparin prophylaxis

Referral and admission details

The next four tables deal with the source of referral and provide information about admission.

Table S71 (q7)
Source of referral

General Medical Practitioner	85
Transfer from another hospital	9
A&E department	5
Self referral by patient	2
Other*	18
Total	**119**

* The "other" sources included outpatients, physicians, surgeons in other specialties, and miscellaneous sources.

Table S72 (q8)
Type of referring hospital (transferred cases only)

District General hospital	4
University/teaching hospital	4
Other acute/partly acute hospital	1
Total	**9**

Table S73 (q12)
Admission category

Elective	57
Urgent	25
Emergency	37
Total	**119**

The high number of elective admissions suggests that time is available for full preoperative assessment and preparation of gynaecological patients.

Table S74 (q13)
Type of area to which patient first admitted

Gynaecological/obstetric ward	79
Surgical ward	19
Medical ward	11
Geriatric ward	6
Mixed medical/surgical ward	1
A&E holding area *(or other emergency admission ward)*	1
Day unit	1
Other	1
Total	**119**

There was no evidence among the records studied of significant delays in admitting patients or transferring them from another specialty into a gynaecological ward.

There was delay between admission and surgery due to non-clinical factors on four occasions. A lack of operating time applied to three cases and one patient chose to delay surgery.

Grade and specialty of operating surgeon

The next table gives the grade of the most senior operating surgeon and shows that this was the consultant in 99 (83%) cases. This reflects excellent practice.

Table S75 (qs 43 and 46)
Grade of most senior operating surgeon

		(locums)	Supervision?
Consultant	99	(7)	-
Associate specialist	4	(1)	1
Senior registrar	5	(1)	1
Registrar	5	(1)	4
Staff grade	3	-	1
Senior house officer	1	-	1
Other	1	-	1
Not answered	1	-	-
Total	**119**	**(10)**	

The occasions on which consultant gynaecological input was lacking were rare, but an example is given below.

> A senior registrar operated on an 86-year-old woman with a poorly differentiated adenocarcinoma of the ovary. During pelvic clearance the left internal iliac vein was damaged and massive intraoperative haemorrhage occurred and a consultant vascular surgeon was called in. There was a forty-minute wait for blood to be cross-matched and the patient ultimately had a 24-unit transfusion. The haemorrhage was controlled with packs which were removed without incident 48 hours later. The patient, in fact, died from carcinomatosis four weeks after surgery.

The question arises as to whether or not this haemorrhage would have occurred had the gynaecologist been more experienced, or if supervision had been available.

The involvement of a gynaecologist with an interest in oncology is desirable for the surgery of genital tract malignancy. Patients with advanced pelvic malignancy often present considerable technical surgical problems. Gynaecologists with special experience of these problems might produce better outcomes. If there is no one with such an interest amongst the gynaecological staff for a given hospital, the gynaecologists should consider whether it might be in a patient's interest to transfer them to the care of another unit.

A 68-year-old woman was operated on by a consultant for a large and advanced ovarian carcinoma involving the bowel. Attempts to remove the tumour failed and both the large and small bowel were damaged during surgery and repaired. The patient died four days later, the cause of death being given as carcinomatosis.

This case underlines the need for additional experience in bowel surgery for gynaecologists operating on patients with pelvic malignancy; a knowledge of gastrointestinal surgical techniques is also invaluable. Failing this, a gastrointestinal surgeon should be involved in the care of the patient.[20]

Anticipated risk of death

The need for applying strict criteria to the selection of cases for surgery is to some extent also shown by the table below. It can be seen that in as many as 64/119 (54%) cases perioperative death was either "not expected" or considered to be a "small, but significant risk".

Table S76 (q35)
Anticipated risk of death related to the proposed operation

Not expected	31
Small but significant risk	33
Definite risk	51
Expected	4
Total	**119**

Classification of final operation and day of operation

Only 13/119 operations in the sample were "urgent" or "emergency" procedures. This suggests that major gynaecological surgery allows ample time for careful preoperative evaluation and preparation.

Table S77 (q37)
Classification of the final operation

Emergency	4
Urgent	9
Scheduled	87
Elective	19
Total	**119**

Only 3/119 procedures were undertaken at a weekend (see table S78) and only four were undertaken "out-of-hours" on a weekday (defined as between 18.01 and 07.59).

Table S78 (q40)
Day of operation

Monday	31
Tuesday	20
Wednesday	22
Thursday	24
Friday	19
Saturday	2
Sunday	1
Total	**119**

Involvement of other specialties

The extent of involvement by specialties from other disciplines is shown in table S79.

Table S79 (q23)
Other specialties sharing care of patient

Medical (oncology), physician	9
General surgery	7
Radiotherapy	6
Geriatrics	2
Palliative medicine	2
Urology	1
Nephrology	1
Neurology	1
Other	2
Total cases *(answers may be multiple)*	**29**

Co-existing problems at the time of the final operation

Table S80 (q29)
Co-existing problems at the time of the final operation

Cardiac	29
Respiratory	27
Renal	17
Gastrointestinal	17
Vascular	14
Haematological	12
Endocrine *(including diabetes mellitus)*	9
Neurological	6
Musculoskeletal	6
Psychiatric	4
Sepsis	3
Alcohol-related problems	1
Drug addiction	1
None	21
Other	22
Not answered	4
Total cases *(answers may be multiple)*	**119**

The table above highlights the need for a multidisciplinary approach to patients who have pelvic malignancy and coexisting problems.

Preoperative preparation

The following table shows the measures taken to improve the patient's preoperative condition and again suggests that a multidisciplinary approach is desirable.

Table S81 (q30)
Preoperative precautions or therapeutic manoeuvres to improve the patient's preoperative condition

None	22
Antibiotics (pre- or intra-operative)	46
Intravenous fluids	39
Urinary catheterisation	28
Anticoagulants	22
Blood transfusion	16
Cardiac support drugs or anti-arrhythmic agents	15
Bowel preparation	14
Chest physiotherapy	13
Diuretics	10
Nutritional support	8
Correction of hypovolaemia	6
Gastric aspiration	4
Oxygen therapy	4
Vitamin K	3
Mechanical ventilation	3
Tracheal intubation	2
Others	23
Not answered	5
Total cases *(answers may be multiple)*	**119**

DVT prophylaxis

DVT prophylaxis is not as widely used in gynaecological surgery as in general surgery or orthopaedic surgery. The practice in this sample is shown below.

Table S82 (q31)
DVT prophylaxis

	Before/during	After
None	20	39
Leg stockings	71	53
Heparin	55	41
Heel support	28	9
Calf compression	26	3
Ripple mattress	9	11
Warfarin	1	2
Electrical stimulation of calves	-	1
Dextran infusion	1	1
Other	1	1
Not answered	1	1
Total cases *(answers may be multiple)*	**119**	***117**

* *(Excluding death in theatre - two cases)*

Of the 119 patients in this sample a total of only 57 (48%) were given heparin. This percentage seems rather low, given the high incidence of malignancy and also the high incidence of the elderly patients in this group. The 1991/92 and 1992/93 NCEPOD Reports,[4, 5] highlighted the inadequate use of thromboprophylaxis. In March 1995, the Royal College of Gynaecologists (RCOG) produced guidelines about thromboprophylaxis.[21] The years covered by this NCEPOD report precede those guidelines, but our findings perhaps underline the importance of their implementation. The RCOG report recommends that patients assessed as "high risk" for venous thrombosis should receive subcutaneous heparin and suggests that leg stockings would also be beneficial.

Use of ICU/HDU

Only 18/117 patients who left theatre were admitted to an intensive care unit or higher dependency unit. Two patients died on the table.

Of the 99 patients who returned to the ward after surgery, seven were described as having been subsequently admitted to ICU/HDU making an overall total of 25 admissions to ICU/HDU after gynaecological surgery. The indications for these 25 admissions are shown in table S82.

Table S83 (q52)
Admission to ICU or HDU

Specialist nursing	10
General monitoring	10
Presence of experienced intensivists	8
Routine for this surgical procedure	5
Ventilation	5
Anaesthetic complications	4
Co-incident medical diseases	4
Metabolic monitoring	3
Surgical complications	3
Inadequate nursing on general wards	1
Transfer from hospital without facilities	1
Other	4
Not answered	1
Total cases *(answers may be multiple)*	**25**

The outcome for patients admitted to ICU/HDU is shown in the following table.

Table S84 (q53)
Discharge from ICU/HDU due to:

Death	17
Elective transfer to ward	7
Other	1
Total	**25**

There were four patients who were not admitted to an ICU/HDU although their condition warranted this. The reasons given in three cases were as follows: no ICU/HDU available in the hospital, no ICU/HDU bed available at the time, and ICU on another site of a split-site hospital. No reason was given in the fourth case.

Table S85 (q56)
Specific postoperative complications:

Cardiac problems	36
Respiratory problems	31
Renal failure	22
Haemorrhage/postoperative bleeding requiring transfusion	9
Generalised sepsis	9
Nutritional problems	9
DVT and/or pulmonary embolus	8
Stroke or other neurological problems	8
Wound infection	7
Other organ failure	5
Persistent coma	4
Urinary tract infection	4
Problems with analgesia	2
Endocrine system failure	2
Miscellaneous *(one each of : wound dehiscence, anastomotic failure, hepatic failure, peripheral ischaemia)*	4
Other	27
Not answered	14
Total cases* *(answers may be multiple)*	**117**

* (Excluding death in theatre - two cases)

Timing and date of perioperative death

The timing is shown in the following table. The number of deaths within the period are shown in the left-hand column of figures and the cumulative totals in the right-hand column.

Table S86 (qs 39 and 58)
Calendar days between operation and death
(i.e. not 24 hour periods)

	Number	Cumulative totals
Same day	10	
Next day	14	24
2 days	10	34
3 days	9	43
4 days	6	49
5 days	9	58
6 to 10 days	27	85
11 to 15 days	11	96
16 to 20 days	10	106
21 to 30 days	13	119
Total	**119**	

The two bar charts which follow illustrate these data.

Figure S3
Calendar days from operation to death
(i.e. not 24 hour periods)

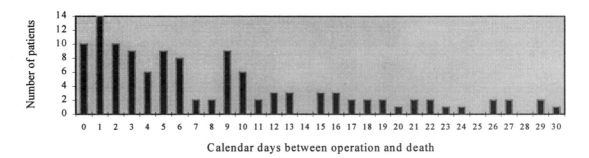

Figure S4
Calendar days from operation to death (cumulative)
(i.e. not 24 hour periods)

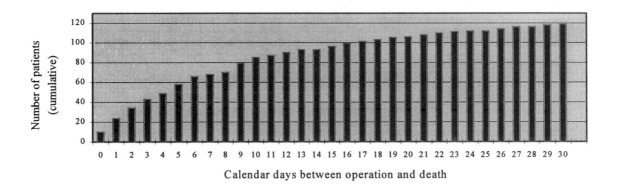

Table S87 (q60)
Place of death

Theatre	2
Recovery room	2
Ward	96
ICU/HDU	17
Home	1
Other	1
Total	**119**

——————— o o o o ———————

Neurosurgery

The advisors in neurosurgery were:

Professor H Coakham   (South and West)
Mr J Vafidis   (Wales)
Mr P Walter   (South Thames)

NCEPOD is very grateful to these advisors for their help and advice.

Point

- Neurosurgeons had the lowest response rate to questionnaires.

Sample

The 1993/94 NCEPOD survey was based on questionnaires concerning the first perioperative death reported for individual consultant surgeons. Thus no consultant surgeon received more than one questionnaire (see page 10). In neurosurgery, 102 cases were selected for the sample, of which 60 questionnaires from 30 hospitals were returned and analysed. A further two questionnaires were returned, but for various reasons (see page 19), were not included in the analysis. The overall return rate was therefore 61%.

Audit

Forty-five (75%) patients were considered at a local audit meeting. The postmortem examination rate was 38/60 (63.3%). In relation to the communication of pathological data, 6/9 hospital postmortem reports were discussed with the surgical team and 20/29 Coroners' postmortem reports were sent to the surgical teams.

List of procedures

Table S88
Final operation performed

Excision of lesion of tissue of brain	15
Exploratory open craniotomy	13
Evacuation of subdural haematoma	9
Reopening of cranium and re-exploration of intracranial operation site	9
Clipping of aneurysm of cerebral artery	6
Creation of ventriculoperitoneal shunt	4
Primary posterior decompression of lumbar spinal cord and fusion of joint of lumbar spine	4
Other specified operation on ventricle of brain	3
Primary decompression operations on cervical spine	2
Miscellaneous	11
Total cases *(answers may be multiple)*	**60**

The total number of procedures is not the same as the total number of cases; two or more procedures may be performed at the same operation.

There were two cases in which the operation was carried out by an inappropriate grade of surgeon.

> A 65-year-old woman was admitted to a university/teaching hospital, with a right fronto-temporal meningioma. She underwent a right frontal temporal craniotomy and excision of the meningioma, done by a registrar. Her condition slowly deteriorated postoperatively and CT scanning confirmed large extra- and subdural haematomas with considerable bleeding in the area of the excised meningioma. The registrar undertook further surgery to evacuate the haematomas but the patient never recovered and she died from cerebral oedema and ischaemia.

Would it have been more appropriate for a consultant to have been available for both operations?

> A 19-year-old woman was seen after an accident. She had a Glasgow Coma Score of 3 with dilated non-reacting pupils. CT scan confirmed a right subdural haematoma and a general surgeon in a DGH undertook a burr hole evacuation of the subdural haematoma. The patient was pronounced brain stem dead twelve hours later.

It was inappropriate for a general surgeon to attempt a burr hole and the evacuation of the haematoma; urgent and rapid transfer to a neurosurgical unit should have been undertaken. However, a transfer which is badly managed may be a guarantee of permanent disability or death.[5]

Whilst the overall standard of neurosurgery was very high, there were instances when inappropriate operations were carried out.

> An 86-year-old woman was admitted to a DGH having sustained an acute left cerebellar infarction. The patient, on transfer to the neurosurgical unit, had become comatose and was graded ASA 5 on admission. She was subjected to a posterior fossa craniectomy and decompression of cerebellum in an operation carried out by a registrar who had been in the grade for six months. The patient died 12 hours later from massive vertebrobasilar infarction.

It was totally inappropriate to subject an 86-year-old patient rated ASA5 on admission, to a major operation.

A 34-year-old woman was admitted to a university/teaching hospital with a known diagnosis of malignant astrocytoma. She had a craniotomy with incomplete excision of her lesion. She developed hydrocephalus and had a ventriculo-peritoneal shunt inserted. She subsequently developed massive gastrointestinal bleeding probably due to steroid medication, and died three days later.

The ventriculo-peritoneal shunt at this stage was not an appropriate operation.

A 58-year-old man was admitted to a university/teaching hospital with a high grade bi-frontal astrocytoma. He was graded ASA 4 and underwent a debulking procedure in an operation lasting three hours. The patient died six days later, as a result of the effects of his tumour.

What was the expected benefit from the debulking procedure?

Patient profile

Table S89 (qs 3 and 4)
Age of patient at final operation

Years	Total	Male	Female
0 to 10	1	1	-
11 to 20	2	-	2
21 to 30	2	-	2
31 to 40	12	4	8
41 to 50	8	6	2
51 to 60	12	10	2
61 to 70	12	7	5
71 to 80	9	7	2
81 to 90	2	-	2
Total	**60**	**35**	**25**

Table S90 (q29)
Co-existing problems (other than main diagnosis) at the time of the final operation

None	17
Respiratory	17
Cardiac	8
Haematological	7
Alcohol-related problems	5
Vascular	5
Renal	2
Gastrointestinal	3
Musculoskeletal	3
Endocrine *(including diabetes mellitus)*	2
Other	2
Sepsis	1
Psychiatric	1
Drug addiction	1
Genetic abnormality	1
Not answered	4
Not known/not recorded	2
Total cases *(answers may be multiple)*	**60**

Table S91 (q28)
ASA Class

ASA Class 1	6
ASA Class 2	11
ASA Class 3	9
ASA Class 4	18
ASA Class 5	15
Not answered	1
Total	**60**

Table S92 (q35)
Anticipated risk of death related to the proposed operation

Not expected	14
Small but significant risk	16
Definite risk	17
Expected	10
Not answered	3
Total	**60**

There was some relationship between the ASA Class and anticipated risk of death; neither appeared to match up with the Glasgow Coma Score where this was mentioned.

> A 26-year-old woman was admitted to a university/teaching hospital with a diagnosis of meningitis. In spite of treatment with antibiotics she became increasingly unresponsive and unconscious, and was transferred to a neurosurgical unit for a CT scan. She was noted to have marked cerebral swelling and was graded ASA 2. The Glasgow Coma Score at this stage was 3 and she was clearly *in extremis*.

> A 56-year-old man was admitted to a university/teaching hospital and found to have a large right parietal grade 3 malignant astrocytoma. The diagnosis was made by burr hole biopsy and he was graded ASA 1 in spite of significant frontal temporal headaches, intellectual deterioration, facial palsies and visual disturbances.

Admission details

Table S93
Admission category

Elective	11
Urgent	10
Emergency	39
Total	**60**

Table S94 (q1)
Type of hospital in which the final operation took place

University/teaching hospital	28
Surgical specialty hospital	18
District General hospital	12
Other acute/partly acute hospital	1
Independent hospital	1
Total	**60**

On occasion, transfer to a neurosurgical unit was delayed.

> A 51-year-old woman was admitted to a DGH following an acute traumatic subdural haematoma. She was detained for five hours before transfer and her ASA grading was 5 on arrival on the neurosurgical unit. A craniotomy was performed, but the patient did not recover.

Would more speedy transfer have resulted in a better outcome?

> A 70-year-old man was admitted to a neurological unit in a DGH in an unconscious state. A CT scan showed an intracerebral right parietal haemorrhage. A neurosurgical opinion was sought two days later, when temporal burr holes were undertaken with aspiration of the haematoma. The patient died 48 hours later following respiratory arrest.

Would a more rapid diagnosis and referral have resulted in a different outcome?

The surgical team

Apart from one case, the patients were looked after by a neurosurgeon at the time of the final operation.

Table S95 (qs 43 and 46)
Grade of most senior operating surgeon

		(locums)	Supervision?
Consultant	25	1	n/a
Associate specialist	1	1	-
Senior registrar	9	-	1
Registrar	25	-	3
Total	**60**		

Preparation for surgery

Table S96 (q30)
Preoperative precautions or therapeutic manoeuvres to improve the patient's preoperative condition

None	6
Intravenous fluids	41
Oxygen therapy	26
Urinary catheterisation	25
Antibiotics (pre- or intra-operative)	24
Mechanical ventilation	21
Tracheal intubation	19
Airway protection *(e.g. in unconscious patients)*	16
Chest physiotherapy	13
Correction of hypovolaemia	11
Gastric aspiration	10
Diuretics	7
Blood transfusion	6
Anticoagulants	3
Vitamin K	2
Cardiac support drugs or anti-arrhythmic agents	2
Nutritional support	1
Others	12
Not answered	1
Total cases *(answers may be multiple)*	**60**

Table S97 (q31)
DVT prophylaxis

	Before/during	After
None	31	35
Leg stockings	22	21
Heel support	9	1
Calf compression	7	3
Ripple mattress	5	1
Electrical stimulation of calves	2	1
Heparin	3	3
Warfarin	-	1
Dextran infusion	-	1
Total cases *(answers may be multiple)*	**60**	

The low use of chemical prophylaxis for venous thromboembolism in neurosurgery is related to a fear of significant intracranial haemorrhage. There were two cases where anticoagulants produced intracranial bleeding for which surgery was required.

Time of surgery

Table S98 (q37)
Classification of the final operation

Emergency	30
Urgent	12
Scheduled	14
Elective	4
Total	**60**

Table S99 (q40)
Day of operation

Monday	15
Tuesday	7
Wednesday	11
Thursday	6
Friday	11
Saturday	2
Sunday	8
Total	**60**

Seventy percent of the operations were classified as emergency or urgent. It is not surprising therefore that sixteen of the weekday operations were performed out of hours and that 10 were performed at the weekend.

Unanticipated intraoperative problems were encountered in nine cases. In six cases the problems related to excessive bleeding and aneurysm rupture. In two cases there was an abnormally difficult dissection and in one case respiratory problems caused difficulties.

Complications

Table S100 (q56)
Specific postoperative complications:

Persistent coma	25
Stroke or other neurological problems	16
Respiratory distress	12
Low cardiac output	4
Other organ failure	4
Cardiac arrest	4
Haemorrhage/postoperative bleeding requiring transfusion	3
DVT and/or pulmonary embolus	2
Upper respiratory obstruction	1
Generalised sepsis	1
Renal failure	1
Urinary tract infection	1
Nutritional problems	1
Other	14
Not answered	7
Total cases *(answers may be multiple)*	**60**

The majority of postoperative complications related to persistent coma and/or other neurological problems. Fifty-three patients were admitted to ICU or HDU immediately postoperatively.

Figure S5
Calendar days between operation and death
(i.e. not 24 hour periods)

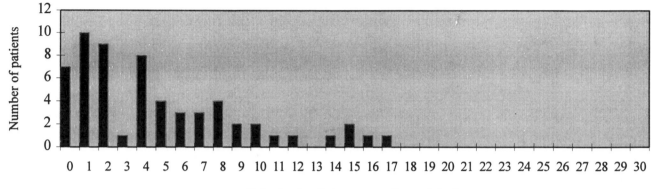

Calendar days between operation and death

_____ o o o o _____

Ophthalmic Surgery

The advisors in ophthalmic surgery were:

Mr S Harding	(North West)
Miss B Harney	(South and West)
Mr N Hawksworth	(Wales)

NCEPOD is very grateful to these advisors for their help and advice.

Point

- Rates of clinical audit and postmortem examination were too low in this specialty, and need to increase.

Sample

The 1993/94 NCEPOD survey was based on questionnaires concerning the first perioperative death reported for individual consultant surgeons (see page 10). In ophthalmic surgery 38 cases were selected for the sample, of which 25 questionnaires from 22 hospitals were returned and analysed. One further questionnaire was returned but not analysed (see page 19). The overall return rate was therefore 68%.

Audit

Table S101 (q74)
Death considered at a local audit meeting

Yes	6
No	18
Not answered	1
Total	**25**

Postmortem examinations were carried out in seven (28%) of the patients. Postmortem reports were received by the surgical teams involved in all of these cases.

List of procedures

Table S102 (q47)
Final operation performed

Cataract extraction and intraocular lens implant	12
Emulsification of cataract and lens implantation	3
Trabeculectomy	3
Cataract extraction	1
Secondary lens implantation	1
Iridectomy	1
Enucleation	1
Evisceration of eye	1
Dacrocystorhinostomy	1
Corneal graft	1
Retinal cryotherapy	1
Total cases *(answers may be multiple)*	**25**

Seventeen of the procedures were performed in District General Hospitals, five in teaching and three in specialty hospitals. All of the hospitals had an intensive care unit, and thirteen had a high dependency unit. One patient was transferred from a DGH for specialist care in a teaching hospital. Eighteen (72%) of the admissions were elective, one was urgent and six were emergency admissions. However, there were no emergency procedures; 22 were scheduled or elective and three were urgent. Six of the cases were performed under local anaesthetic (three in the presence of an anaesthetist).

Patient profile

Table S103 (qs 3 and 4)
Age of patient at final operation

Years	Total	Male	Female
Under 61	1	-	1
61 to 70	2	1	1
71 to 80	10	5	5
81 to 90	9	4	5
91 to 100	3	1	2
Total	**25**	**11**	**14**

Table S104 (q30)
Preoperative precautions or therapeutic manoeuvres to improve the patient's preoperative condition

None	13
Gastric aspiration	4
Antibiotics (pre- or intra-operative)	4
Cardiac support drugs or anti-arrhythmic agents	2
Diuretics	2
Chest physiotherapy	1
Oxygen therapy	1
Tracheal intubation	1
Mechanical ventilation	1
Nutritional support	1
Others	1
Not answered	1
Total cases (answers may be multiple)	**25**

In some cases it was felt that preoperative precautions, whilst appearing satisfactory, could have been improved. Patients did not always have a complete preoperative workup and investigation.

Table S105 (q29)
Co-existing problems at the time of the final operation

None	1
Cardiac	18
Respiratory	10
Vascular	6
Endocrine *(including diabetes mellitus)*	5
Neurological	4
Renal	3
Musculoskeletal	3
Gastrointestinal	2
Haematological	1
Sepsis	1
Psychiatric	1
Other	3
Total cases *(answers may be multiple)*	**25**

Five of the patients were graded by the surgeon as ASA Class 1 at the time of the procedure; 14 were graded as Class 2.

Table S106 (q35)
Anticipated risk of death related to the proposed operation

Not expected	21
Small but significant risk	2
Definite risk	1
Expected	-
Not answered	1
Total	**25**

The surgical team

All patients were under the care of ophthalmic surgeons and all decisions to operate were made by consultants or associate specialists.

Table S107 (qs 43 and 46)
Grade of most senior operating surgeon

		Supervision?
Consultant	19	n/a
Associate specialist	1	-
Senior registrar	2	2
Registrar	3	2
Total	**25**	

The grades of surgeon were appropriate for the operations performed.

Unanticipated intra-operative problems

An 84-year-old man was admitted on a Friday for cataract surgery on the following day. He was known to have cardiac problems but was graded ASA 2. No specific precautions or therapeutic manoeuvres were undertaken preoperatively. A-V heart block occurred during the operation and the patient required transfer immediately postoperatively to the ICU at the main hospital site. Death occurred from cardiac failure 26 days after surgery.

Would more accurate assessment, including an ECG, have altered the management in this case?

Postoperative complications

Table S108 (q56)
Specific postoperative complications:

Respiratory distress	6
Stroke or other neurological problems	3
Cardiac arrest	2
Other organ failure	2
Urinary tract infection	2
Haemorrhage/postoperative bleeding requiring transfusion	1
Wound dehiscence	1
Low cardiac output	1
Renal failure	1
DVT and/or pulmonary embolus	1
Urinary retention/catheter blockage	1
Other	1
Not answered	9
Total cases *(answers may be multiple)*	**25**

Table S109 (q51)
Was the patient admitted immediately to an ICU or HDU postoperatively?

ICU	3
HDU	-
Neither of the above	22
Total	**25**

Figure S6
Calendar days between operation and death
(i.e. not 24 hour periods)

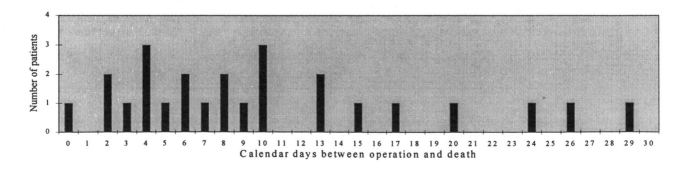

———— o o o o ————

Oral/Maxillofacial Surgery

The advisors in oral/maxillofacial surgery were:

Mrs S E Fisher	(Trent)
Mr P A Johnson	(South Thames)

NCEPOD is very grateful to these advisors for their help and advice

Point

> • There was a low rate of clinical audit in this specialty.

Sample

The NCEPOD report for 1993/94 was based on questionnaires concerning the first perioperative death reported for individual consultant surgeons (see page 10). In oral/maxillofacial surgery 21 cases were selected for the sample, of which 16 questionnaires from 15 hospitals were returned and analysed. One further questionnaire was returned but not analysed (see page 19). The overall return rate was therefore 81%.

Audit

Ten cases were considered at a local audit meeting and 12 postmortem examinations were carried out ; four were carried out at the request of the surgical staff and eight were carried out by the Coroner's pathologist.

List of procedures

Table S110
Final operation performed

One each of:

Exploration and biopsies
Evacuation haematoma L neck
Post-nasal packing
Cryoanalgesia to right inferior alveolar nerve (mandibular nerve)
Haemostasis including temporary fixation of fractures, tracheostomy
Open reduction and internal fixation right Le fort III fracture, left Le fort II fracture
Open reduction and plating of bilateral fractures mandible
Internal fixation Le fort II fracture and tracheostomy
Hemimandibulectomy with block dissection of neck and pectoralis major flap reconstruction
Cryosurgery to carcinoma lip and chin
Resection of squamous cell carcinoma of tongue and fauces and full flap reconstruction
Tracheostomy, bilateral neck dissection, resection of tumour, pectoralis major myocutaneous flap repair
Resection of tumour of floor of mouth and ventral tongue with bilateral supra-omohyoid neck dissections, reconstruction using radical free forearm flaps and attempts to establish anastomosis of RFFF.
Extraction of deciduous molar tooth
Multiple dental extractions, scaling of remaining teeth
Dental clearance

There were no instances of apparently inappropriate surgery.

Patient profile

Table S111 (qs 3 and 4)
Age of patient at final operation

Years	Total	Male	Female
0 to 10	1	1	-
11 to 20	1	-	1
21 to 30	1	-	1
31 to 40	-	-	-
41 to 50	2	2	-
51 to 60	-	-	-
61 to 70	6	4	2
71 to 80	5	3	2
Total	**16**	**10**	**6**

Seven of the patients were admitted as emergencies; the remainder were elective admissions. All of the operations were performed in District General or teaching hospitals. A five-year old child was appropriately managed by a consultant in paediatric dentistry.

Table S112 (q29)
Co-existing problems at the time of the final operation

None	1
Respiratory	5
Cardiac	5
Gastrointestinal	4
Neurological	3
Haematological	2
Musculoskeletal	2
Alcohol-related problems	2
Renal	1
Endocrine *(including diabetes mellitus)*	1
Psychiatric	1
Other	3
Not answered	1
Total cases *(answers may be multiple)*	**16**

Table S113 (q28)
ASA Class

ASA Class 1	4
ASA Class 2	5
ASA Class 3	3
ASA Class 4	2
ASA Class 5	2
Total	**16**

Preparation for surgery

Table S114 (q30)
Preoperative precautions or therapeutic manoeuvres to improve the patient's preoperative condition

None	7
Antibiotics (pre- or intra-operative)	6
Intravenous fluids	5
Blood transfusion	4
Oxygen therapy	4
Airway protection *(e.g. in unconscious patients)*	3
Cardiac support drugs or anti-arrhythmic agents	2
Correction of hypovolaemia	2
Tracheal intubation	2
Nutritional support	2
Gastric aspiration	1
Urinary catheterisation	1
Diuretics	1
Anticoagulants	1
Mechanical ventilation	1
Others	1
Not answered	1
Total cases *(answers may be multiple)*	**16**

Table S115 (q31)
DVT prophylaxis

	Before/during	After
None	7	10
Heel support	6	2
Leg stockings	4	3
Heparin	3	3
Calf compression	3	1
Ripple mattress	3	-
Dextran infusion	1	-
Total cases *(answers may be multiple)*	**16**	***15**

* *(Excluding death in theatre - one case)*

> A 70-year-old man was admitted with bilateral facial fractures which were treated by open reduction and internal fixation. He was known to have hypertension for which he was receiving treatment. Postoperatively he became drowsy and irritable and was thought to be suffering from apnoeic attacks. The patient died six days postoperatively and at postmortem examination there was evidence of massive pulmonary emboli and deep venous thrombosis affecting both legs.

No DVT prophylaxis had been used.

The surgical team

Twelve of the procedures (including four at weekends) were performed by consultant surgeons, and one by an associate specialist. A registrar was the most senior operating surgeon for the other three procedures.

Postoperative complications

Table S116 (q56)
Specific postoperative complications:

Respiratory distress	4
Generalised sepsis	3
Cardiac arrest	3
Renal failure	2
Persistent coma	2
Nutritional problems	2
Wound dehiscence	1
Anastomotic failure	1
Hepatic failure	1
Stroke or other neurological problems	1
Pressure sores	1
Urinary retention/catheter blockage	1
Other	4
Total cases* *(answers may be multiple)*	**15**

* *(Excluding death in theatre - one case)*

Availability of facilities

Table S117 (q2)
Availability of facilities

	Available in the hospital	Available 24hrs per day, 7 days per week
Theatre recovery area	16	13
Adult ICU	15	14
Adult HDU	5	3
Paediatric ICU/HDU	4	4
Emergency theatre	13	9
Total cases *(answers may be multiple)*	**16**	

———— o o o o ————

Orthopaedic Surgery

The advisors in orthopaedic surgery were:

Mr J M Barnes	(Wales)
Mr N J Fiddian	(South and West)
Mr J R Johnson	(North Thames)
Mr M L Porter	(North West)
Mr T W D Smith	(Trent)

NCEPOD is very grateful to these advisors for their help and advice.

Points

- Seventy-five percent of the deaths in this sample followed femoral neck fracture.
- There remain considerable organisational problems in dealing with increasing numbers of elderly unfit patients.
- The role of chemical prophylaxis in venous thromboembolism remains uncertain.
- There was an inadequate provision of critical care services for these patients.
- The low rate (26%) of operations performed by consultants is clearly unsatisfactory.

Sample

The 1993/94 NCEPOD survey was based on questionnaires concerning the first death reported for individual surgeons in that year. Thus no consultant received more than one questionnaire (see page 10). In orthopaedic surgery 716 cases were selected for the sample, of which 543 questionnaires from 220 hospitals were returned and analysed. A further eight questionnaires were returned, but for various reasons, (see page 19), not analysed. The overall return rate was therefore 77%.

Audit

Four hundred (74%) patients were considered at a local audit meeting. Of those deaths not considered (126), 124 were associated with a femoral neck fracture. Research is still needed in the very difficult area of femoral neck fracture management. A total of 285 (52%) postmortem examinations were carried out.

List of procedures

Table S118 (q47)
Final operation performed

Dynamic hip screw, etc. for fractured neck of femur	219		
Revision of dynamic hip screw, etc. for fractured neck of femur	3		
Hemiarthroplasty for fractured neck of femur	166	407	*75.0%*
Revision/removal/attention to above	13		
Total hip replacement for fractured neck of femur	6		
Total hip replacement for arthritis	24		
Revision of total hip replacement for arthritis	12	56	*10.3%*
Total knee replacement for arthritis	15		
Revision of total knee replacement for arthritis	5		
Operations for fractured shaft of femur	28		
Operations for fractured humerus	11		
Operations for fractured acetabulum/dislocated hip	4		
Operations for fractured tibia/fibula	2	51	*9.4%*
Operations for fractured ankle	2		
Operations for fractured wrist	2		
Operations for fractured olecranon	1		
Operations for multiple fractures	1		
Spinal operations	7		
Amputation of limb (any site)	4		
Carpal tunnel decompression	2	29	*5.3%*
Attention to pressure sores	2		
Miscellaneous	14		
Total	**543**		

Fifty-six (10%) of the deaths in this sample followed surgery for arthritis of the hip or knee. It was noted that there were instances of inappropriate surgery, most often apparent in the management of difficult fractures of the proximal femur in elderly unfit patients.

Admission details

Table S119 (q12)
Admission category

		%
Elective	60	*11.0*
Urgent	56	*10.3*
Emergency	426	*78.5*
Not answered	1	*0.2*
Total	**543**	

Table S120 (q1)
Type of hospital in which the final operation took place

District General hospital	417
University/teaching hospital	108
Surgical specialty hospital	10
Independent hospital	6
Defence Medical Services hospital	2
Total	**543**

The type of hospital in which the final operation took place was appropriate in all cases.

Table S121 (q2)
Availability of facilities

	Available in the hospital	Available 24hrs per day, 7 days per week
Theatre recovery area	541	405
Adult ICU	510	474
Adult HDU	172	140
Emergency theatre	490	362
Total cases (answers may be multiple)	**543**	

There was an unacceptable deficiency in terms of operating theatres, recovery areas and adult ICU/HDU facilities based on a 24-hour, seven day a week availability.

Where facilities are not available the management of the elderly surgical patient may suffer and it is clear that more resources must be made available to create further high dependency units.

Patient profile

Table S122 (qs 3 and 4)
Age of patient at final operation

Years	Total	%	Male	%	Female	%
11 to 20	1	0.2	1	0.6	0	0.0
21 to 30	4	0.7	3	1.7	1	0.3
31 to 40	2	0.4	1	0.6	1	0.3
41 to 50	5	0.9	2	1.1	3	0.8
51 to 60	9	1.7	6	3.4	3	0.8
61 to 70	38	7.0	17	9.7	21	5.7
71 to 80	143	26.3	55	31.4	88	23.9
81 to 90	246	45.3	68	38.9	178	48.4
91 to 100	95	17.5	22	12.6	73	19.8
Total	**543**		**175**		**368**	

Ninety-two percent of the female patients were aged between 71 and 100, and 83% of the males were in the same band. Twenty-one patients were less than 60 years old at the time of their final operation.

Table S123 (q29)
Co-existing problems at the time of the final operation

		%
None	32	5.9
Cardiac	289	53.2
Respiratory	220	40.5
Neurological	95	17.5
Musculoskeletal	92	16.9
Psychiatric	87	16.0
Haematological	70	12.9
Gastrointestinal	64	11.8
Vascular	61	11.2
Endocrine	60	11.0
Renal	59	10.9
Sepsis	26	4.8
Alcohol-related problems	12	2.2
Genetic abnormality	2	0.4
Drug addiction	1	0.2
Other	75	13.8
Not answered	11	2.0
Total cases *(answers may be multiple)*	**543**	

Co-existing problems at the time of the final operation were considerable and diverse in this group. There were significant problems in relation to the cardiorespiratory and neurological systems.

Table S124 (q28)
ASA Class

		%
ASA Class 1	31	5.7
ASA Class 2	157	28.9
ASA Class 3	208	38.3
ASA Class 4	106	19.5
ASA Class 5	8	1.5
Not answered	32	5.9
Not known/not recorded	1	0.2
Total	**543**	

Fifty-eight percent of the sample were in ASA Classes 3 or 4.

> An 87-year-old woman was admitted with a pathological fracture of the shaft of left femur. She was known to have a left hemiplegia, senile dementia and osteoporosis. She was grossly obese, and graded ASA 4. She underwent a very difficult intramedullary nailing of the left femur. Postoperatively she developed renal failure and died five days after surgery.

This is an example of the type of patient who would have benefited from a team approach.

The surgical team

At the time of the final operation, 542 of the patients were under the care of consultants in orthopaedic surgery and trauma and one patient was under the care of an accident and emergency surgeon. There was an appropriate consultant in charge of all patients.

Table S125 (qs 24 and 34)
Most senior surgeon involved in decision-making prior to surgery

		%	(locums)
Consultant	417	76.8	(12)
Associate specialist	22	4.1	-
Senior registrar	32	5.9	(2)
Registrar	60	11.0	(9)
Staff grade	7	1.3	-
Senior house officer	5	0.9	-
Total	**543**		

It is encouraging that only a very small percentage (0.9%) of decisions were taken by senior house officers.

> A 90-year-old woman was admitted to a DGH with a subtrochanteric fracture of the left femur. She was known to have cardiorespiratory problems and a senior house officer made the final decision to operate. Intra-operatively there were unanticipated problems in reducing the fracture which was being carried out by an SHO.

Subtrochanteric fractures are often very difficult to reduce and internally fix. The decision to operate was correct, but a more senior colleague should have been involved in the operation.

Table S126 (qs 43 and 46)
Grade of most senior operating surgeon

		%	(locums)	Supervision?
Consultant	144	26.5	(10)	n/a
Associate specialist	47	8.7	-	13
Senior registrar	74	13.6	(8)	16
Clinical assistant	5	0.9	-	-
Registrar	195	35.9	(19)	56
Staff grade	35	6.4	(1)	10
Senior house officer	41	7.6	(1)	18
Other	2	0.4	-	1
Total	**543**			

These figures may reflect working practices involving both traumatic and elective orthopaedic surgery, but there remain a number of examples where inappropriate and injudicious surgery was carried out by doctors in sub-consultant grades. The quality of surgical management was, in many instances, further jeopardized by inexperienced anaesthetists (see anaesthetic section). This problem was exacerbated by anaesthetic staffing difficulties.

A 90-year-old man was admitted with an intratrochanteric fracture of the left femoral neck. The ASA grade was 3 and he was noted to have a significant cardiorespiratory problem. The final decision to operate was taken by an SHO and the most senior operating surgeon was also an SHO. The patient died of a presumed myocardial infarct.

A 90-year-old woman was admitted with a fracture of the neck of the left femur. She was known to have psoriatic polyarthopathy on admission, was drowsy and dehydrated with a chest infection. There was evidence of transient ischaemic attacks. She was graded ASA 3 and the decision to operate was taken by an SHO. The operation was carried out by an SHO who had spent less than one year in the grade. The patient died on the same day.

It is inappropriate for senior house officers to operate on elderly patients with difficult problems.

Preparation for surgery

Table S127 (q30)
Preoperative precautions or therapeutic manoeuvres to improve the patient's preoperative condition

		%
None	66	*12.2*
Antibiotics (pre- or intra-operative)	299	*55.1*
Intravenous fluids	281	*51.7*
Urinary catheterisation	116	*21.4*
Chest physiotherapy	115	*21.1*
Diuretics	96	*17.7*
Correction of hypovolaemia	94	*17.3*
Cardiac support drugs or antiarrhythmic agents	85	*15.7*
Anticoagulants	82	*15.1*
Oxygen therapy	73	*13.4*
Blood transfusion	64	*11.8*
Nutritional support	24	*4.4*
Gastric aspiration	9	*1.7*
Tracheal intubation	8	*1.5*
Vitamin K	6	*1.1*
Airway protection *(e.g. in unconscious patients)*	6	*1.1*
Mechanical ventilation	6	*1.1*
Bowel preparation	4	*0.7*
Others	63	*11.6*
Not answered	14	*2.6*
Total cases *(answers may be multiple)*	**543**	

The majority of patients received adequate preoperative therapeutic measures appropriate to their preoperative conditions.

Table S128 (q31)
DVT prophylaxis

	Before/during	After
None	247	237
Heparin	166	167
Leg stockings	146	155
Heel support	57	44
Ripple mattress	37	39
Calf compression	16	4
Dextran infusion	9	6
Warfarin	4	10
Electrical stimulation of calves	4	1
Other†	14	21
Total cases *(answers may be multiple)*	**543**	***535**

* (Excluding death in theatre - eight cases)
† Including aspirin (8), exercise/mobilisation, foot pump, plaquenil, hydoxychloroquine, elevation of foot of bed, "Pegasus bed".

The question of prophylaxis for venous thromboembolism remains uncertain and no conclusions can be drawn. Forty-five percent of patients received no prophylaxis either before, during or after surgery. The use of chemical or physical prophylaxis did not appear to follow any rational programme and the clinical diagnosis of venous thromboembolism was only made in 34/534 cases. This figure reflects the inaccuracy of clinical diagnosis since in cases where a postmortem examination was carried out, venous thromboembolism was confirmed as the cause of death in 59 (20%) cases. Further research is required to develop a rational prophylaxis of thromboembolism.

Table S129 (q37)
Classification of the final operation

		%
Emergency	15	*2.8*
Urgent	353	*65.0*
Scheduled	122	*22.5*
Elective	53	*9.8*
Total	**543**	

Ten percent of procedures were delayed due to non-clinical factors, the majority of these being delayed due to lack of theatre facilities including equipment and/or staff.

> A 92-year-old woman was admitted with a spiral fracture of the femoral shaft, distal to the fixation plate of a trochanteric fracture on the ipsilateral side. Operation was postponed, due to the equipment for the reconstruction nailing not being immediately available.

> A 92-year-old woman was admitted with a fracture of the right femoral neck. Operation was delayed for five days as a result of lack of theatre space and closure of the intensive care unit. A surgeon noted the lack of an efficient trauma theatre for emergency and urgent cases, inevitably leading to a delay in operation with increased morbidity and mortality.

Table S130 (q40)
Day of operation

Monday	62
Tuesday	75
Wednesday	97
Thursday	89
Friday	93
Saturday	76
Sunday	51
Total	**543**

Twenty-seven (6.5%) of the weekday operations were carried out between 18.01 and 07.59 hrs.

Table S131 (q49)
Unanticipated problems during operation

None stated	497
Cardiovascular problems including hypotension, bradycardia	20
Unsatisfactory fracture reduction	12
Unexpected blood loss	4
Unexpected severe osteoporosis	3
Others - unspecified	7
Total	**543**

Eight percent of cases demonstrated unanticipated problems during operation; the majority was associated with cardiovascular problems and blood loss. This small percentage suggests a general high standard of preoperative preparation and surgical planning in this sample.

Postoperative care and management

Table S132 (q51)
Was the patient admitted immediately to an ICU or HDU postoperatively?

		%
ICU	26	*4.8*
HDU	26	*4.8*
Neither of the above	476	*89.0*
Not answered	7	*1.3*
Total*	**535**	

* (Excluding death in theatre - eight cases)

Table S133 (q51a)
If neither, was the patient admitted to an ICU/HDU after an initial period on a routine postoperative ward?

Yes	19
No	448
Not answered	9
Total	**476**

Given the nature of the sample, it seems unlikely that 84% (448/535) of all patients were fit enough postoperatively to be readmitted to a ward without any admission to either ICU or HDU. It has already been noted (see table S121) that adult HDU facilities were only available over a 24 hour basis in 140/543 cases. Better provision of HDU facilities might improve the management of these patients.

Postoperative complications

Table S134 (q56)
Specific postoperative complications:

Respiratory distress	168
Low cardiac output	114
Cardiac arrest	109
Renal failure	70
Haemorrhage/postoperative bleeding requiring transfusion	39
Stroke or other neurological problems	39
Nutritional problems	36
DVT and/or pulmonary embolus	34
Pressure sores	26
Generalised sepsis	25
Urinary tract infection	23
Urinary retention/catheter blockage	22
Wound infection	20
Other organ failure	14
Orthopaedic prosthetic complication	14
Wound dehiscence	13
Upper respiratory obstruction	9
Persistent coma	8
Endocrine system failure	7
Problems with analgesia	6
Hepatic failure	4
Fat embolus	4
Peripheral ischaemia	3
Anastomotic failure	2
Other	97
Total cases* *(answers may be multiple)*	**535**

* *(Excluding deaths in theatre - eight cases)*

There was a preponderance of cardiorespiratory problems associated with renal failure, postoperative haemorrhage, neurological problems, sepsis and urinary retention. The high level of postoperative complications might be addressed by increasing HDU facilities.

Figure S7 (qs 39 and 58)
Calendar days between operation and death
(i.e. not 24 hour periods)

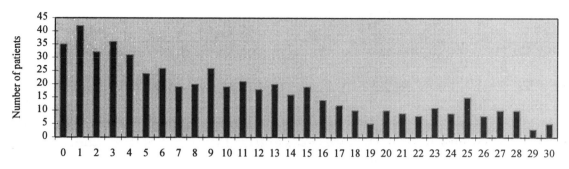

Otorhinolaryngological Surgery

The advisors in otorhinolaryngological (ENT) surgery were:

Mr W Primrose	(Northern Ireland)
Mr R Slack	(South and West)
Mr M P Stearns	(North Thames)

NCEPOD is very grateful to these advisors for their help and advice.

Points

- Senior surgeons had operated on 87% of the patients in the sample.
- Patients with respiratory problems should receive adequate preoperative chest assessment and appropriate postoperative treatment.
- Deaths after epistaxis are more common than is generally supposed.
- There was an inadequate provision of HDU beds.
- The level of clinical audit was low and unsatisfactory.

Sample

The 1993/94 NCEPOD survey was based on questionnaires concerning the first perioperative death reported for individual consultant surgeons. Thus, no consultant surgeon received more than one questionnaire (see page 10). In ENT there were 56 cases in the sample, of which 47 questionnaires, from 39 hospitals, were returned and analysed. One further questionnaire was returned but not analysed (see page 19). The overall return rate was therefore 86%.

Audit

Thirty (64%) deaths were considered at a local audit meeting. This is a lower figure than is reported for other specialties and leaves room for improvement. Twenty-four patients had a postmortem examination. There were five hospital postmortems and 19 Coroners' postmortems. One hospital postmortem report failed to reach the surgeon and seven of the Coroners' reports were not received by the surgical team. There is scope for improved communication here.

List of procedures

This information relates to the final operation done. There were 28 operations for malignant and 19 for benign disease. The list below includes all procedures done; many operations included more than one procedure.

Table S135 (q47)
Surgery for malignancy

Endoscopies (+/- biopsy)	13
Radical head and neck surgery (including reconstruction)	10
Debulking of various tumours (surgical, laser or diathermy)	5
Ligature of external carotid artery	2
Tracheostomy	1
Miscellaneous (one each of: debridement of necrotic flap, drainage of intra-abdominal and intrathoracic abscesses, biopsy of maxillary tumour, excision of pinna, total thyroidectomy, insertion of feeding tube)	6

Surgery for benign conditions

Nasal packing for epistaxis	3
Submucous resection	2
Change of tracheostomy tube	2
Radical mastoidectomy	2
Drainage of cervical abscess	2
Miscellaneous (one each of: Teflon injection of vocal cord, tracheostomy, antral washouts, diathermy for epistaxis, nasal biopsy, revision mastoidectomy, EUA nose, ethmoidectomy, insertion of ventricular drain, tonsillectomy and oesophagoscopy)	11
Total cases *(answers may be multiple)*	**47**

Admission details

Table S136 (q12)
Admission category

Elective	26
Urgent	9
Emergency	12
Total	**47**

Many of the elective admissions were for advanced head and neck malignancy.

Table S137 (q1)
Type of hospital in which the final operation took place

District General hospital	28
University/teaching hospital	17
Surgical specialty hospital	1
Independent hospital	1
Total	**47**

Table S138 (q2)
Availability of essential services

	Available in the hospital	Available 24hrs per day, 7 days per week
Theatre recovery area	46	33
Adult ICU	43	38
Adult HDU	21	18
Emergency theatre	40	27
None of the above	1	n/a
Total cases (answers may be multiple)	**47**	

The provision of high dependency units was low (45%) despite the fact that many of these patients require specialised care of the airway and careful monitoring rather than the more specialised form of care available in an intensive care unit. One 85-year-old patient underwent a direct laryngoscopy, biopsy and tracheostomy in a unit which was said to have none of those specialised services.

Patient profile

Table S139 (qs 3 and 4)
Age of patient at final operation

Years	Total	Male	Female
31 to 40	1	1	-
41 to 50	-	-	-
51 to 60	6	2	4
61 to 70	19	14	5
71 to 80	13	9	4
81 to 90	8	1	7
Total	**47**	**27**	**20**

Forty (85%) of these patients were over 60 years of age. The population of patients undergoing ENT surgery is, in general, much younger; the ages of these patients who died after surgery reflect the sampling technique (one death per surgeon) and also the number of cases undergoing surgery for malignancy.

Table S140 (q28)
ASA Class

ASA Class 1	5
ASA Class 2	20
ASA Class 3	6
ASA Class 4	8
ASA Class 5	4
Not answered	4
Total	**47**

Table S141 (q35)
Anticipated risk of death related to the proposed operation

Not expected	24
Small but significant risk	9
Definite risk	10
Expected	4
Total	**47**

Surgeons stated that 24 patients were not expected to die. Given that something unexpected happened, what did the surgical team do afterwards to find out the reason for the patient's death? Fifteen of the 24 patients had a postmortem examination; four of these were hospital-based and 11 were ordered by a Coroner. Of the remaining nine cases, a postmortem was refused on four occasions and was not even requested for five patients. For two of these it was felt that the cause of death was clear; no explanation was given for the other three.

Many of the patients had coexisting diseases, and respiratory problems were common.

Table S142 (q29)
Co-existing problems at the time of the final operation

Respiratory	22
Cardiac	16
Vascular	8
Gastrointestinal	8
Neurological	7
Sepsis	6
Haematological	5
Renal	4
Musculoskeletal	4
Endocrine *(including diabetes mellitus)*	3
Alcohol-related problems	3
Psychiatric	2
Other	3
None	6
Not answered	2
Total cases *(answers may be multiple)*	**47**

In view of these co-existing problems and the complex nature of some cases it was wholly appropriate that many were managed jointly with other specialties.

Table S143 (q23)
Was care undertaken on a formal shared basis with another specialty (excluding anaesthesia)?
This was answered "yes" in 16 cases.

General surgery	3
General medicine	3
Plastic surgery	2
Chest medicine	2
Intensive care	2
Head and neck surgery	1
Neurosurgery	1
Neurosurgery	1
Renal medicine	1
Haematology	1
Radiotherapy	1
Total cases (answers may be multiple)	**16**

The surgical team

Table S144 (q22)
Specialty of consultant surgeon in charge at time of final operation

Otorhinolaryngology	45
General surgery with special interest in head and neck surgery	1
General surgery with special interest in vascular surgery	1
Total	**47**

In all cases the care was delivered by a surgeon with an appropriate specialty or special interest.

Table S145 (qs 34 and 24)
The most senior surgeon involved in decision-making prior to surgery

		(locums)
Consultant	44	(1)
Associate specialist	1	(1)
Senior house officer	2	-
Total	**47**	

A senior house officer made all the decisions on two occasions. Both these cases were reviewed by the advisors; the doctors in question were experienced and the level of decision-making was appropriate for the patients concerned.

Table S146 (qs 43 and 46)
Grade of most senior operating surgeon

		(locums)	Supervision?
Consultant	32	(1)	n/a
Associate specialist	2	(1)	-
Senior registrar	7	-	4
Registrar	4	-	2
Senior house officer	2	-	-
Total	**47**		

Consultants operated on 32 (68%) cases; if associate specialists and senior registrars are included, then senior surgeons operated on 87% of the patients. On occasions even senior registrars should be supervised.

> A 70-year-old man underwent a laryngectomy by a consultant after irradiation of a laryngeal carcinoma. A large fistula developed following a bout of vomiting in the early postoperative period. An unsupervised senior registrar then re-operated and attempted to close the fistula with a sternomastoid flap. Six days later the consultant re-operated, a pharyngo-oesophagectomy was done and the stomach pulled up into the neck for reconstruction. The patient died four days later. The cause of death was disseminated intravascular coagulopathy and adult respiratory distress syndrome.

The senior registrar did an unconventional operation; should he have been asked to do the case at all?

On two occasions an SHO operated alone. In one case an SHO did an antral washout on an alcoholic patient with liver disease; death was not related to surgery. In the second case an experienced SHO performed a submucous resection and anterior nasal packing for recurrent epistaxis (see comment regarding epistaxis on page 168).

Preparation for surgery

Table S147 (q30)
Preoperative precautions or therapeutic manoeuvres to improve the patient's preoperative condition

None	15
Antibiotics (pre- or intra-operative)	16
Intravenous fluids	13
Chest physiotherapy	9
Oxygen therapy	9
Correction of hypovolaemia	8
Blood transfusion	8
Cardiac support drugs or anti-arrhythmic agents	6
Urinary catheterisation	6
Diuretics	5
Tracheal intubation	5
Mechanical ventilation	5
Nutritional support	5
Airway protection (e.g. in unconscious patients)	2
Gastric aspiration	1
Anticoagulants	1
Vitamin K	1
Others	6
Not answered	3
Total cases (answers may be multiple)	**47**

Routine pre-operative chest physiotherapy is of debatable benefit and prophylaxis against postoperative respiratory complications is best commenced immediately postoperatively. ENT surgeons should not underestimate the importance of chest disease; it has been suggested that an ASA Class of more than 1 and an age of more than 60 years are helpful indicators of the risk of postoperative respiratory complications.[22]

Table S148 (q31)
DVT prophylaxis

	Before/during	After
None	33	34
Leg stockings	10	9
Heel support	6	2
Not answered	2	2
Dextran infusion	1	2
Heparin	2	-
Ripple mattress	1	1
Electrical stimulation of calves	1	-
Other	1	2
Total cases *(answers may be multiple)*	**47**	**47**

The use of venous thromboembolic prophylaxis was low. Heparin was rarely used (presumably because many procedures were short and because of the fear of haemorrhage) and compression stockings were the most common method of prevention. It is important that surgeons think about the relevance of venous thromboembolism in the specialty and develop an appropriate protocol for prophylaxis based on the best available methods according to current knowledge.

> A consultant with an interest in major head and neck surgery operated on a 66-year-old man with an advanced malignant goitre (papillary carcinoma of thyroid). Venous thromboembolic prophylaxis consisted of stockings and electrical calf stimulation during surgery. A total thyroidectomy, laryngectomy and partial pharyngectomy were done. All went well until the eighth postoperative day when the patient died of a massive pulmonary embolism.

The consultant surgeon who operated in this case wrote to NCEPOD explaining that his protocol for prophylaxis did not include heparin. In view of this death his policy was to be reviewed and a questionnaire was being circulated to other consultants to enquire about their practice. This is an example of audit in action and an attempt to close the audit loop based on the observation of practice and the surgeon is to be congratulated on these actions.

Table S149 (q37)
Classification of the final operation

Emergency	2
Urgent	15
Scheduled	25
Elective	5
Total	**47**

The majority of work done was scheduled or elective (64%). These terms are defined in the Glossary in Appendix B.

Table S150 (q40)
Day of operation

Monday	8
Tuesday	8
Wednesday	13
Thursday	7
Friday	8
Saturday	2
Sunday	1
Total	**47**

Only seven operations were done "out-of-hours". Three were done at a weekend and four between the hours of 18.01 and 07.59 during the week.

Table S151 (q56)
Specific postoperative complications:

Respiratory distress	13
Cardiac problems	10
Stroke or other neurological problems	6
Haemorrhage/postoperative bleeding requiring transfusion	5
Generalised sepsis	3
DVT and/or pulmonary embolus	3
Anastomotic failure	2
Wound infection	2
Renal failure	2
Hepatic failure	2
Endocrine system failure	1
Peripheral ischaemia	1
Urinary tract infection	1
Nutritional problems	1
Other	9
Not answered	14
Total cases *(answers may be multiple)*	**47**

Reference has already been made to the management of respiratory disease; respiratory complications were the most common postoperative problem.

Table S152 (qs 39 and 58)
Calendar days between operation and death
(i.e. not 24 hour periods)

Same day	2
Next day	7
2 days	7
3 days	1
4 days	6
5 days	5
6 to 10 days	7
11 to 15 days	4
16 to 20 days	4
21 to 30 days	4
Total	**47**

Special problems

A surgical dilemma

On occasions surgeons must trust their experience when attempting to help a patient with distressing symptoms.

> A 58-year-old woman had a posterior postpharyngeal wall squamous carcinoma and was treated with radiotherapy and chemotherapy. A recurrence appeared to have developed but this was difficult to diagnose and repeated biopsies of a necrotic mass were negative. Eventually a pharyngolaryngectomy was done. Histology showed necrotic tissue only. All was well for 18 days but then chest symptoms occurred and the posterior tracheal wall necrosed as a consequence of irradiation damage. Intrathoracic sepsis followed and despite surgical drainage the patient died.

The surgeon operated believing there to be a recurrent tumour and that resection was necessary to remove the painful necrotic mass. The diagnosis was incorrect but surgery was done for relief of the patient's symptoms. Unfortunately the irradiated tissues failed to heal.

Post-tonsillectomy bleeding

> A mildly obese (67.2kg) normotensive 54-year-old woman was admitted for an elective tonsillectomy. Three years previously she had been treated for acute myeloid leukaemia and was in remission. The indication for surgery was obstructive sleep apnoea and was recommended after consultation between an otorhinolaryngologist, a haematologist and a physician with a special interest in sleep abnormalities. The operation was done by a senior registrar who noted large tonsils. The patient went home the following day. On the fifth postoperative day the patient re-presented with a secondary tonsillar haemorrhage but was found to be dead on arrival at the hospital. A postmortem examination confirmed clots and adherent debris in both tonsillar fossae.

The surgery was appropriate and competently done. Secondary haemorrhage from the tonsillar bed is potentially life-threatening. It is not as dangerous as reactionary haemorrhage, but fatalities do occur from this condition and secondary haemorrhage should be considered to be a serious complication.[23] Death from a post-tonsillectomy haemorrhage is apparently rare,[24] but it may be that under-recording occurs due to early discharge from hospital. When such haemorrhage does occurs it is often sudden and torrential.

Epistaxis

Four deaths occurred after surgery and packing for epistaxis; these deaths are more common than other specialists and the public might think. Acute blood loss is not the main cause of death; low haemoglobin levels and hypoxia may be associated with myocardial infarction. Nasal packs are known to produce a significant hypoxaemia within the first 48 hours after surgery.[25]

———— o o o o ————

Plastic Surgery

The advisors in plastic surgery were:

Mr F S C Browning	(Northern and Yorkshire)
Mr G Lamberty	(Anglia and Oxford)
Mr M A P Milling	(Wales)

NCEPOD is very grateful to these advisors for their help and advice.

Points

- The operative procedures illustrate the wide range of cases under the care of plastic surgeons. Nine of the procedures were for major malignancies of the head and neck, and one for malignant melanoma.
- All patients received the specialist care of a plastic surgery team.

Sample

The 1993/94 NCEPOD survey was based on questionnaires concerning the first perioperative death reported for individual consultant surgeons. Thus no consultant surgeon received more than one questionnaire (see page 10). In plastic surgery 36 cases were selected for the sample, of which 29 questionnaires from 22 hospitals were returned and analysed. The overall return rate was therefore 81%.

List of procedures

Table S153

	Sex	Age of patient	ASA Class	Grade of most senior operating surgeon	Classification of admission/operation
Burns					
Excision and graft (70%)	M	20	4	Consultant	Emergency/Scheduled
Excision of slough and skin grafts (15%)	F	36	4	Consultant	Emergency/Scheduled
Debridement (60%)	M	38	4	Senior registrar	Urgent/Urgent
Escharotomy (hands) (25%)	M	48	4	Registrar	Emergency/Emergency
Tracheostomy, excision and skin grafts (upper limbs)	M	65	4	Consultant	Urgent/Scheduled
Excision and skin grafts, both legs (14%) - transferred from overseas	F	75	3	Consultant	Urgent/Scheduled
Shaving and grafting (both legs)	M	82	3	Senior registrar	Emergency/Elective
Debridement and contralateral below knee amputation	F	83	3	Consultant	Urgent/Scheduled
Procedures for malignancy					
Excision multiple cutaneous and subcutaneous metastatic melanoma nodules (from scalp)	M	27	5	Consultant	Elective/Scheduled
Orbitectomy, cranial base resection, free flap	M	74	2	Consultant	Urgent/Scheduled
Radical excision scapula and chest wall, graft and flap	F	75	Not answered	Consultant	Elective/Scheduled
Trimming amputation stump and resuture groin (previous below knee amputation and block dissection)	M	75	Not answered	Consultant	Elective/Urgent
Wound debridement, split skin graft (melanoma on foot)	F	76	4	Registrar (supervised by Consultant)	Elective/Scheduled
Excision squamous cell ca., mastoid region	M	78	2	Consultant	Elective/Scheduled
Revision arterial anastomosis (previous squamous cell ca. left cheek, neck dissection, free flap)	F	85	2	Consultant	Elective/Emergency

	Sex	Age of patient	ASA Class	Grade of most senior operating surgeon	Classification of admission/operation
Procedures for malignancy (cont'd.)					
Excision and grafting basal cell carcinoma (face)	F	85	2	Senior registrar (supervised by Consultant)	Elective/Scheduled
Excision and grafting basal cell carcinoma, inner canthus	F	85	3	Consultant	Elective/Scheduled
Excision lesion (upper eyelid), orbital exenteration, flap reconstruction	F	90	3	Consultant	Elective/Scheduled
Other procedures					
Debridement of tibia, change of gentamicin beads, skin graft and flap (osteomyelitis)	M	52	2	Consultant	Elective/Elective
Debridement fasciotomy wound	F	54	4	Senior house officer (supervised by consultant)	Urgent/Scheduled
Debridement of necrotising fasciitis	F	60	4	Consultant	Emergency/Emergency
Radio-cephalic shunt revision (Cimino procedure)	F	63	4	Registrar	Urgent/Urgent
Skin graft (ankle) and contralateral above knee amputation	M	65	4	Staff grade	Emergency/Scheduled
Debridement necrotic lymphoedematous tissue (leg)	F	65	1	Senior house officer	Elective/Scheduled
Radical debridement of necrotising fasciitis/gas gangrene	M	69	4	Senior Registrar	Emergency/Urgent
Skin grafting (pre-tibial laceration)	F	71	2	Registrar	Emergency/Urgent
Excision necrotic muscle and opening of sinus in sacral pressure sore	F	72	3	Senior Registrar	Elective/Urgent
Excision and graft pre-tibial laceration	F	80	3	Registrar	Emergency/Urgent
Debridement and flap reconstruction (sacral sore)	F	89	Not answered	Locum registrar (re-explored by consultant later the same day)	Elective/Scheduled

Burns surgery

All of the eight procedures were carried out in specialist burns units. In one case (schizophrenia) the care was managed jointly with a psychiatrist.

Procedures for malignancy (M) and other procedures (OP)

Table S154 (q12)
Type of hospital in which the final operation took place

	M	OP
District General hospital	6	4
University/teaching hospital	4	6
Independent hospital	-	1
Total	**10**	**11**

Inter-hospital transfer preceded four of the procedures for malignancy and five of the other procedures. In all but one case transfer was <u>from</u> a DGH for specialist care in either another DGH or a teaching hospital. In one case the transfer was from an independent hospital to a teaching hospital because of the patient's deteriorating condition. The consultant surgeon involved identified a delay between admission and the surgical procedure in one case where a 75-year-old man was transferred from a DGH to a teaching hospital. The patient was admitted electively eight days after the initial referral (the Christmas period intervened) and the first procedure (below knee amputation and groin dissection for Stage II malignant melanoma) was performed by a consultant two days after admission. The stump was trimmed and the groin re-sutured as an urgent procedure 20 days later. The patient died 13 days postoperatively. The consultant stated that he had "instructed the trainee staff to inform the Coroner, and they failed to do this"; a hospital postmortem examination was not requested.

Table S155 (q29)
Co-existing problems at the time of the final operation

	M	OP
None	3	-
Cardiac	5	3
Respiratory	3	3
Psychiatric	2	1
Endocrine *(including diabetes mellitus)*	1	3
Neurological	1	1
Dehydration	1	-
Renal	-	3
Vascular	-	4
Sepsis	-	3
Gastrointestinal	-	1
Musculoskeletal	-	2
Not answered	1	2
Total cases *(answers may be multiple)*	**10**	**11**

Table S156 (q23)
Was care undertaken on a formal shared basis with another specialty?

Care shared with:	M	OP
Care of the elderly	1	2
Renal medicine	-	2
General medicine	-	1
Neurosurgery	1	-
Oncology	1	-
Radiotherapy	1	-
Not specified	1	-
Total cases *(answers may be multiple)*	**5**	**5**

Table S157 (q30)
Preoperative precautions or therapeutic manoeuvres to improve the patient's preoperative condition

	M	OP
None	4	4
Antibiotics (pre- or intra-operative)	3	3
Cardiac support drugs or anti-arrhythmic agents	3	2
Chest physiotherapy	2	1
Diuretics	2	1
Intravenous fluids	1	2
Urinary catheterisation	1	2
Anticoagulants	-	2
Blood transfusion	-	2
Correction of hypovolaemia	-	2
Gastric aspiration	-	2
Mechanical ventilation	-	2
Tracheal intubation	-	2
Airway protection	-	1
Oxygen therapy	-	1
Nutritional support	1	1
Other	2	1
Not answered	-	1
Total cases *(answers may be multiple)*	**10**	**11**

Table S158 (q2)
Availability of services

	M	OP
Theatre recovery area	10	11
Adult ICU	10	11
Adult HDU	2	4
Emergency theatre	8	10
Total cases *(answers may be multiple)*	**10**	**11**

In one case, the recovery area was only available from 9.00am to 5.00pm on weekdays. The urgent procedure (pre-tibial laceration) was carried out on a Sunday, under local anaesthetic administered by the registrar who performed the procedure. The patient, aged 80 years, died 24 days later from bronchogenic carcinoma of the lung.

In three of the malignancy cases, the emergency theatre was only available between 5.00pm and 9.00am and at weekends. Only one of the cases was classified as an emergency (revision of arterial thrombosis) and was performed at 10.00pm on a Monday by a consultant. Two previous procedures had been carried out earlier on the same day.

Five of the patients were admitted immediately to an ICU or HDU, and three patients were admitted for special care after an initial period on a ward.

All cases

Table S159
What was the anticipated risk of death related to the proposed operation?

Not expected	10
Small but significant risk	8
Definite risk	10
Expected	1
Total	**29**

Table S160
Calendar days from operation to death
(i.e. not 24 hour periods)

Same day	-
1 to 5	9
6 to 10	4
11 to 15	8
16 to 20	2
21 to 25	3
27	3
Total	**29**

Discussion took place at audit meetings about all but one of the burns cases, eight (80%) of the procedures for malignancy and seven (64%) of the other procedures.

Coroners' postmortem examinations were performed for all of the burns cases, four of the malignancy cases and one of the other procedures. Hospital postmortem examinations were carried out for two of the other procedures.

———— o o o o ————

Urology

The advisors in urology were:

Mr G F Abercrombie	(South and West)
Mr K N Bullock	(Anglia and Oxford)
Mr P N Matthews	(Wales)
Mr K T H Moore	(Trent)

NCEPOD is very grateful to these advisors for their help and advice.

Points

- There was a high (97%) consultant input in decision-making.
- Eighty-nine percent of patients were over 60 years of age.
- Fifty-six percent of patients were in ASA classes 3 and 4.
- The value of prophylaxis against venous thromboembolism is uncertain in urology and deserves further investigation.
- The rate of postmortem examination was unacceptably low.

Sample

The 1993/94 NCEPOD survey was based on questionnaires concerning the first perioperative death reported for individual consultant surgeons. Thus, no consultant surgeon received more than one questionnaire (see page 10). Two-hundred-and-two cases were selected for the sample, of which 166 questionnaires, from 114 hospitals, were returned and analysed. A further five questionnaires were returned but for various reasons (see page 19), not analysed. The overall return rate was therefore 85%.

Audit

One-hundred-and-forty patients (84%) were considered at a local audit meeting. The postmortem examination rate was only 40% (66/166) and this level is clearly unacceptable. Postmortem examinations are an important form of audit. At least 49% of postmortem examinations demonstrate, despite clinicians' scepticism, significant new and unexpected findings which are relevant. Considerable emphasis must be placed on improving the rate of these examinations to enable valid conclusions to be made (see pathology section).

Communication problems between clinician and pathologist remain. A copy of the postmortem examination report was received by the surgical team in 8/10 cases where a hospital postmortem examination was done and in 46/56 cases where a Coroner's postmortem examination was done.

List of procedures

Table S161 (q47)
Final operation performed

Transurethral resection of prostate (benign or malignant)	56
Transurethral resection of bladder tumour	21
Laparotomy (+/- procedure)	20
Nephrectomy	19
Orchidectomy (single or bilateral)	9
Urethrotomy (+/- other operations for urethral stricture)	8
Ileal conduit	7
Cystoscopy (flexible or rigid; +/- bladder washout)	5
Retropubic prostatectomy	4
Bladder neck incision	4
Insertion of ureteric stent	3
Total cystectomy	3
Circumcision	3
Percutaneous renal surgery	2
Open operations on bladder	2
Endoscopic litholopaxy	2
Penile operations (excluding circumcision)	2
Wound resuture	2
Miscellaneous (one each of: drainage of kidney, prostatic biopsy, urethrectomy, ureterolysis, nephrostomy)	5
Total cases *(answers may be multiple)*	**166**

There were instances of inappropriate surgery.

> A 92-year-old man known to have a carcinoma of the prostate and renal failure presented with haematuria and retention. He also had cardiomegaly with ventricular failure and bilateral pulmonary congestion. There was no evidence that he had metastatic disease from his prostate carcinoma. Transurethral resection of the prostate was done and the patient died with renal failure nine days later.

Would hormonal treatment have been more appropriate initially?

> A 65-year-old man was admitted to a DGH under the care of a urological surgeon. He had prostatic carcinoma invading the vesicoureteric area of the bladder. He was a Jehovah's Witness; risks of surgery and the alternatives were explained to him. The transurethral prostatectomy and bilateral orchidectomy were done. He began to bleed heavily on the day following surgery, refused blood and despite admission to the intensive care unit for cardiopulmonary support and large volumes of intravenous crystalloids, colloids and albumin, died within 48 hours of surgery.

Jehovah's Witnesses are difficult to manage.[26] Should the surgeon have persevered with non-operative treatment? Altogether there were three examples of Jehovah's Witnesses who bled to death after prostatectomy. This is a particularly dangerous operation for this group of patients.[27]

Admission details

Table S162 (q12)
Admission category

Elective	90
Urgent	9
Emergency	67
Total	**166**

Table S163 (q1)
Type of hospital in which the final operation took place

District General hospital	114
University/teaching hospital	48
Other acute/partly acute hospital	1
Defence Medical Services hospital	2
Independent hospital	1
Total	**166**

With one exception, all urological operations occurred in appropriate hospitals. One District General hospital had no intensive care or high dependency unit on site.

> An 82-year-old man, rated ASA 3, was admitted for a transurethral prostatectomy and orchidectomy for carcinoma of the prostate. There were no ICU or HDU services in the hospital. Postoperative bleeding occurred and re-operation was required at 24 hours. A cardiac arrest occurred 36 hours after the second procedure. The cardiac arrest team comprised a urologist and gynaecologist; no anaesthetist attended.

It is not essential, although perhaps desirable, for an anaesthetist to attend cardiac arrests. All doctors should be versed in resuscitation skills as recommended in the guidelines published by the Resuscitation Council.[28] Although ICU and HDU services were deemed to be satisfactory, only 73% of all hospitals had a theatre recovery area available 24 hours a day, seven days a week (table S164).

Table S164 (q2)
Availability of essential services

	Available in the hospital	Available 24hrs per day, 7 days per week
Theatre recovery area	166	122
Adult ICU	155	147
Adult HDU	45	41
Emergency theatre	132	81
Total cases *(answers may be multiple)*	**166**	

Fifty (30%) patients were admitted to an ICU or HDU and it is clear that in circumstances where elderly and infirm patients are undergoing major surgery (see later), ICU and HDU facilities are of extreme importance. Likewise, a dedicated emergency theatre is important and was only available in 49% of instances in this survey, but this did not appear to be a major practical problem. There are clear guidelines pointing out that, where acute surgical practice is undertaken, an emergency theatre must be available at all times.

Patient profile

Table S165 (qs 3 and 4)
Age of patient at final operation

Years		Male	Female
11 to 20	1	1	-
21 to 30	1	1	-
31 to 40	1	1	-
41 to 50	3	-	3
51 to 60	13	9	4
61 to 70	30	22	8
71 to 80	66	60	6
81 to 90	45	38	7
91 to 100	6	5	1
Total	**166**	**137**	**29**

One-hundred-and-seventeen (70%) patients were over the age of 70. Where there are pre-existing medical problems in elderly patients who need special preparation preoperatively, there will be a significant risk of perioperative complications.

Table S166 (q29)
Co-existing problems at the time of the final operation

None	20
Cardiac	77
Respiratory	48
Renal	38
Endocrine *(including diabetes mellitus)*	21
Musculoskeletal	19
Neurological	17
Vascular	17
Haematological	13
Gastrointestinal	13
Sepsis	13
Psychiatric	5
Alcohol-related problems	1
Genetic abnormality	1
Other	18
Not answered	5
Total cases *(answers may be multiple)*	**166**

Table S167 (q28)
ASA Class

ASA Class 1	14
ASA Class 2	53
ASA Class 3	63
ASA Class 4	30
ASA Class 5	-
Not answered	4
Not known/not recorded	2
Total	**166**

Table S168 (q35)
Anticipated risk of death related to the proposed operation

Not expected	59
Small but significant risk	54
Definite risk	49
Expected	3
Not answered	1
Total	**166**

Surgeons stated that 59 patients were not expected to die. Given that something unexpected happened, what did the surgical team do to find out the reason for the patient's death?

Of these 59 patients 33 were subjected to a postmortem examination. Of the remaining 26 cases, 22 were considered at a local audit meeting. Despite the fact that the patients were not expected to die, there remained four cases who did not have a postmortem examination and were not discussed at an audit meeting. These patients may represent a missed educational opportunity.

The surgical team

Table S169 (q22)
Specialty of consultant surgeon in charge at time of final operation

Urology	155
General with a special interest in urology	10
Gynaecology	1
Total	**166**

The above table shows that an appropriately experienced surgeon was in charge of the care of all these patients.

Table S170 (qs 24 and 34)
The most senior surgeon involved in decision-making prior to surgery

		(locums)
Consultant	162	(6)
Senior registrar	4	(4)
Total	**166**	

Ninety-eight percent of all patients had a consultant urological opinion prior to operation.

Table S171 (qs 43 and 46)
Grade of most senior operating surgeon

		(locums)	Supervision?
Consultant	112	(9)	n/a
Associate specialist	2	-	-
Senior registrar	28	(2)	17
Clinical assistant	2	-	2
Registrar	15	(1)	7
Staff grade	4	-	2
Senior house officer	1	-	1
Not answered	2	-	1
Total	**166**		

Eighty-six percent of all patients were operated on by a senior surgeon (consultant, associate specialist or senior registrar). In 15 cases more senior supervision was not provided in the operating theatre.

The input of consultant urologists was high. There was evidence of registrars undertaking surgical treatment in elderly unfit patients.

There was one case in the series in which consultant input and supervision were lacking.

> A 58-year-old woman was admitted as an emergency to a teaching hospital under the care of a urologist. There was large a left sided hydronephrosis and bladder tumour. She was obese and there was a left pulmonary effusion. Surgery was therefore delayed for nine days until an ICU bed became available. At operation, done by a consultant urologist, a ureteric tumour was found in addition to the bladder tumour and there were large para-aortic nodes. There was considerable bleeding from the nephrectomy site which required packing to stabilise the patient's condition. The patient was managed in intensive care in order that the lungs could be ventilated and 48 hours after initial surgery a registrar operated without supervision to remove the packs. Fortunately there was no further bleeding but the patient remained unconscious and died a week after the second operation without regaining consciousness.

Removal of a pack can be a hazardous procedure and consultant supervision should have been available.

Preparation for surgery

Table S172 (q30)
Preoperative precautions or therapeutic manoeuvres to improve the patient's preoperative condition

None	37
Antibiotics (pre- or intra-operative)	78
Bladder catheterisation	54
Intravenous fluids	41
Chest physiotherapy	34
Blood transfusion	26
Cardiac support drugs or anti-arrhythmic agents	25
Anticoagulants	20
Diuretics	19
Bowel preparation	13
Oxygen therapy	13
Correction of hypovolaemia	10
Gastric aspiration	8
Nutritional support	6
Tracheal intubation	2
Mechanical ventilation	2
Airway protection *(e.g. in unconscious patients)*	2
Others	14
Not answered	2
Total cases *(answers may be multiple)*	**166**

This table shows the various means used to prepare patients for their operations. The table below specifically focuses on methods of venous thromboembolic prophylaxis.

Table S173 (q31)
DVT prophylaxis

	Before/during	After
None	62	84
Leg stockings	85	62
Heparin	45	34
Heel support	15	6
Calf compression	14	2
Ripple mattress	2	1
Dextran infusion	1	2
Electrical stimulation	1	1
Warfarin	-	1
Other	2	3
Total cases *(answers may be multiple)*	**166**	***162**

* *(Excluding death in theatre - four cases)*

Venous thromboembolic complications remain a difficult and uncertain area to evaluate, and owing to the low postmortem examination rate, no conclusions can be drawn regarding the use of prophylactic measures. Eleven patients were considered to have had a proven pulmonary embolus (table S177). Seven of these patients had had venous thromboembolic prophylaxis. It thus remains impossible to make any useful statement about prophylaxis from these data.

Time of surgery

Table S174 (q37)
Classification of the final operation

Emergency	2
Urgent	24
Scheduled	95
Elective	44
Not answered	1
Total	**166**

The majority of work done, in this sample of patients who died, was scheduled or elective (84%). Even patients who were admitted as emergencies subsequently had scheduled or elective surgery (see table below); this reflects the workload produced by urinary outflow obstruction and acute retention. Those patients who had elective admissions but whose final operation was an emergency were those with postoperative complications requiring a return to the operating theatre.

Table S175 (qs 12 and 37)
Admission category by classification of final operation

Admission category	Classification of final operation					
	Emergency	Urgent	Scheduled	Elective	Not stated	**Total**
Emergency	-	18	43	5	1	67
Urgent	-	1	7	1	-	9
Elective	2	5	45	38	-	90
Total	**2**	**24**	**95**	**44**	**1**	**166**

Table S176 (q40)
Day of operation

Monday	20
Tuesday	37
Wednesday	42
Thursday	29
Friday	29
Saturday	6
Sunday	3
Total	**166**

Nine procedures were performed at weekends, and four were reported to have taken place out-of-hours on weekdays.

Unanticipated intra-operative problems

When unanticipated intra-abdominal problems occurred they were associated with previous sepsis or tumour removals. The occurrence of these problems was not related to the grade of the surgeon.

Complications

Sixty-seven per cent of all patients were managed in a ward environment without receiving ICU or HDU management. This figure must be placed against the fact that only 20 (12%) patients had no recognised co-existing problems at the time of surgery (table S166) and only 37 (22%) patients required no specific preoperative therapeutic manoeuvre to improve their condition (table S172).

There were three instances where the surgeon wished to admit the patient to an ICU or HDU but no bed was available.

Table S177 (q56)
Specific postoperative complications

Cardiac problems	68
Respiratory distress	37
Renal failure	26
Haemorrhage/postoperative bleeding requiring transfusion	25
Stroke or other neurological problems	21
Generalised sepsis	17
Urinary tract infection	9
Urinary retention/catheter blockage	8
DVT and/or pulmonary embolus†	6
Nutritional problems	6
Hepatic failure	4
Other	48
Total cases* *(answers may be multiple)*	**162**

* *(Excluding death in theatre - four cases)*
† In the postmortem reports received, there were 11 confirmed pulmonary emboli.

Significant hyponatraemia was not reported. The problem of the TUR syndrome appears to have been overstated. There were many anticipated perioperative problems as might have been expected, since 93 (56%) patients in ASA Class 3 and 4 (table S166).

Figure S8 (qs 39 and 58)
Calendar days between operation and death
(i.e. not 24 hour periods)

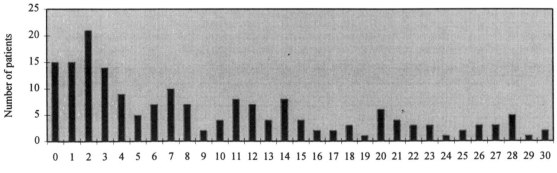

Calendar days between operation and death

———— o o o o ————

Vascular Surgery

The advisors in vascular surgery were:

Mr R B Galland	(Anglia and Oxford)
Mr G Hamilton	(North Thames)
Mr P M Lamont	(South and West)

Professor C McCollum (Manchester) was nominated but was unable to attend any meetings.

NCEPOD is very grateful to these advisors for their help and advice.

Points

- Thirty-six percent of emergency or urgent vascular surgery in this sample was done by surgeons with no regular vascular practice.
- Surgeons managing acute limb ischaemia must have the support of vascular interventional radiologists.
- Any hospital receiving major vascular emergencies or trauma must maintain an immediately available on-call surgical team, and must have adequate ICU/HDU services.
- Anaesthetists should be fully involved in the care of vascular patients, particularly those undergoing embolectomy, when this is being done with local anaesthesia or sedation.

Sample

The 1993/94 NCEPOD survey was based on questionnaires concerning the first perioperative death reported for individual consultant surgeons. Thus, no consultant surgeon received more than one questionnaire (see page 10). Two-hundred-and-eighty-one cases made up the sample in vascular surgery, of which 209 questionnaires, from 146 hospitals, were returned and analysed. A further four questionnaires were returned but for various reasons (see page 19), not analysed. The overall return rate was therefore 76%.

Audit

One-hundred-and-eighty-three patients (86%) were considered at a local audit meeting. The postmortem examination rate was 39% (82/209). There were 16 hospital postmortem examinations and 66 Coroners' postmortem examinations. A copy of the report was received by the surgical team in 14 of the hospital examinations and 53 of the Coroners' cases.

A postmortem examination might reveal information which would be instructive and point to improvements in management and surgical technique. There were cases in which there was some disagreement between the anaesthetist and surgeon as to the postoperative complications and cause of death. A postmortem examination might have clarified the situation in these cases and provided information for education and audit.

List of procedures

Table S178 (q47)
Final operation performed

Aneurysm surgery

Repair of ruptured abdominal aortic aneurysm	88
Surgery for abdominal aortic aneurysm (not ruptured)	13
Laparotomy for bleeding following aneurysm surgery	3
Repair ruptured iliac aneurysm	1
Repair femoral aneurysm	1

Reconstruction for occlusive aortic disease

Aortofemoral bypass	3
Axillobifemoral bypass	2

Lower limb revascularisation

Femoral embolectomy (may be bilateral)	26
Embolectomy for saddle embolus	4
Femoropopliteal bypass (all techniques)	3
Exploration of femoral and popliteal arteries	2
Exploration of wound (bleeding)	1
Revision of anastomosis	1

Amputations

Amputation - above knee	26
Amputation - below knee	13
Refashioning/revision/debridement of stump	5
Amputation - through knee	3
Amputation - toe/foot	3

Others

Debridement and/or fasciotomy (main procedure)	2
Brachial embolectomy	2
Carotid surgery	2
Varicose vein surgery	2
Evacuation of haematoma (main procedure)	1
Miscellaneous	5

Total cases *(answers may be multiple)*   **209**

There were 13 examples of inappropriate surgery. These concerned:

- Surgery where death seemed inevitable
- The management of abdominal aortic aneurysms
- The management of acutely ischaemic legs

There were instances of patients with abdominal aortic aneurysms who were operated on by general surgeons without a vascular interest. The outcome may have been improved had a specialist vascular surgeon been involved with the case. Examples included technical difficulties during the elective repair of an inflammatory aneurysm which contributed to the patient's death, and a decision to operate on a patient who had suffered a rupture of an abdominal aortic aneurysm and who presented in a pulseless state with no detectable oxygen saturation prior to surgery.

The management of acute ischaemia of the leg may require the use of diagnostic radiology, thrombolysis, reconstructive surgery or even the consideration of a primary amputation. There were several patients who presented with acute limb ischaemia, where a clinical diagnosis of embolism was made without arteriography, and embolectomy was attempted, but was unsuccessful because the true diagnosis was thrombosis or atheroma. The optimum management of this latter condition requires specialist vascular expertise and a vascular opinion would have been helpful in these cases prior to embolectomy.

Admission details

Table S179 (q12)
Admission category

Elective	41
Urgent	15
Emergency	153
Total	**209**

Of these patients who died after surgery, only 41 were elective admissions whilst 168 (80%) were urgent or emergency admissions. Vascular emergencies are associated with a high morbidity and mortality and ideally require the services of an appropriately experienced vascular surgeon.

Table S180 (q1)
Type of hospital in which the final operation took place

District General hospital	152
University/teaching hospital	53
Independent hospital	3
Defence Medical Services hospital	1
Total	**209**

Not all these hospitals were appropriate for the operations done since ICU and HDU services were not always available or adequate. Hospitals which do not have adequate ICU services and are unable to offer haemofiltration should not be treating vascular emergencies which might cause renal problems. In one case a 69-year-old woman presented initially to a DGH with a ruptured iliac aneurysm. There was no vascular expertise at this hospital so she was transferred to a second hospital where an emergency operation was done successfully by a specialist vascular surgeon. The patient then developed acute tubular necrosis; the ICU did not have facilities to deal with this so she was transferred to a third hospital for haemodialysis. The patient died at the third hospital after a laparotomy to evacuate a perigraft haematoma.

Table S181 (q2)
Availability of services

	Available in the hospital	Available 24hrs per day, 7 days per week
Theatre recovery area	208	152
Adult ICU	201	186
Adult HDU	71	57
Emergency theatre	176	88
Total cases (*answers may be multiple*)	**209**	

Lack of angiography

Acute ischaemia of the leg is rarely due to an embolus, and an arteriogram can be crucial in the diagnosis and management of acute ischaemia. Thrombolysis or suction thrombectomy may prevent the need for surgery and arteriography can demonstrate the extent of arterial disease and the need for more extensive surgery. Hospitals receiving and treating patients for ischaemia must have access to an angiographic and interventional radiological service and must use it. Failing this the patient should be transferred to a hospital that does provide these services.

A typical example of such failure to properly investigate patients concerns a 71-year-old man with known arterial disease. He presented with acutely ischaemic legs, no arteriography was done and a right femoral artery embolectomy was attempted by an SHO (supervised by a senior registrar). The embolectomy catheter would not pass down the femoral artery because of an atheromatous stricture. Surgery was abandoned, the patient was managed with symptom control and died 36 hours after presentation.

Patient profile

Table S182 (qs 3 and 4)
Age of patient at final operation

Years		Male	Female
11 to 20	1	-	1
21 to 30	-	-	-
31 to 40	-	-	-
41 to 50	-	-	-
51 to 60	11	7	4
61 to 70	44	31	13
71 to 80	92	63	29
81 to 90	55	29	26
91 to 100	6	1	5
Total	**209**	**131**	**78**

Most patients were over 50 years of age and 197 (94%) were aged over 60 years. There was one death in a young patient who developed insurmountable vascular complications following viral myocarditis.

Table S183 (q29)
Co-existing problems at the time of the final operation

None	17
Cardiac	135
Vascular	71
Respiratory	67
Renal	35
Neurological	31
Sepsis	26
Endocrine *(including diabetes mellitus)*	25
Musculoskeletal	16
Gastrointestinal	15
Haematological	10
Psychiatric	7
Alcohol-related problems	2
Drug addiction	1
Other	21
Not answered	5
Not known/not recorded	2
Total cases *(answers may be multiple)*	**209**

In view of the many general problems which co-existed with the vascular pathology it was to be expected that other specialties provided some input into the care of these patients. This was the case on 38 occasions and some surgeons cooperated with another surgeon in managing patients.

Table S184 (q23)
Was care undertaken on a formal shared basis with another specialty (excluding anaesthesia)?

Physician/general medicine/medicine	9
Care of the elderly/geriatrics	6
Cardiology	5
Intensive care	4
Diabetic medicine	4
Vascular surgery	2
Nephrology	2
General surgery with interest in vascular surgery	1
General surgery with interest in gastroenterology	1
General surgery	1
Urology	1
Neurosurgery	1
Rheumatology	1
Dermatology	1
Bacteriology	1
Chest medicine	1
Radiology	1
Dietetics	1
Continuing medical care	1
Total cases *(answers may be multiple)*	**38**

Table S185 (q28)
ASA Class

ASA Class 1	-
ASA Class 2	28
ASA Class 3	57
ASA Class 4	79
ASA Class 5	38
Not answered	6
Not known/not recorded	1
Total	**209**

There was a high proportion of patients in ASA classes 3 to 5 (174/209, 83%) and there were no patients who were thought by the surgeons to be ASA 1.

Table S186 (q35)
Anticipated risk of death related to the proposed operation

Not expected	12
Small but significant risk	29
Definite risk	140
Expected	28
Total	**209**

Surgeons stated that 12 patients were not expected to die. Something unexpected happened so what did the surgical team do to find out the cause? Only five of these patients had a hospital postmortem examination. How did the surgeons audit the outcome for the remaining seven patients?

The surgical team

Table S187 (q22)
Specialty of consultant surgeon in charge at time of final operation

Vascular	15
General with special interest in vascular surgery	130
Transplantation	2
General surgery	25
General with special interest in gastroenterology	24
General with special interest in urology	4
General with special interest in breast surgery	4
General with special interest in transplantation	3
General with special interest in colorectal surgery	1
General with special interest in laparoscopic surgery	1
Total	**209**

One hundred and forty-seven (70%) patients were treated by surgeons with an appropriate interest. This means, however, that 30% of patients who died following vascular procedures were under the care of surgeons who did not have a regular practice in vascular surgery. These surgeons had other special interests and, whilst they were specialists by day, they were required to be generalists at night as part of the on-call rota. This can be seen from the table below.

Table S188

Specialty of consultant surgeon in charge by classification of operation

	Classification of final operation	
	Emergency or urgent	Scheduled or elective
Vascular	9	6
General with special interest in vascular surgery	92	38
Transplantation	-	2
General surgery	21	4
General with special interest in gastroenterology	23	1
General with special interest in urology	4	-
General with special interest in breast surgery	4	-
General with special interest in transplantation	3	-
General with special interest in colorectal surgery	1	-
General with special interest in laparoscopic surgery	1	-
Total	**158**	**51**

Whilst 86% (44/51) of the scheduled and elective vascular cases were done under a surgeon with a vascular interest, 36% (57/158) of those patients who required emergency or urgent operations, were operated on by surgeons with no regular practice in vascular surgery. Was this in the patients' best interests?

Many patients with complex vascular problems require a specialist opinion. The clinical profile below describes a patient who was appropriately managed by two surgeons.

> A 70-year-old man presented to a general surgeon with a probable ruptured abdominal aortic aneurysm. The patient was known to have pulmonary, cardiac and renal disease and was taking warfarin. He was stable enough to allow a CT scan which confirmed the diagnosis. The general surgeon called in a vascular surgeon and they operated together; the operation commenced at 5.00pm on a Friday. In addition to repairing the aneurysm it was necessary to perform an embolectomy on one leg. At some point (possibly at induction) the patient suffered a myocardial infarction and problems with poor myocardial function and peripheral perfusion became obvious in the postoperative period. Death occurred 24 hours after surgery; a postmortem confirmed an intact graft and a recent myocardial infarction.

Despite the outcome, this is an example of good practice with two surgeons operating together.

Specialist referral and organisation of vascular services

When a patient is transferred between hospitals, ostensibly for a vascular opinion, it is important that such an opinion is available. This did not always happen. On several occasions patients were transferred from one DGH to another, only to be seen at the second hospital by the receiving surgeon who was a general surgeon with no declared interest in vascular surgery. There should be a recognised arrangement for transfer of patients to the care of specialist vascular surgeons.

Similarly, surgeons without a vascular expertise should refer patients to a colleague when a vascular opinion is needed. This may avoid unnecessary and inappropriate operations.

Table S189 (qs 24 and 34)
Most senior surgeon involved in decision-making prior to surgery

		(locums)
Consultant	175	(7)
Associate specialist	2	-
Senior registrar	20	(1)
Registrar	10	-
Staff grade	1	-
Senior house officer	1	-
Total	**209**	

Table S190 (qs 43 and 46)
Grade of most senior operating surgeon

		(locums)	Supervision?
Consultant	126	(8)	n/a
Associate specialist	3	-	1
Senior registrar	33	(3)	10
Registrar	38	(1)	10
Staff grade	1	-	-
Senior house officer	7	(1)	3
Not answered	1	-	-
Total	**209**		

Seventy-eight percent of all patients were operated on by a senior surgeon (consultant, associate specialist or senior registrar). Senior house officers operated on seven patients; senior supervision was provided in three cases. The four procedures where supervision was not given were all amputations. In two of these cases anaesthetic and surgical SHOs were working together, without senior support, treating elderly frail patients out of hours. This is not acceptable.

Availability of surgical on-call teams

In one case an SHO and an associate specialist were operating on a ruptured abdominal aortic aneurysm but found that they needed consultant help, and eventually had to call in the on-call consultant from a neighbouring hospital, because none of the consultants from their own hospital were available.

There was no anaesthetic questionnaire for this case. The co-operation of the consultant who finally came to help is to be applauded. **Any hospital receiving major surgical emergencies or trauma must maintain an on-call team on site.** Duty rotas must also be regularly revised and updated to ensure that the designated on-call staff are available.

There were instances when a registrar managed a patient's care without any referral or discussion with a senior surgeon. This sometimes led to inappropriate care and discussion with a senior might have altered the management and avoided inappropriate surgery.

Preparation for surgery

Table S191 (q30)
Preoperative precautions or therapeutic manoeuvres to improve the patient's preoperative condition

None	13
Intravenous fluids	147
Antibiotics (pre- or intra-operative)	110
Urinary catheterisation	107
Oxygen therapy	87
Correction of hypovolaemia	77
Cardiac support drugs or anti-arrhythmic agents	46
Blood transfusion	46
Anticoagulants	29
Diuretics	27
Gastric aspiration	25
Chest physiotherapy	25
Tracheal intubation	12
Mechanical ventilation	11
Airway protection (e.g. in unconscious patients)	9
Nutritional support	7
Vitamin K	2
Bowel preparation	1
Others	21
Not answered	2
Total cases (answers may be multiple)	**209**

This table shows the various means used to prepare patients for their operations. The table below specifically focuses on methods of venous thromboembolic prophylaxis. The reader should bear in mind that prophylaxis in the form of anticoagulants, e.g. heparin, would be inappropriate in cases of active haemorrhage such as a ruptured abdominal aortic aneurysm.

Table S192 (q31)
DVT prophylaxis

	Before/during	After
None	90	88
Heparin	87	66
Leg stockings	27	23
Heel support	30	10
Calf compression	18	2
Ripple mattress	6	10
Warfarin	2	6
Dextran infusion	1	1
Electrical stimulation of calves	1	-
Other	4	-
Total cases (answers may be multiple)	**209**	***174**

* (Excluding death in theatre - 35 cases)

Time of surgery

Table S193 (q37)
Classification of the final operation

Emergency	102
Urgent	56
Scheduled	38
Elective	13
Total	**209**

The majority (76%) of operations , in this sample of patients who died, were emergencies or urgent procedures. Vascular disease continued to generate a heavy demand for emergency surgical services which was still incompletely and inappropriately met (see sections on the surgical team and essential services).

Delays

There were 13 cases where delays occurred, between admission and surgery, which were due to non-clinical factors. There were four instances where patients delayed surgery before finally agreeing to the procedure, three occasions where a theatre was not available, three cases where investigations, such as arteriography or ultrasonography, caused delay, two patients who were initially misdiagnosed leading to a delay in surgery and one patient whose operation was delayed due to the lack of a bed in the intensive care unit.

Table S194 (q40)
Day of operation

Monday	32
Tuesday	31
Wednesday	37
Thursday	35
Friday	33
Saturday	24
Sunday	17
Total	**209**

There were 49 (23%) operations done between 18.01 and 07.59 on weekdays and a further 41 operations were performed at weekends. Thus a total of 90 (43%) patients had operations "out of hours". This is a reflection of the urgent or emergency nature of the procedures in this specialty.

Unanticipated intra-operative problems

There were 51 (24%) operations where there were unanticipated problems during the surgery.

Table S195 (q49)
Unanticipated intra-operative problems

Haemorrhage	18
Cardiac arrest (whether successfully resuscitated or not)	12
Difficulties with control or suturing at the neck of an abdominal aortic aneurysm	7
Aortocaval fistula	3
Intra-abdominal adhesions	2
Need for "inflow" procedure	2
Inadequate provision from blood transfusion service	2
Miscellaneous *(one each of: respiratory arrest, unsuspected arterio-venous fistula, technical problems with anastomosis, abnormal anatomy, unspecified)*	5
Total cases *(answers may be multiple)*	**51**

Use of local anaesthesia and/or sedation

Fourteen patients died after a procedure which was done solely under local anaesthesia or sedation administered by the surgeon. On several occasions an anaesthetist was not present. NCEPOD recommends the presence of an anaesthetist in order to give sedation and analgesia, monitor the patient's condition and manage fluid and blood replacement as appropriate.

All the procedures were to extract arterial emboli; 11 were femoral, one brachial, one iliac and there was one saddle embolus of the aorta. Many of these patients seemed not to have experienced an embolic episode at all but rather thrombosis of an artery with pre-existing atherosclerosis; the operations were, therefore, inappropriate. There was also less use of arteriography and thrombolysis than would be expected.

Complications

Table S196 (q56)
Specific postoperative complications:

Cardiac problems	114
Renal failure	54
Respiratory distress	36
Haemorrhage/postoperative bleeding requiring transfusion	28
Peripheral ischaemia	20
Generalised sepsis	20
Neurological problems	16
Wound infection	10
Other organ failure	9
DVT and/or pulmonary embolus	6
Hepatic failure	5
Nutritional problems	4
Endocrine system failure	3
Wound dehiscence	3
Urinary tract infection	3
Urinary retention/catheter blockage	3
Other	31
Not answered	9
Total cases * *(answers may be multiple)*	**174**

* *(Excluding death in theatre - 35 cases)*

Table S197 (q51)
Was the patient admitted immediately to an ICU or HDU postoperatively?

ICU	79
HDU	6
Neither of the above	89
Total cases * *(answers may be multiple)*	**174**

* *(Excluding death in theatre - 35 cases)*

Thus 49% of the patients who survived their surgery (85/174) required the services of either an ICU or an HDU. NCEPOD cannot say, from the information available, whether these admissions to ICU/HDU were planned or unexpected; the high rate of emergency admissions and emergency/urgent operations suggests that much of the use of the critical care services was unforeseen which must have implications for the provision and management of these services. An additional 10 patients were admitted to an ICU/HDU after an initial period on a general postoperative ward. This increases the number of these patients who needed critical care services to 55%.

Surgeons reported that it was impossible to admit seven patients to an ICU/HDU despite the need. The main reason was the lack of an available bed (five cases). One patient was refused admission, on clinical grounds, by an intensivist in charge of the ICU and one patient died in the recovery area before admission to the ICU had taken place.

It is not good practice to embark upon elective aneurysm surgery without prior arrangements for an admission of the patient to an ICU/HDU bed. Even in good risk cases unexpected intraoperative difficulties may arise and in higher risk cases the added factor of the absence of an ICU may make the risks of surgery unacceptable. Occasionally the ICU resource was inappropriately used, as in the case of an 81-year-old man who suffered a myocardial infarction two days after a below knee amputation. He was known to suffer from carcinoma of the prostate, poorly controlled diabetes mellitus, ischaemic heart disease and asthma. Following the myocardial infarction he was transferred to the ICU for treatment, but the decision was made not to resuscitate him if his condition deteriorated.

Table S198 (q53)
Discharge from ICU/HDU due to:

Death	76
Elective transfer to ward	15
Pressure on beds	1
Other	4
Not answered	1
Total cases *(answers may be multiple)*	**95**

Five patients were subsequently re-admitted to an ICU/HDU because of deterioration in their condition.

Figure S9 (qs 39 and 58)
Calendar days between operation and death
(i.e. not 24 hour periods)

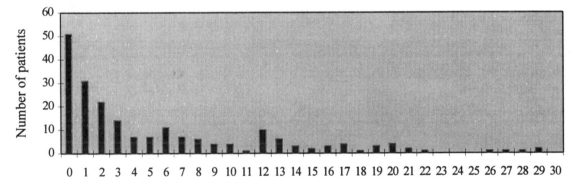

Calendar days between operation and death

Table S199 (qs 39 and 58)
Calendar days between operation and death
(i.e. not 24 hour periods)

Same day	51
Next day	31
2 days	22
3 days	14
4 days	7
5 days	7
6 to 10 days	32
11 to 15 days	22
16 to 20 days	15
21 to 30 days	8
Total	**209**

Special problems

Critical limb ischaemia

Patients with critical limb ischaemia often received less than optimal treatment. Surgeons without a regular vascular practice may not be aware of the nature of critical limb ischaemia and there is poor organisation of services; patients are not being treated by doctors with special expertise and interest. Vascular surgeons need to be supported by specialist anaesthetists, vascular interventional radiologists and diabetologists.[29]

Throughout this section there have been several references to inappropriate embolectomy. It has also been recommended that an anaesthetist be present at the procedure despite the fact that local anaesthesia is used. Even when embolectomy was appropriate, the administration of local anaesthesia and sedation was occasionally managed poorly by surgeons. In one incident a 72-year-old woman had an embolectomy by a surgical registrar who also administered intravenous sedation and local anaesthesia. This patient had a respiratory arrest and needed to be resuscitated by an anaesthetist who was called urgently to the operating theatre. An anaesthetist, if present from the start of surgery, could advise on the most appropriate anaesthetic techniques.

Ruptured abdominal aortic aneurysm

(see also Anaesthetic section page 66)

Some referrals with ruptured abdominal aortic aneurysms were inappropriate. Local protocols for the referral of patients with suspected ruptured abdominal aortic aneurysms could be drawn up and some patients could be given symptom relief by local practitioners if they do not fulfil criteria for referral.

Intra-operative and postoperative bleeding due to a coagulopathy is a not uncommon cause of death in these patients. The presentation of a patient with a ruptured abdominal aortic aneurysm can place a considerable strain on a haematology department, especially out of hours, and there is a need for generally accepted standards and local protocols governing the provision of blood, blood products and platelets. In one such case a 59-year-old man presented to a general surgeon with a ruptured abdominal aortic aneurysm. A consultant surgeon and senior registrar operated together with a registrar anaesthetist. A coagulopathy developed and in all there was a blood loss of 22 litres. Two further laparotomies were done in the next 48 hours in attempts to arrest haemorrhage; at both of these operations no specific bleeding point was found. The patient died of multi-organ failure nine days after surgery.

Cardiac assessment for patients prior to elective aneurysm surgery

There is little uniformity of practice at present. There ought to be well publicised and accepted protocols for cardiac assessment prior to elective surgery for abdominal aortic aneurysm. Calculation of a clinical index is a simple and reliable way of selecting patients who are at risk of developing adverse postoperative cardiac outcomes.[30] Currently it appears that being more than 65 years of age, having a history of myocardial infarction and/or coronary artery disease are better predictors of postoperative problems than a thallium scan.[31]

———— o o o o ————

Pathology

Pathology

Advisors:

Dr E W Benbow	(Manchester)
Dr J Burns	(Liverpool)
Dr S S Cross	(Sheffield)
Dr N J E Marley	(Portsmouth)
Dr A W Popple	(Carlisle)

NCEPOD is very grateful to these advisors for their help and advice.

Points

- The number of postmortem examinations performed was too low.
- The overall quality of postmortem examinations was generally satisfactory; early signs of improvement following the publication of the Royal College of Pathologists' "Guidelines for Post Mortem Reports" were evident.
- Communication between surgeons and pathologists was sometimes poor.
- Pre-printed formats for postmortem reports are undesirable since they limit the space available for description and interpretation. Flexible pre-formatted frameworks on word processors are recommended.
- There should be greater adherence to the standard format of the death certificate. Some clarification of the guidelines is needed.
- A clinico-pathological correlation should be included in all postmortem reports.
- Introduction of a system of audit, which includes Coroners' postmortem examinations, should be considered.

Review of surgical questionnaire

This section of the analysis is based on the total of 1913 surgical questionnaires returned to NCEPOD and analysed for the 1993/94 survey. The surgical cases were sampled on the basis of one per surgeon (normally the first death in the period) and included all age groups and specialties. Some procedures were excluded e.g. endoscopy, tracheostomy. In all, 840 (44%) postmortem examinations were recorded in the surgical questionnaires of which 707 were Coroners' cases and the remaining 133 were hospital postmortem examinations. The advisors reviewed those 429 Coroners' and 85 hospital postmortem reports which were enclosed with the questionnaires.

Table P1 (q64)
Was the death reported to the Coroner?

		%
Yes	1220	64
No	600	31
Not answered	53	3
Not known/not recorded	40	2
Total	**1913**	

If yes, was a postmortem examination ordered (and performed) under the Coroner's authority?

		%
Yes	707	58
No	486	40
Not answered/ Not known	27	2
Total	**1220**	

Failure on the part of doctors to recognize cases that should be reported to the Coroner may create administrative difficulties and additional distress for bereaved relatives. Other cases may evade medico-legal investigation altogether because they are not recognized as death due to unnatural causes. All doctors should be aware of the various categories of cases which require referral to the Coroner. Failure to identify reportable deaths has been a theme in previous NCEPOD reports.[5] Hospital consultants have recently been reminded of the guidelines for referral to the Coroner.[32]

Any case should be referred to the Coroner if the medical practitioner cannot readily certify death as being due to natural causes within the forms of regulation 41 of the "Registration of Birth and Deaths Regulations 1987". The following are some of the major categories:

◊   The cause of death appears to be unknown.
◊   There is any element of suspicious circumstances or a history of violence.
◊   The death may be linked to an unnatural event.
◊   The death may be due to industrial disease or related in some way to the deceased's occupation.
◊   The death is linked with an abortion.
◊   The death occurred during an operation or before full recovery from the effects of anaesthesia, or was in some way related to the anaesthesia.
◊   The death was related to a medical procedure or treatment.
◊   The actions of the deceased may have contributed to his or her own death, for example by suicide, self-neglect or drug abuse.
◊   The death occurred in police or prison custody.

Not statutory but desirable:

◊   The deceased was detained on a criminal charge under the Mental Health Act.
◊   The death occurred within 24 hours of admission to hospital.

If doubt persists, discussion with the Coroner is always advisable.

Table P2 (q65)
If a Coroner's postmortem examination was not performed, was a hospital postmortem examination requested?

Yes	286
No	692
Not answered/not known	228
Total	**1206**

In only 23.7% of possible hospital postmortem examinations was one requested (excluding no answer/not known), but overall (hospital and Coroners') the postmortem examination rate was 44%.

Table P3 (q65a)
The reasons for not requesting a hospital postmortem examination were:

		%
Cause of death known	164	24
Diagnosis already known	132	19
No clinical indication/not necessary	116	17
Relative-related*	33	5
Coroner felt not necessary	29	4
Age of patient	16	2
Patient under care of physician	11	2
Surgeon neglected to ask	8	1
Other	17	2
Not answered†	120	17
Not known/not recorded	77	11
Total cases *(answers may be multiple)*	**692**	

* This is separate from those cases where permission was requested, but denied by the patient's relatives.
† Many of these were cases that had been reported to the Coroner, but where a Coroner's postmortem examination was not performed.

The main reason why a postmortem examination was not requested was because the cause of death was already thought to be known. Many published studies, however, have shown that in a very substantial proportion of cases significant discrepancies are found between the clinical diagnosis and the postmortem findings (see also page 211).

Table P4 (q65b)
If a hospital postmortem examination was requested, was it performed?

		%
Yes	133	*47*
No	151	*53*
Not answered	2	*1*
Total	**286**	

If no, why not?

		%
Relatives refused permission	148	*98*
"Patient's size precluded postmortem"	1	*1*
Not answered	2	*1*
Total	**151**	

Permission for a hospital postmortem examination by the relatives of the deceased was refused in 52% of cases requested. Relatives should not feel unduly pressurized into granting permission for a postmortem examination. In particular, the threat of referral to the Coroner if permission is refused should be deprecated. It appears that between clinical specialties there is considerable variation in success in obtaining permission for a postmortem examination. Commonly the responsibility falls to the most junior member of the surgical team. Through publications like "The Autopsy and Audit"[33] clinicians should be regularly reminded of the value of the postmortem examination. It appears that the appropriate communication skills required when approaching bereaved relatives are sometimes lacking; few clinicians have received formal training.[34] It is recommended that there should be more formal training and that more senior doctors should be involved in obtaining permission for postmortem examinations.

Communication between surgeons and pathologists

Table P5 (q66)
Was the surgical team informed of the date and time of the postmortem examination?

	Hospital PMs		Coroners' PMs		All PMs	
		%		%		%
Yes	66	*50*	233	*33*	299	*36*
No	52	*39*	409	*58*	461	*55*
Not answered	6	*5*	28	*4*	34	*4*
Not known/not recorded	9	*7*	37	*5*	46	*5*
Total	**133**		**707**		**840**	

If yes, which member of the surgical team attended the postmortem examination?

	Hospital PMs	Coroners' PMs	All PMs
None	23	109	132
Consultant	9	33	42
Associate specialist	-	1	1
Senior registrar	6	10	16
Staff grade	1	2	3
Registrar	11	32	43
Senior house officer	6	37	43
House officer	19	21	40
Other	-	1	1
Not answered	1	5	6
Not known/not recorded	1	6	7
Total cases *(answers may be multiple)*	**66**	**233**	**299**

All efforts should be made to encourage clinico-pathological correlation in postmortem examinations. In only 36% of cases was the surgical team informed of the date and time of the postmortem examination. Surgeons cannot be expected to attend without this information. On the other hand, in 44% of those cases when the surgeons were supplied with this information, none of the surgical team attended. Clinicians should ensure that the Coroner or hospital pathologist is aware that they wish to attend. There are probably many other reasons why clinicians fail to attend postmortem examinations. Inconvenient timing of the postmortem examination and pressure of work were factors mentioned in the questionnaires.

Problems may arise from Coroners' postmortem examinations. Those which are of interest to hospital clinicians should ideally be carried out in the hospital mortuary. However, the Coroners' rules state that if the conduct of any member of hospital staff is likely to be called into question then the pathologist performing the postmortem examination should not be a colleague of the clinician involved. Under those circumstances, the Coroner may well arrange for an "independent" outside pathologist to perform the postmortem examination. Every effort should then be made to encourage the "independent" pathologist to attend the local hospital, rather than have the body removed to a second mortuary where the postmortem examination would be performed. It may be necessary to transport the body to a second mortuary if full facilities are not available in the first mortuary, or because of constraints on specialist pathologists' time. What is most undesirable is the routine transporting of bodies to a public mortuary which may be an inconvenient distance away.

It is important that good local communication occurs between pathologists and surgeons before the postmortem examination, and that the clinician is fully informed of the postmortem examination findings.

Table P6 (q68)
Did the consultant surgeon and his/her team receive a copy of the postmortem report?

	Hospital PMs	%	Coroners' PMs	%	All PMs	%
Yes	110	83	538	76	648	77
No	18	14	155	22	173	21
Not answered	4	3	12	2	16	2
Not known/not recorded	1	1	2	-	3	-
Total	**133**		**707**		**840**	

In 77% of these cases the surgeon received a written postmortem report. It is essential that written reports are produced and distributed. Each report should be filed in the patient's case notes, and a copy sent to the hospital consultant involved. The patient's general practitioner should also receive a copy of the report. Ideally this distribution of reports should also apply to Coroners' postmortem examinations. The Schedules to the Coroners' Rules note that the postmortem examination report is confidential and should not be disclosed to a third party without the Coroner's consent; however, communication at a local level between medical staff and the Coroner should enable dissemination to those with a valid interest. A small statutory charge may be levied by the Coroner for these reports, although in many instances this is waived. Occasionally there may be particular reasons why a report should remain confidential. These cases should be the exception rather than the rule.

Table P7 (q72)
Who performed the postmortem examination?

	Hospital PMs	%	Coroners' PMs	%	All PMs	%
Consultant/specialist pathologist	98	74	618	87	716	85
Junior pathologist	22	17	20	3	42	5
Not answered	12	9	48	7	60	7
Not known/not recorded	1	1	21	3	22	3
Total	**133**		**707**		**840**	

From the questionnaires it is evident that consultant pathologists perform the majority of postmortem examinations. It is of interest that junior doctors perform a higher proportion of hospital than Coroners' postmortem examinations. These data also reveal that three postmortem examinations were not performed by histopathologists. These were performed by a haematologist, a chemical pathologist and a microbiologist. All postmortem examinations should be performed by trained histopathologists. Some should be carried out by histopathologists with training and expertise in specialized areas, e.g. unexpected deaths in childhood.

Review of postmortem reports

The postmortem reports were returned with the surgical questionnaires in 61% (514/840) of those cases where a postmortem examination was indicated on the questionnaire. Of these, 429 were Coroners' postmortem examinations, the remaining 85 were hospital cases. Surgeons should make every effort to include the postmortem report: 326 reports were not included with the surgical questionnaires.

Those postmortem reports returned were reviewed by a group of pathologists representing district general, academic and forensic practice. In the analysis a check list was used which was similar to those used by the 1991/92 and 1992/93 review panels. Some modifications were made, but in the interests of continuity, these were only of a minor degree. The format of the check list employed is reproduced in Appendix E.

The group examined the postmortem reports using, as a "gold standard", the Guidelines from the Royal College of Pathologists,[35] published in August 1993, a time within the period under review. Since the postmortem reports were generally from the first death within the year, it appears unlikely that these guidelines had a major impact on the standards of the postmortem reports under review.

It was the view of the group that the Royal College guidelines should apply to all postmortem reports, whether hospital, Coroners' or forensic. These guidelines state that a postmortem report should normally include the following:

1. Demographic details.
2. History.
3. External examination.
4. Internal examination.
5. Histology report.
6. Summary of findings.
7. Commentary/conclusions.
8. Cause of death (standard format, previously OPCS).

Table P8
Is the report typewritten?

	Coroners'	Hospital	**Total**
Yes	427	85	**512**
No	2	-	**2**

Handwritten reports are becoming exceptional. Unavoidable circumstances may have accounted for the two recorded. Pre-printed formats, that restricted the space for all parts of the postmortem reports, were not unusual. These formats may be required by the Coroner, but impose excessive brevity, where longer descriptions would be more appropriate. We strongly recommend that they be replaced with more flexible pre-formatted frameworks on word processors.

Table P9
Is a clinical history provided?

	Coroners'	Hospital	**Total**
Yes	331	73	**404**
No	98	12	**110**

The history should be an integral part of the report and reference to notes or letters is unsatisfactory. The pathologist should obtain a full clinical history. The absence of a clinical history may indicate little or no prior knowledge of the case. Clinico-pathological correlation then becomes impossible and full value cannot be obtained from the postmortem examination. In addition, concern was expressed that in the absence of a history, the pathologist and mortuary staff may not be aware of potential hazards e.g. Hepatitis B, HIV, and Creutzfeldt-Jakob disease.

Less than 1% of clinical histories, when present, were unacceptable. There were instances when the details of the anaesthetic management were absent. In 2%, the external description was unacceptably brief or badly organized. Scars and incisions were measured in 54% of cases.

The gross description of the internal organs was deemed unacceptable in 1% of cases. In general the gross description of internal organs was satisfactory although in 10% no organs were weighed at all. The weighing of six organs, paired organs counting as one, remains the norm. In 9% the skull and brain were not examined. This represents a significant number of cases where the cause of death could wrongly be attributed to another organ system. In our survey there was no indication, in any case reviewed, of a request for a limited postmortem. This alternative should be exploited, and may be a very useful option when relatives are unwilling to agree to a full postmortem examination.

The serous cavities were described in 71% and intravascular cannulae in 18% of cases. When a serous effusion was present this was measured in 63% of cases. The position of intravascular cannulae, when present, was recorded in 9% of cases. Unless measurements of effusions are made it is difficult for the surgeon to determine the importance of the finding. The position of intravascular cannulae and catheters, especially the siting of the tip of these structures, can be of considerable value in assessing the significance of measurements made during life. All staff should be encouraged not to remove these devices before the patient is taken to the mortuary.

Table P10
Is the gross examination appropriate to the clinical problems?

	Coroners'	Hospital	Total
Yes	413	59	**472**
No	38	4	**42**

The correlation between the gross examination and the clinical problems was very difficult to assess in some cases, most often as a result of the absence of a thorough clinical history. The operation site must be described in detail even though it may have no direct relevance to the cause of death.

Table P11
Samples were taken for:

Answers may be multiple	Coroners'	Hospital	Total
Histology	79	37	**116**
Microbiology	5	1	**6**
Toxicology	3	-	**3**
Other	7	1	**8**
None of these investigations	341	47	**388**

Table P12
Is a histological report included with the PM report?

	Coroners'	Hospital	Total
Yes	47	32	**79**
No	382	53	**435**

When present, the histological report is:

	Coroners'	Hospital	Total
Unacceptably brief, obscure, not relevant to clinical need in this case	2	-	**2**
Poor	5	2	**7**
Satisfactory	13	7	**20**
Good	16	9	**25**
Fully detailed, informative, relevant to clinical need in this case	11	14	**25**

It appeared that histology reports continue to become separated from the macroscopic descriptions. It would be helpful for future NCEPOD reports if surgeons made greater efforts to submit both with the surgical questionnaires. It is also recommended that pathologists record in their reports whether samples have been taken for further tests. In the Royal College of Pathologists' guidelines, histology reports, excepting neuropathology, should be made within two to three weeks. Neuropathology will require four to six weeks for completion. When these guidelines are followed it is less likely that the histology report will become separated from the rest of the report.

Table P13
When absent, does the lack of histology detract significantly from the value of this report?

	Coroners'	Hospital	**Total**
Yes	209	37	**246**
No	173	16	**189**

The Royal College of Pathologists' guidelines emphasize the desirability of histology in all postmortem examinations. It can be used to confirm the impression of naked eye examination of organs, acting as an internal quality control. Even the most simple abnormality, noted macroscopically, may be misinterpreted.[36] In addition it provides evidence which can be used alongside the clinical and gross postmortem examination findings.

In some cases, the advisors recognized that histology would not have provided further insight into the clinical problem. However, in 57%, the lack of histology detracted significantly from the value of the report. Significantly more hospital postmortem examinations than Coroners' postmortem examinations had a histological report included with the postmortem report.

The provisions of the Human Tissue Act and the Coroners Act are set out in such a way that problems have arisen relating to histological examination in some Coroners' cases. Where there have been problems relating to histology in non-inquest cases, or histology that would be desirable to clarify clinical problems rather than absolutely necessary to determine the actual cause of death, then, as with matters relating to confidentiality, these may be resolved by communication at a local level.

Table P14
Is a summary of lesions present?

	Coroners'	Hospital	**Total**
Yes	74	41	**115**
No	355	44	**399**

When present, does this correspond accurately to the text report?

	Coroners'	Hospital	**Total**
Yes	74	37	**111**
No	-	4	**4**

Surgeons, general practitioners and Coroners find summaries valuable. Long lists of pathological findings are better presented in a systematic form. Many pathologists now code their postmortem findings and this helps in the retrieval of material for teaching and research purposes.

Table P15
Is a certified cause of death present?

	Coroners'	Hospital	Total
Yes	408	58	466
No	21	27	48

When present, does it correspond accurately to the text report?

	Coroners'	Hospital	Total
Yes	362	51	413
No	46	7	53

Does it follow standard formatting rules?

	Coroners'	Hospital	Total
Yes	343	44	387
No	65	14	79

Coroners usually require a cause of death in the standard format. There appeared to be a different approach in hospital postmortem examinations where fewer were expressed in this way.

Table P16
Summary of lesions/certified cause of death

	Both	%	Lesions only	%	Certified only	%	Neither	%	Total
Coroners'	59	14	15	3	349	81	6	1	429
Hospital	16	19	25	29	42	49	2	2	85

From the above table it appears that pathologists are to a certain extent using summaries of lesions and certified causes of death interchangeably, choosing the former more frequently in hospital rather than in Coroners' postmortem examinations. Rarely are both absent.

In general the certified cause of death corresponds to the text, but in more than 10% it did not. It was not unusual to find no reference to the preceding surgical procedure in the cause of death. The mode of death is not the same as the cause of death, and problems arise when this distinction is not made clearly. Useful guidance for doctors on differentiating mode and cause was given in "The Completion of Medical Certificates of Cause of Death"[37] and there is also helpful information to be found in the notes accompanying books of Medical Certificates of Cause of Death.

Table P17

Is a clinico-pathological correlation present?

	Coroners'	Hospital	**Total**
Yes	184	41	**225**
No	245	44	**289**

If yes, the clinico-pathological correlation is:

	Coroners'	%	Hospital	%	**Total**
Unacceptably brief, obscure, uninformative	2	1	2	5	**4**
Poor	12	7	2	5	**14**
Satisfactory	57	31	8	20	**65**
Good	58	32	14	34	**72**
Clear, concise, fully informative, accurate	55	30	15	37	**70**

Correlation of clinical and pathological findings is one of the most important aspects of a postmortem examination and therefore it is disappointing that it was found in less than half of our cases. When present, 8% were either poor or unacceptable.

Table P18

When the history, ante-mortem clinical diagnosis and cause of death are compared with the postmortem findings, this postmortem examination demonstrates:

	Coroners'	%	Hospital	%	Total
A discrepancy in the cause of death or in a major diagnosis, which if known, might have affected treatment, outcome or prognosis	49	11	10	12	59
A discrepancy in the cause of death or in a major diagnosis, which if known, would probably _not_ have affected treatment, outcome or prognosis	80	19	24	28	104
A minor discrepancy	10	2	0	0	10
Confirmation of essential clinical findings	**334**	78	**64**	75	**398**
An interesting incidental finding	28	7	7	8	35
A failure to explain some important aspect of the clinical problem despite a satisfactory autopsy	11	3	4	5	15
A failure to explain some important aspect of the clinical problem as a result of an unsatisfactory autopsy	17	4	1	1	18
Some other feature	10	2	3	3	13
Total (answers may be multiple)	**429**		**85**		**514**

(Based on identification of diagnostic discrepancies in Hill and Anderson[38])

In over 11% of postmortem examinations, a discrepancy in the cause of death or in a major diagnosis, which if known, might have affected treatment, outcome or prognosis, was found. These results compare closely with previously reported studies.[39, 40, 41]

Confirmation of essential clinical findings was found in 77% of cases. Positive value can be gained by confirmation of clinical findings at postmortem, in terms of audit, education, training and research. In addition, death statistics will be improved.

Table P19
Overall score for the postmortem examination

	Coroners'	Hospital	**Total**
Excellent, an exemplary report, meeting the highest standards of practice	15	13	**28**
Good	164	38	**202**
Satisfactory	189	22	**211**
Poor	53	12	**65**
Unacceptable, laying the pathologist open to serious professional criticism	8	-	**8**

Two percent of reports were considered unacceptable. The total of unacceptable and poor reports was 73, representing 14% of all cases reviewed. This is a considerable improvement on the figure of 28% in the 1992/93 sample year, but it is important to remember that the study populations were not strictly comparable. It is hoped, however, that this may indicate a trend in improvement of standards. This may further improve when the influence of the Royal College of Pathologists' guidelines is seen. This can be expected in future NCEPOD studies.

References

References

1 Buck N, Devlin H B, Lunn J N. *The Report of a Confidential Enquiry into Perioperative Deaths.* Nuffield Provincial Hospitals Trust and The King Edward's Hospital Fund for London. London, 1987.

2 Campling E A, Devlin H B, Lunn J N. *The Report of the National Confidential Enquiry into Perioperative Deaths 1989.* London, 1990.

3 Campling E A, Devlin H B, Hoile R W, Lunn J N. *The Report of the National Confidential Enquiry into Perioperative Deaths 1990.* London, 1992.

4 Campling E A, Devlin H B, Hoile R W, Lunn J N. *The Report of the National Confidential Enquiry into Perioperative Deaths 1991/1992.* London, 1993.

5 Campling E A, Devlin H B, Hoile R W, Lunn J N. *The Report of the National Confidential Enquiry into Perioperative Deaths 1992/1993.* London, 1995.

6 Haynes S R, Lawler P G P. *An assessment of the consistency of ASA Physical Status Classification.* Anaesthesia 1995; **50:**105-9.

7 King's Fund Organisational Audit, 1992.

8 *Assistance for the Anaesthetist.* Association of Anaesthetists of Great Britain and Ireland, 1988.

9 *Guidelines for Purchasers.* Royal College of Anaesthetists.

10 *Specialist Training in Anaesthesia - Guidelines for Educational Approval.* Royal College of Anaesthetists, June 1996.

11 *Anaesthetic Record Set; Suggestions as to a reasonable content.* Royal College of Anaesthetists, Association of Anaesthetists of Great Britain and Ireland, Society for Computing and Technology in Anaesthetics. April 1996.

12 Patterson B M, Healey J H, Cornell C N, Sharrock N E. *Cardiac arrest during arthroplasty with a cemented long-stem component.* Journal of Bone and Joint Surgery. February 1991. **73-A No 2:** 271-277.

13 *Fractured Neck of Femur. Prevention and management.* The Royal College of Physicians of London. January 1989.

14 Audit Commission. *United they stand. Co-ordinating care for elderly patients with hip fracture.* HMSO 1995.

15 Todd C J, Freeman C J, Camilleri-Ferrante C, Palmer C R, Hyder A, Laxton C E, Parker M J, Payne B V, Rushton N. *Differences in mortality after fracture of hip: the East Anglian audit.* BMJ 1995. **310:** 904-908.

16 Kreibach et al. *Geriatricians and perioperative care.* Health Trends 1995; **27:** 43.

17 Bowling A. *Health care rationing: the public's debate.* BMJ 1996; **312:** 670-674.

18 Gillies T E, Ruckley C V, Nixon S J. *Fatal pulmonary embolism: still missing the boat.* Br J Surg, June 1996; **83 Suppl. 1**: 33.

19 Charlton J E. *Monitoring and supplemental oxygen during endoscopy.* BMJ 1995; **310:**886-7.

20 Standing Medical Advisory Committee: *Report on the management of ovarian cancer, current clinical practices.* 1991.

21 *Report of the RCOG Working Party on Prophylaxis Against Thromboembolism in Gynaecology and Obstetrics.* March 1995.

22 Hall J C, Tarala R A, Tapper J, Hall J L. *Prevention of respiratory complications after abdominal surgery: a randomised clinical trial.* BMJ 1996; **312:** 148-153

23 Zalzal G H, Cottom R T. *Pharyngitis and Adenotonsillar Disease.* In: Cummings C W, Frederickson J M, Harker L A, Krause C J, Schuller D E,. eds. Otolaryngology - Head and Neck Surgery. 2nd New York: Mosby Year Books 1993; 1180-98.

24 Yardley M. *Is it appropriate to perform adenoidectomy tonsillectomy or adenotonsillectomy on a day case basis?* Clin. Otolaryngol. 1995, **20,** 95-96.

25 Kalogjera L, Pegan B, Petric V. *Adaptation to oral breathing after anterior nasal packing.* Acta Otolaryngol, (Stockh) 1995; **115:** 304-306.

26 *The Surgical Management of Jehovah's Witnesses.* The Royal College of Surgeons of England, 1996.

27 Cox M, Lumley J. *No blood or blood products.* Anaesthesia, 1995; **50:** 583-585

28 *Guidelines for Resuscitation.* European Resuscitation Council Secretariat, Belgium, 1994.

29 Dormandy J A. *Who should deal with patients with critical leg ischaemia?* Critical Ischaemia 1995; **5:** 79-81.

30 Krupski W C, Bensard D D. *Preoperative cardiac risk management.* Surgical Clinics of North America, August 1995; **Vol 75 No 4:** 647-663.

31 Baron J F, Mundler O, Bertrand M et al. *Dipyridamole-thallium scintigraphy and gated radionuclide angiography to assess cardiac risk before abdominal aortic surgery.* N. Engl. J. Med 1994; **330 No 10:** 663-669.

32 Coleman MP. *Death certification and referral to the Coroner.* Office for National Statistics. 1 July 1996.

33 *The Autopsy and Audit.* Report of the Joint Working Party of the Royal College of Pathologists, the Royal College of Physicians of London and the Royal College of Surgeons of England. London 1991.

34 Sherwood S J, Stuart R D, Birdi K S, Cotton D W, Bunce D. *How do clinicians learn to request permission for autopsies?* Med Educ 1995; **29 (3):** 231-4.

35 *Guidelines for Post Mortem Reports.* The Royal College of Pathologists. London 1993.

36 Hunt C R, Benhow E W, Knox WF , McMahon R F T, McWilliam L J. *Can histopathologists diagnose bronchopneumonia?* J Clin Pathol 1995; **48**: 120-123.

37 *The Completion of Medical Certificates of Cause of Death.* Dr J S A Ashley MB FFCM, Deputy Chief Medical Statistician, OPCS, 1990.

38 Hill R B, Anderson R E. *The Autopsy - Medical Practice and Public Policy*. Butterworth, London 1988.

39 Cameron H M, McGoogan E. *A prospective study of 1152 hospital autopsies: I. Inaccuracies in death certification.* Journal of Pathology 1981; **133:** 273-283.

40 Cameron H M, McGoogan E. *A prospective study of 1152 hospital autopsies: II. Analysis of inaccuracies in clinical diagnoses and their significance.* Journal of Pathology 1981; **133:** 285-300.

41 National Advisory Committee for Scientific Services. *Autopsy Services in Scotland*. Edinburgh, SHHD, 1994.

Appendices

Appendix A - Abbreviations

A&E	Accident and Emergency
ASA	American Society of Anesthesiologists
BP	Blood pressure
CFAM	Cerebral function analysing monitor
CT	Computerised tomography
CVP	Central venous pressure
DA	Diploma in Anaesthetics
D&C	Dilatation and currettage
DGH	District General Hospital
DIC	Disseminated intravascular coagulation
DVT	Deep vein thrombosis
ECG	Electrocardiogram
ERCP	Endoscopic retrograde cholangio-pancreatogram
EUA	Examination under anaesthesia
FRCA	Fellow of the Royal College of Anaesthetists
HDU	High Dependency Unit
ICU	Intensive Care Unit
IPPV	Intermittent positive pressure ventilation
ODA	Operating Department Assistant
OPCS	Office of Population Censuses and Surveys (now the Office for National Statistics)
NSAID	Non-steroidal anti-inflammatory drug
PEG	Percutaneous endoscopic gastrostomy
SHO	Senior house officer
SLE	Systemic lupus erythematosus

Appendix B - Glossary

ADMISSION

Elective - at a time agreed between the patient and the surgical service.

Urgent - within 48 hours of referral/consultation.

Emergency - immediately following referral/consultation, when admission is unpredictable and at short notice because of clinical need.

AMERICAN SOCIETY OF ANESTHESIOLOGISTS (ASA) CLASSIFICATION OF PHYSICAL STATUS

Class 1

The patient has no organic, physiological, biochemical or psychiatric disturbance. The pathological process for which operation is to be performed is localised and does not entail a systemic disturbance. Examples: a fit patient with inguinal hernia, fibroid uterus in an otherwise healthy woman.

Class 2

Mild to moderate systemic disturbance caused either by the condition to be treated surgically or by other pathophysiological processes. Examples: non- or only slightly limiting organic heart disease, mild diabetes, essential hypertension, or anaemia. Some might choose to list the extremes of age here, either the neonate or the octogenarian, even though no discernible systemic disease is present. Extreme obesity and chronic bronchitis may be included in this category.

Class 3

Severe systemic disturbance or disease from whatever cause, even though it may not be possible to define the degree of disability with finality. Examples: severely limiting organic heart disease, severe diabetes with vascular complications, moderate to severe degrees of pulmonary insufficiency, angina pectoris or healed myocardial infarction.

Class 4

Severe systemic disorders that are already life-threatening, not always correctable by operation. Examples: patients with organic heart disease showing marked signs of cardiac insufficiency, persistent angina, or active myocarditis, advance degrees of pulmonary, hepatic, renal or endocrine insufficiency.

Class 5

The moribund patient who has little chance of survival but is submitted to operation in desperation. Examples: burst abdominal aneurysm with profound shock, major cerebral trauma with rapidly increasing intracranial pressure, massive pulmonary embolus. Most of these patients require operation as a resuscitative measure with little if any anaesthesia.

CAUSE OF DEATH - OFFICE OF POPULATION CENSUSES AND SURVEYS FORMAT

The condition thought to be the "Underlying Cause of Death" should appear in the lowest completed line of Part I.

I   (a)   Disease or condition directly leading to death*

       (b)   Other disease or condition, if any, leading to I (a)

       (c)   Other disease or condition, if any, leading to I (b)

II   Other significant conditions CONTRIBUTING TO DEATH but not related to the disease or condition causing it.

* This does not mean the mode of dying, such as heart failure, asphyxia, asthenia, etc.: it means the disease, injury or complication which caused death.

(NCEPOD) CLASSIFICATION OF OPERATIONS

Emergency

Immediate life-saving operation, resuscitation simultaneous with surgical treatment (e.g. trauma, ruptured aortic aneurysm). Operation usually within one hour.

Urgent

Operation as soon as possible after resuscitation (e.g. irreducible hernia, intussuception, oesophageal atresia, intestinal obstruction, major fractures). Operation within 24 hours.

Scheduled

An early operation but not immediately life-saving (e.g. malignancy). Operation usually within three weeks.

Elective

Operation at a time to suit both patient and surgeon (e.g. cholecystectomy, joint replacement).

DAY CASE

A patient who is admitted for investigation or operation on a planned non-resident basis (i.e. no overnight stay).

OUT OF HOURS

NCEPOD's definition of out-of-hours operating includes all operations started between 18.01 and 07.59 on a weekday, as well as operations performed at any time on a Saturday, Sunday or Bank Holiday.

GLASGOW COMA SCALE

Eye opening	Pts	Verbal response	Pts	Motor response to pain (best limb)	Pts
Spontaneous	4	Orientated verbal response	5	Obeys commands	5
Eye opening to speech	3	Confused verbal response	4	Localisation	4
Eye opening to pain	2	Inappropriate words	3	Flexion normal/abnormal	3
None	1	Incomprehensible sounds	2	Extension	2
		No verbal response	1	No motor response	1

RECOVERY AND SPECIAL CARE AREAS

(Definitions used by the Association of Anaesthetists of Great Britain and Ireland)

High dependency unit

A high dependency unit (HDU) is an area for patients who require more intensive observation and/or nursing care than would normally be expected on a general ward. Patients who require mechanical ventilation or invasive monitoring would not be admitted to this area.

Intensive care unit

An intensive care unit (ICU) is an area to which patients are admitted for treatment of actual or impending organ failure who may require technological support (including mechanical ventilation of the lungs and/or invasive monitoring).

Recovery area

A recovery area is an area to which patients are admitted from an operating room, where they remain until consciousness is regained and ventilation and circulation are stable.

STANDARDS, GUIDELINES AND PROTOCOLS

A **Standard of Practice** is the level of modern good practice to which all clinicians aspire.

A **Clinical Guideline** is a nationally agreed set of evidence based principles to guide endeavours to achieve the standard.

A **Protocol** is a locally derived plan to direct trainees and aid all practitioners to achieve the standard within the limits established in the guideline.

The differences between these terms are intentional but *legally* there may be no distinction to be made.

Appendix C

Anaesthetic Questionnaire

1993/94

NATIONAL CONFIDENTIAL ENQUIRY INTO PERIOPERATIVE DEATHS

35-43 Lincoln's Inn Fields, London, WC2A 3PN

ANAESTHETIC QUESTIONNAIRE (DEATHS) 1993/94

QUESTIONNAIRE No.   [A] [ ][ ][ ][ ]

DO NOT PHOTOCOPY ANY PART OF THIS QUESTIONNAIRE

QUESTIONNAIRE COMPLETION

The information you supply is important. It must be accurate if valid conclusions are to be drawn.

Neither the questions nor the choices for answers are intended to suggest standards of practice.

Please **enclose** a copy of the ANAESTHETIC record and of the fluid balance chart(s). Any identification will be removed in the NCEPOD office.

Many of the questions can be answered by "Yes" or "No".
Please insert the relevant **number** in the appropriate box eg

[1] for Yes

[2] for No

Where multiple choices are given, please insert the relevant letter(s) of your answer in the box(es), and leave the remaining boxes blank.

Eg question 12b

C
D

indicates that advice was sought from both a Senior Registrar and a Consultant.

Where more details are requested, please write in BLOCK CAPITALS.

Consultants or junior staff may write to the NCEPOD office under separate cover, quoting the questionnaire number.

All original copies of correspondence will be confidential (**but do not retain copies of your correspondence**).

The whole questionnaire will be shredded when data collection is complete.

In case of difficulty, please contact the NCEPOD office on:

071-831-6430

HAVE YOU ENCLOSED COPIES OF THE ANAESTHETIC RECORD AND FLUID BALANCE CHARTS?

PROXY ANAESTHETISTS

1. If you were not involved in any way with this anaesthetic and have filled out this questionnaire on behalf of someone else, please indicate your position.

   A   Chairman of Division
   B   College Tutor
   C   Duty Consultant
   D   Other Consultant
   E   Other (please specify)

   [ ] 1

HOSPITAL

2. In what type of hospital did the anaesthetic take place?

   A   District General Hospital or equivalent
   B   University/Teaching Hospital
   C   Surgical Specialty Hospital
   D   Other Acute/Partly Acute Hospital
   E   Community Hospital
   F   Defence Medical Services Hospital
   G   Independent Hospital
   H   Other (please specify)

   [ ] 2

THE ANAESTHETIST(S)

3. Grade(s) of all anaesthetist(s) who were present at the start of this anaesthetic. Enter the appropriate letter for each person present.

   A   Senior House Officer
   B   Registrar
   C   Senior Registrar
   D   Consultant
   E   Staff Grade
   F   Associate Specialist
   G   Clinical Assistant
   H   General Practitioner
   I   Hospital Practitioner
   J   Other (please specify)

   [ ][ ][ ][ ][ ][ ][ ][ ][ ][ ] A B C D E F G H I J   3

We want to know about the experience of the **most senior anaesthetist** in the operating room at the **start** of this procedure.

Questions 4 to 11 inclusive refer to **this** anaesthetist

4. Year of primary medical qualification

   [ ][ ] 4a

   Please state country: _____

   [ ] 4b

5. Year of first full-time anaesthetic training post ⬚⬚⬚⬚ 5a

Which higher diploma in **anaesthesia** is held? 5b

		Year of award
A	none	⬚
B	Fellowship (Royal College, College or Faculty)	⬚⬚⬚⬚
C	DA (or Part 1 FCAnaes)	⬚⬚⬚⬚
D	other (please specify)	⬚⬚⬚⬚

6. Was this anaesthetist employed in a locum capacity?

Yes = 1   No = 2   ⬚ 6

7. Is this locum post part of a recognised training programme?

Yes = 1   No = 2   ⬚ 7

8. How long had this locum anaesthetist been in this post at the time of this operation?

⬚⬚ months   8

9. Is this locum post an exchange one with another country?

Yes = 1   No = 2   ⬚ 9

10. Is this locum anaesthetist accredited by the Royal College of Anaesthetists?

Yes = 1   No = 2   ⬚ 10

11. If the most senior anaesthetist present was **not** in a training grade, please enter the appropriate letters in the boxes provided if he/she has regular weekly (ie more than 50 operations per year) NHS commitments in anaesthesia for the following:

⬚⬚⬚ 11

A cardiac surgery
B children under 3 years old
C neurosurgery

12. Did the anaesthetist (of whatever grade) **seek advice** at any time from another anaesthetist (not mentioned in question 3)?

Yes = 1   No = 2   ⬚ 12a

If **yes**, grade(s) of anaesthetist(s) from whom advice sought:

⬚⬚⬚⬚⬚⬚⬚⬚⬚⬚ 12b

A Senior House Officer
B Registrar
C Senior Registrar
D Consultant
E Staff Grade
F Associate Specialist
G Clinical Assistant
H General Practitioner
I Hospital Practitioner
J Other (please specify)

13. Did any colleague(s) (not mentioned in question 3) **come to help** at any time?

Yes = 1   No = 2   ⬚ 13a

If **yes**, grade(s) of anaesthetist(s) who came to help:

⬚⬚⬚⬚⬚⬚⬚⬚⬚⬚ 13b

A Senior House Officer
B Registrar
C Senior Registrar
D Consultant
E Staff Grade
F Associate Specialist
G Clinical Assistant
H General Practitioner
I Hospital Practitioner
J Other (please specify)

THE PATIENT

14. Date of patient's birth:

[ ][ ][ ][ ][ ][ ] 14
D D M M Y Y

15. Age of patient at time of operation:

——— Y ——— M 15

16. Date of admission to hospital in which final operation took place eg 05 04 93 (5 April 1993):

[ ][ ][ ][ ][ ][ ] 16
D D M M Y Y

17. Time of admission:

[ ][ ][ ][ ] 17
(use 24 hour clock)

18. Date of final operation:

[ ][ ][ ][ ][ ][ ] 18
D D M M Y Y

19. Date of death:

[ ][ ][ ][ ][ ][ ] 19
D D M M Y Y

20. Was the patient transferred from another hospital?

Yes = 1   No = 2   [ ] 20

21. If **yes**, had the patient's condition apparently deteriorated during transfer?

Yes = 1   No = 2   Not known = 3   [ ] 21

If **yes**, please explain:

———————————————————
———————————————————

THE OPERATION

22. Primary pre-operative diagnosis:

———————————————————
———————————————————

23. What operation was planned?

———————————————————
———————————————————

24. What operation was performed, if different?

———————————————————
———————————————————

25. If this operation was the most recent in a sequence, please list the previous procedures.

Procedure: Date

———————————————   ————————
———————————————   ————————
———————————————   ————————
———————————————   ————————

Please enclose a copy of all anaesthetic records

26. Classification of operation (last before death). See definitions below.

A   Emergency
B   Urgent
C   Scheduled
D   Elective

[ ] 26

DEFINITIONS

A   **Emergency**
Immediate life-saving operation, resuscitation simultaneous with surgical treatment (eg trauma, ruptured aortic aneurysm). Operation usually within one hour.

B   **Urgent**
Operation as soon as possible after resuscitation (eg irreducible hernia, intussusception, oesophageal atresia, intestinal obstruction, major fractures). Operation within 24 hours.

C   **Scheduled**
An early operation, but not immediately life-saving (eg malignancy). Operation usually within 3 weeks.

D   **Elective**
Operation at a time to suit both patient and surgeon (eg cholecystectomy, joint replacement).

27. Was a record of the patient's weight available?

Yes = 1   No = 2   ☐ 27

If **yes**, what was this weight?

If **no**, the estimated weight was _____ kg

_____ kg

28. Was a record of the patient's height available?

Yes = 1   No = 2   ☐ 28

If **yes**, what was this height? _____ cm

If **no**, estimated height was _____ cm

29. Was an anaesthetist **consulted** by the surgeon (as distinct from informed) **before the operation?**

Yes = 1   No = 2   ☐ 29

30. Where did the anaesthetist assess the patient before the operation?

A   Ward
B   Outpatient department
C   Theatre suite
D   Accident and Emergency Department
E   ICU/HDU
F   Other (please specify)

☐☐☐☐☐☐ 30a
A B C D E F

_____

G   Patient not assessed   ☐ G

30b. Was **this** anaesthetist present **at the start of the operation?**

Yes = 1   No = 2   ☐ 30b

31. Were any investigations done before the operation? (Including tests carried out in the referral hospital and available before the operation.)

Yes = 1   No = 2   ☐ 31a

If **yes**, which of the following?

PLEASE WRITE RESULTS IN THE SPACE NEXT TO THE TEST NAME

Indicate which test(s) by insertion of the appropriate letter in each box.

31b

A   Haemoglobin _____ $gm.litre^{-1}$ ☐ A

B   Packed cell volume (haematocrit) _____   ☐ B

C   White cell count _____ $x10^9.litre^{-1}$ ☐ C

D   Sickle cell test (eg Sickledex) _____   ☐ D

E   Coagulation screen _____   ☐ E

F   Plasma electrolytes   Na _____ $m\,mol.litre^{-1}$ ☐ F

G   K _____ $m\,mol.litre^{-1}$ ☐ G

H   Cl _____ $m\,mol.litre^{-1}$ ☐ H

I HCO_3 _____ $m\,mol.litre^{-1}$ ☐ I

J   Blood urea _____ $m\,mol.litre^{-1}$ ☐ J

K   Creatinine _____ $micro\,mol.litre^{-1}$ ☐ K

L   Serum albumin _____ $g.litre^{-1}$ ☐ L

M   Bilirubin (total) _____ $micro\,mol.litre^{-1}$ ☐ M

N   Glucose _____ $m\,mol.litre^{-1}$ ☐ N

O   Amylase _____   ☐ O

P   Urinalysis (ward or lab) _____   ☐ P

Q   Blood gas analysis _____   ☐ Q

R   Chest x-ray _____   ☐ R

S   Electrocardiography _____   ☐ S

T   Respiratory function tests _____   ☐ T

U   Special cardiac investigation (eg cardiac catheterization) _____   ☐ U

V   Special neurological investigation (eg imaging) _____   ☐ V

W   Others relevant to anaesthesia (please specify) _____   ☐ W

_____

32. Coexisting medical diagnoses (please enter the appropriate letter in a box, **and specify the disorder in the space next to the category**).

A none

B respiratory _____

C cardiac _____

D neurological _____

E endocrine _____ 32

F alimentary _____

G renal _____

H musculoskeletal _____

I haematological _____

J genetic abnormality _____

K obesity _____

L other (please specify) _____

A	B	C	D	E	F	G	H	I	J	K	L

_____
_____
_____

33. What drug or other therapy was the patient receiving regularly at the time of operation (but excluding premedication or drugs for anaesthesia)?

Please specify drugs in the space below.

_____
_____
_____
_____

34. Was there any history of a drug reaction?

Yes = 1   No = 2   [ ] 34

If **yes**, specify drug and reaction:

_____
_____
_____

35. ASA status (enter class number) 1 to 5 (Note we do not use the E subclassification)   [ ] 35

ASA GRADES

AMERICAN SOCIETY OF ANESTHESIOLOGY CLASSIFICATION OF PHYSICAL STATUS

CLASS 1

The patient has no organic, physiological, biochemical, or psychiatric disturbance. The pathological process for which the operation is to be performed is localized and does not entail a systemic disturbance.

Examples: a fit patient with inguinal hernia;
fibroid uterus in an otherwise healthy woman.

CLASS 2

Mild to moderate systemic disturbance caused either by the condition to be treated surgically or by other pathophysiological processes.

Examples: non-, or only slightly limiting organic heart disease
mild diabetes
essential hypertension
anaemia.

Some might choose to list the extremes of age here, either the neonate or the octogenarian, even though no discernible systemic disease is present. Extreme obesity and chronic bronchitis may be included in this category.

CLASS 3

Severe systemic disturbance or disease from whatever cause, even though it may not be possible to define the degree of disability with finality.

Examples: severely limiting organic heart disease
severe diabetes with vascular complications
moderate to severe degrees of pulmonary insufficiency
angina pectoris or healed myocardial infarction.

CLASS 4

Severe systemic disorders that are already life threatening, not always correctable by operation.

Examples: patients with organic heart disease showing marked signs of cardiac insufficiency
persistent angina or active myocarditis
advanced degree of pulmonary, hepatic, renal or endocrine insufficiency.

CLASS 5

The moribund patient who has little chance of survival but is submitted to operation in desperation.

Examples: the burst abdominal aneurysm with profound shock
major cerebral trauma with rapidly increasing intracranial pressure
massive pulmonary embolus.

Most of these patients require operation as a resuscitative measure with little if any anaesthesia.

PREPARATION OF PATIENT BEFORE OPERATION

36. When was the last fluid given by mouth? ☐ 36

- A   more than 6 hours before operation
- B   between 4-6 hours before operation
- C   less than 4 hours before operation
- D   not known/not recorded

Please specify nature and volume if known.

_____

37. Indicate measures taken to reduce gastric acidity and volume, as prophylaxis against acid aspiration.

☐A ☐B ☐C ☐D ☐E ☐F ☐G 37

- A   none
- B   antacids
- C   H₂ antagonists
- D   metoclopramide
- E   proton pump inhibitor (eg omeprazole)
- F   nasogastric/stomach tube
- G   other (please specify)

38. Did the patient receive intravenous fluid therapy in the 12 hours before induction? ☐ 38

Yes = 1   No = 2

If **yes**, please send copies of the fluid balance charts.

39. Were measures taken to improve or protect the cardiorespiratory system **before** induction of anaesthesia? ☐ 39a

Yes = 1   No = 2

If **yes**, please indicate which measure(s) by entering a letter for each.

☐A ☐B   ☐C ☐D ☐E ☐F ☐G 39b

- A   antibiotic therapy
- B   bronchodilators (specify nature and dose)

_____

- C   chest physiotherapy
- D   airway management eg oral airway, tracheostomy
- E   inotropes or vasoactive drugs
- F   steroids
- G   other (please specify)

_____

40. Were premedicant drugs prescribed? ☐ 40a

Yes = 1   No = 2

If **yes**, please enter the appropriate letter in each box, and specify drugs and dose in the space next to each category.

☐A ☐B ☐C ☐D ☐E ☐F ☐G ☐H ☐I ☐J ☐K ☐L ☐M ☐N ☐O ☐P ☐Q ☐R ☐S 40b

- A   Atropine _____
- B   Chloral hydrate _____
- C   Diazepam (eg Valium) _____
- D   Droperidol _____
- E   Fentanyl _____
- F   Glycopyrronium (Robinul) _____
- G   Hyoscine (Scopolamine) _____
- H   Lorazepam (eg Ativan) _____
- I   Ketamine _____
- J   Metoclopramide _____
- K   Midazolam (Hypnovel) _____
- L   Morphine _____
- M   Papaveretum (Omnopon) _____
- N   Pethidine _____
- O   Prochlorperazine (eg Stemetil) _____
- P   Temazepam _____
- Q   Promethazine (eg Phenergan) _____
- R   Trimeprazine (Vallergan) _____
- S   Other (please specify) _____

_____

THE ANAESTHETIC

41. Was **non-invasive** monitoring established just **before** the induction of anaesthesia?

Yes = 1   No = 2   ☐ 41a

If **yes**, please indicate

A   ECG
B   BP
C   pulse oximetry
D   other (please specify)

☐☐☐☐ A B C D 41b

_____

42. Was **invasive** monitoring established **before** induction of anaesthesia eg CVP, arterial line?

Yes = 1   No = 2   ☐ 42a

If **yes**, please indicate;

A   CVP
B   Arterial line
C   Pulmonary arterial line
D   Other (please specify)

☐☐☐☐ A B C D 42b

43. Were any measures taken (before, during or after operation) to prevent venous thrombosis?

Yes = 1   No = 2   ☐ 43a

If **yes**, please enter letter for each measure taken;

	Before or during	After
A aspirin	☐	☐ A
B heparin	☐	☐ B
C dextran infusion	☐	☐ C
D leg stockings	☐	☐ D 43b
E calf compression	☐	☐ E
F electrical stimulation of calves	☐	☐ F
G warfarin	☐	☐ G
H heel supports	☐	☐ H
I ripple mattress	☐	☐ I
J other (please specify)	☐	☐ J

_____

44. Time of start of anaesthetic:

☐☐☐☐ 44
(use 24 hour clock)

(enter "X" in boxes if times not recorded)

45. Time of start of surgery:

☐☐☐☐ 45
(use 24 hour clock)

46. Time of transfer out of operating room:
(ie to recovery, ICU etc)

☐☐☐☐ 46
(use 24 hour clock)

If you are not able to provide the **times**, please indicate total duration of operation
(ie time of start of anaesthetic to time of transfer):

_____ hours _____ mins

47. What was the grade of the most senior **surgeon** in the operating room?

A   House Officer
B   Senior House Officer
C   Registrar
D   Senior Registrar
E   Associate Specialist
F   Clinical Assistant
G   Staff Grade
H   Consultant
I   Other (please specify)

☐ 47

48. Was there a trained anaesthetist's assistant (ie ODA, SODA, anaesthetic nurse) present for this case?

Yes = 1   No = 2   ☐ 48

If **no**, please explain

_____
_____

FLUIDS DURING OPERATION

49. Is there an anaesthetic record for this operation in the notes?

Yes = 1   No = 2

□ 49

If **yes**, please send a complete copy of it with this questionnaire to the NCEPOD office. (We will delete/remove identification marks).

If **no**, please give as full an account as possible of the anaesthetic below. Please include details of anaesthetic agents, drugs, routes of administration, breathing systems, and tube size.

50. What was the assessed blood loss during operation?

□□□□ 50
ml

51. Did the patient receive intravenous fluids **DURING** the operation?

Yes = 1   No = 2

□ 51a

If **yes**, please indicate which;

51b **Crystalloid**

Fluid (indicate type by inserting appropriate letter)	Total volume during operation (mls)

A   Dextrose 5%

B   Dextrose 4% saline 0.18%

C   Dextrose 10%

D   Saline 0.9%

E   Hartmann's (compound sodium lactate)

F   Other (please specify)

51c **Colloid**

A   Modified gelatin (Gelofusine, Haemaccel)

B   Human albumin solution

C   Starch (HES)

D   Dextran

E   Mannitol (Please specify concentration)

F   Other (please specify)

51d **Blood**

A   Whole blood

B   Red cell component

C   Other component (please specify)

52. Were monitoring devices used during the management of this anaesthetic?

Yes = 1   No = 2   ☐ 52a

If **yes**, please indicate which monitors were used.

Please enter appropriate letter(s) in boxes:

	Anaesthetic Room	Operating Room
A ECG		A
B pulse oximeter		B 52b
C indirect BP		C
D pulse meter		D
E oesophageal or precordial (chest wall) stethoscope		E
F fresh gas O$_2$ analyser		F
G inspired gas O$_2$ analyser		G
H inspired anaesthetic vapour analyser		H
I expired CO$_2$ analyser		I
J airway pressure gauge		J
K ventilation volume		K
L ventilation disconnect device		L
M peripheral nerve stimulator		M
N temperature (state site)		N
O urine output		O
P CVP		P
Q direct arterial BP (invasive)		Q
R pulmonary arterial pressure		R
S intracranial pressure		S
T EEG/CFAM/evoked responses		T
U other (please specify)		U

V anaesthetic room not used   ☐ V

53. Was there any malfunction of monitoring equipment?

Yes = 1   No = 2   ☐ 53

If **yes**, please specify:

54. Did anything hinder full monitoring?

Yes = 1   No = 2   ☐ 54

If **yes**, please specify: (eg bilateral arm surgery, radiotherapy, skin pigmentation, inaccessibility, non-availability of monitors)

POSITION OF PATIENT

55. What was the position of the patient during surgery?   ☐ 55

A   supine
B   lateral
C   prone
D   sitting
E   knee-elbow
F   lithotomy (inc. Lloyd-Davies)
G   jack knife
H   head down
I   head up
J   other (please specify)

TYPE OF ANAESTHESIA

56. What type of anaesthetic was used?   ☐ 56

A   general alone (57-63)
B   local infiltration alone
C   regional alone (64-65, and 67)
D   general and regional (57-65)
E   general and local infiltration (57-63)
F   sedation alone (66-67)
G   sedation and local infiltration (66-67)
H   sedation and regional (64-67)

Please now answer the questions indicated in brackets, and then continue from question 68.

GENERAL ANAESTHESIA

57. Did you take precautions **at induction** to minimise pulmonary aspiration?

   Yes = 1   No = 2   ☐ 57a

   If **yes**, please indicate which;

   A   cricoid pressure
   B   postural changes – head up
   C   postural changes – head down
   D   postural changes – lateral
   E   preoxygenation without inflation of the lungs
   F   aspiration of nasogastric tube
   G   trachea already intubated on arrival in theatre
   H   other (please specify)

   [A B C D E F G H] 57b

58. How was the airway established during anaesthesia?

   A   face mask (with or without oral airway)
   B   laryngeal mask
   C   orotracheal intubation
   D   nasotracheal intubation
   E   endobronchial
   F   tracheostomy
   G   patient already intubated prior to arrival in theatre suite
   H   other (please specify)

   [A B C D E F G H] 58

59. If the trachea was intubated, how was the position of the tube confirmed?

   A   tube seen passing through cords
   B   chest movement with inflation
   C   auscultation
   D   expired CO_2 monitoring
   E   oesophageal detector device
   F   other (please specify)

   [A B C D E F] 59

60. What was the mode of ventilation during the operation?

   A   spontaneous
   B   controlled

   [A B] 60

---

61. Were muscle relaxants used during the anaesthetic?

   Yes = 1   No = 2   ☐ 61a

   If **yes**, please indicate which;

   A   depolarising
   B   non-depolarising

   [A B] 61b

62. Were there any problems with airway maintenance or ventilation?

   Yes = 1   No = 2   ☐ 62

   If **yes**, please specify

   _____

63. How was general anaesthesia maintained?

   A   nitrous oxide
   B   volatile agent
   C   narcotic agent
   D   intravenous infusions

   [A B C D] 63

REGIONAL ANAESTHESIA

64. If the anaesthetic included a regional technique, which method was used?

   A   epidural – caudal
   B   lumbar
   C   thoracic
   D   interpleural
   E   intravenous regional
   F   peripheral, nerve block, eg paravertebral, sciatic, intercostal
   G   plexus block (eg brachial, 3-in-1 block)
   H   subarachnoid (spinal)
   I   surface (eg for bronchoscopy)

   [A B C D E F G H I] 64

65. Which agent was used? Please specify drug(s) and dosage(s);

   A   local _____
   B   narcotic _____
   C   other (please specify) _____

   [A B C] 65

SEDATION (as opposed to General Anaesthesia)

66. Which sedative drugs were given for this procedure (excluding premedication)?

   A   inhalant

   B   narcotic analgesic   66

   C   benzodiazepine

   D   sub-anaesthetic doses of IV anaesthetic drugs

   E   other (please specify)

   [ ][ ][ ][ ][ ]   A B C D E

67. Was oxygen given?

   Yes = 1   No = 2   ☐ 67a

   If **yes**, for what reason?

   A   routine   [ ][ ] 67b   A B

   B   otherwise indicated (please specify indications)

   _____

RECOVERY FROM ANAESTHESIA

Definitions

(as used by the Association of Anaesthetists of Great Britain and Ireland)

A recovery area is an area to which patients are admitted from an operating room, where they remain until consciousness is regained and ventilation and circulation are stable.

A high dependency unit (HDU or area A) is an area for patients who require more intensive observation and/or nursing care than would normally be expected on a general ward. Patients who require mechanical ventilation or invasive monitoring would not be admitted to this area.

An intensive care unit (ICU) is an area to which patients are admitted for treatment of actual or impending organ failure who may require technological support (including mechanical ventilation of the lungs and/or invasive monitoring).

68. Which special care areas (see definitions above) **exist** in the hospital in which the operation took place?

   A   recovery area or room equipped and staffed for this purpose

   B   high dependency unit

   C   intensive care unit   68

   D   other (please specify) _____

   E   none of the above

   [ ][ ][ ][ ][ ]   A B C D E

69. Where did this patient go on leaving theatre?

   A   recovery area or room equipped and staffed for this purpose

   B   high dependency unit

   C   intensive care unit

   D   specialised ICU

   E   ward

   F   another hospital

   G   other (please specify) _____

   H   died in theatre

   ☐ 69

If the patient died in theatre please move to question 77.

70. Was that an optimal location for this patient?

   Yes = 1   No = 2   ☐ 70

   If **no**, please explain.

   _____

71. Would this destination represent your normal practice?

   Yes = 1   No = 2   ☐ 71

   If **no**, please explain.

   _____

72. Were you unable at any time to transfer the patient into an ICU, HDU, etc?

   Yes = 1   No = 2   ☐ 72a

   If **yes**, why?

   A   closed at night

   B   closed at weekend

   C   understaffing   72b

   D   lack of beds

   E   no ICU or HDU in hospital

   F   other (please specify)

   [ ][ ][ ][ ][ ][ ]   A B C D E F

   _____

RECOVERY AREA/ROOM

If the patient did not enter a recovery room, please move to question 76.

73. Were monitoring devices used during the management of this patient in the recovery room?

Yes = 1   No = 2   ☐ 73a

If **yes**, please indicate which monitors were used.

Enter the letter(s) in each appropriate box;

A   ECG
B   pulse oximeter
C   indirect BP
D   pulse meter
E   oesophageal or precordial (chest wall) stethoscope
F   inspired gas O_2 analyser
G   expired CO_2 analyser
H   airway pressure gauge
I   ventilation volume
J   ventilator disconnect device
K   peripheral nerve stimulator
L   temperature (state site) _____
M   urine output
N   CVP
O   direct arterial BP (invasive)
P   pulmonary arterial pressure
Q   intracranial pressure
R   other (please specify)

☐☐☐☐☐ 73b (A B C D E)
☐☐☐☐☐ 73c 73d (F G H I J)
☐☐☐ 73e (K L M)
☐☐☐☐☐ 73f (N O P Q R)

74. Time of transfer from recovery area:

☐☐☐☐ 74

(use 24 hour clock)

(enter "X" in boxes if not recorded)

75. Where did this patient go next (ie after the recovery room)?   ☐ 75

A   ward
B   high dependency unit
C   intensive care unit
D   specialised ICU
E   home
F   another hospital
G   died in recovery area
H   other (please specify)

76. Was controlled ventilation used postoperatively?

Yes = 1   No = 2   ☐ 76a

If **yes**, why?

A   routine management
B   respiratory inadequacy
C   control of intracranial pressure or other neurosurgical indications
D   part of the management of pain
E   other reasons (please specify) _____

☐☐☐ 76b (A B C)
☐☐ (D E)

CRITICAL EVENTS DURING ANAESTHESIA OR RECOVERY

77. Did any of the following events, which required specific treatment, occur during anaesthesia or immediate recovery (ie the first few hours after the end of the operation)?

Yes = 1   No = 2   ☐ 77a

If **yes**, please specify nature by insertion of the appropriate letter(s) in a box.

A   air embolus
B   airway obstruction
C   anaphylaxis
D   arrhythmia
E   bradycardia (to or less than 50% of resting)
F   bronchospasm
G   cardiac arrest (unintended)
H   convulsions

☐☐☐☐☐☐☐☐ A B C D E F G H 77b

I   disconnection of breathing system
J   hyperpyrexia (greater than 40°C or very rapid increase in temperature)
K   hypertension (increase of more than 50% resting systolic)
L   hypotension (decrease of more than 50% resting systolic)

☐☐☐☐ I J K L 77b

M   hypoxaemia (please state oxygen saturation)
N   misplaced tracheal tube
O   pneumothorax
P   pulmonary aspiration
Q   pulmonary oedema
R   respiratory arrest (unintended)
S   tachycardia (increase of 50% or more)
T   unintentional delayed recovery of consciousness

☐☐☐☐☐☐☐☐ M N O P Q R S T

U   ventilatory inadequacy
V   total spinal
W   wrong dose or overdose of drug
X   other (please specify)

☐☐☐☐ U V W X

Please specify location of patient, treatment and outcome.

_____
_____
_____
_____
_____

78. Was there any mechanical failure of equipment during anaesthesia or recovery (excluding that for monitoring)?

Yes = 1   No = 2   ☐ 78a

If **yes**, please specify:

A   equipment for IPPV
B   suction equipment
C   syringe drivers
D   infusion pump
E   other (please specify)

☐☐☐☐☐ A B C D E 78b

If the patient died in the theatre please move to question 83.

79. Were there **early** (ie up to 7 days) complications or events after this operation?

Yes = 1   No = 2   ☐ 79a

Please enter a letter for each, and specify in the space below each category:

A   ventilatory problems (eg pneumonia, pulmonary oedema)   ☐ A 79b

B   cardiac problems (eg acute LVF, intractable arrhythmias, post-cardiac arrest)   ☐ B

C   hepatic failure   ☐ C

D   septicaemia   ☐ D

E   renal failure   ☐ E

F   central nervous system failure (eg failure to recover consciousness)   ☐ F

G   other (please specify)   ☐ G

Please give an account of any adverse events during this period.

_____
_____
_____
_____

DEATH

80. Were narcotic analgesic drugs given in the first 48 hours after operation?

Yes = 1   No = 2   ☐ 80

If **yes**, please specify drug(s), dose(s), frequency and route(s):

_____

81. Did complications occur as a result of these analgesic methods?

Yes = 1   No = 2   ☐ 81

If **yes**, please specify

_____

_____

82. Were other sedative/hypnotic or other analgesic (non-narcotic) drugs given?

Yes = 1   No = 2   ☐ 82

If **yes**, please specify drug(s), dose(s), times and routes

_____

_____

83. Date of death:

☐☐ ☐☐ ☐☐ 83
D D M M Y Y

84. Time of death:

☐☐ ☐☐ 84

(use 24 hour clock)

85. Place of death:

A   theatre
B   recovery area
C   intensive care unit
D   high dependency unit
E   ward
F   home
G   another hospital
H   other (please specify)

☐ 85

_____

86. Cause of death:

_____

_____

87. Do you have morbidity/mortality review meetings in your department?

Yes = 1   No = 2   ☐ 87a

If **yes**, will this case be, or has it been discussed at your departmental meeting?

Yes = 1   No = 2   ☐ 87b

88. Has a consultant anaesthetist seen and agreed this form?

Yes = 1   No = 2   ☐ 88

REMINDER

**Have you enclosed copies of the
anaesthetic record and fluid balance charts?**

**THANK YOU FOR TAKING THE TIME TO COMPLETE THIS
QUESTIONNAIRE**

YOU MUST NOT KEEP A COPY OF THIS QUESTIONNAIRE

Please return it in the reply-paid envelope provided to:

NCEPOD
35-43 Lincoln's Inn Fields
LONDON
WC2A 3PN

If you wish to inform the NCEPOD office of any other details of this case,
please do so on a separate sheet.

CONSULTANT ANAESTHETISTS ONLY

We would like to publish the names of all
consultants who have returned completed questionnaires.

Please help us by providing your initials and surname.

This page will be removed from the questionnaire on receipt.

Initials _____ Surname _____

Appendix D

Surgical Questionnaire

1993/94

NATIONAL CONFIDENTIAL ENQUIRY INTO PERIOPERATIVE DEATHS
35-43 Lincoln's Inn Fields, London, WC2A 3PN

SURGICAL QUESTIONNAIRE (DEATHS) 1993/94

QUESTIONNAIRE No.   S

DO NOT PHOTOCOPY ANY PART OF THIS QUESTIONNAIRE

QUESTIONNAIRE COMPLETION

This questionnaire has been redesigned. We would like to know how much time you have taken to complete the questionnaire (excluding finding the notes).

Please note the time when you start.

Time taken: _____ hours _____ minutes

This questionnaire should be completed with reference to the last operation before the death of the patient specified by the NCEPOD office. If you feel that this was not the **main** operation in the period before the patient's death, you may give additional information.

The whole questionnaire will be shredded when data collection is complete. The information will be filed anonymously.

Neither the questions nor the choices for answers are intended to suggest standards of practice.

Please enclose a copy of all the relevant surgical operation notes, the postmortem reports and the postmortem request form if available. Any identification will be removed in the NCEPOD office.

Many of the questions can be answered by "yes" or "no". **Please insert a tick (✓) in the appropriate box.**

Where multiple choices are given, please insert the tick(s) in the appropriate box(es).

Where more details are requested for an answer, please write in **BLOCK CAPITALS.**

In case of difficulty, please contact the NCEPOD office on:

071-831-6430

Please use this section to provide a brief summary of this case, adding any comments or information you feel are relevant: **(Please write clearly for the benefit of the specialist group who will be reviewing the questionnaire).**

If you wish to inform the NCEPOD office of any further details of this case, please do so on a separate sheet, quoting the questionnaire number.

1   In which type of hospital did the <u>final operation</u> take place?

a   District General (or equivalent)
b   University/Teaching
c   Surgical Specialty
d   Other Acute/Partly Acute
e   Community
f   Defence Medical Services
g   Independent
h   Other (please specify)

[a][b][c][d][e][f][g][h]   1

Definitions

(As used by the Association of Anaesthetists of Great Britain and Ireland)

A **recovery area** is an area to which patients are admitted from an operating room, where they remain until consciousness is regained and ventilation and circulation are stable.

A **high dependency unit (HDU)** is an area for patients who require more intensive observation and/or nursing care than would normally be expected on a general ward. <u>Patients who require mechanical ventilation or other organ support would not be admitted to this area.</u>

An **intensive care unit (ICU)** is an area to which patients are admitted for treatment of actual or impending organ failure who may require technological support (including mechanical ventilation of the lungs and/or invasive monitoring).

2   Are the following areas available in the hospital in which the final operation took place? (see definitions above):

a   Theatre recovery area   Yes ☐ No ☐   2a

If **yes**, is this available <u>and staffed</u> 24 hours per day, 7 days per week?   Yes ☐ No ☐

If **no**, please specify times when available

_____

b   Adult ICU   Yes ☐ No ☐   2b

If **yes**, is this available and staffed 24 hours per day, 7 days per week?   Yes ☐ No ☐

If **no**, please specify times when available

_____

c   Adult HDU   Yes ☐ No ☐   2c

If **yes**, is this available and staffed 24 hours per day, 7 days per week?   Yes ☐ No ☐

If **no**, please specify times when available

_____

d   Paediatric ICU/HDU   Yes ☐ No ☐   2d

If **yes**, is this available and staffed 24 hours per day, 7 days per week?   Yes ☐ No ☐

If **no**, please specify times when available

_____

e   Emergency theatre   Yes ☐ No ☐   2e

If **yes**, is this available and staffed 24 hours per day, 7 days per week?   Yes ☐ No ☐

If **no**, please specify times when available

_____

PATIENT DETAILS

3   Date of birth   [ ][ ] [ ][ ] [ ][ ]   3
          D D M M Y Y

4   Date of final operation   [ ][ ] [ ][ ] [ ][ ]   4
          D D M M Y Y

5   Sex   Male ☐ a   Female ☐ b   5

11 Date of admission to hospital in which final operation took place:

D D M M Y Y   11

12 Admission category:

a **Elective**   – at a time agreed between patient and surgical service   a

b **Urgent**   – within 48 hours of referral/consultation   b   12

c **Emergency**   – immediately following referral/consultation   c

13 To what type of area was the patient **first** admitted?

a Surgical ward (including surgical specialties)   a
b Gynaecological/Obstetric ward   b
c Medical ward   c
d Mixed medical/surgical ward   d
e Geriatric ward   e   13
f Admission ward   f
g A&E holding area (or other emergency admission ward)   g
h Day unit   h
i Direct to theatre   i
j ICU   j
k Coronary care unit (CCU)   k
m HDU   m
n Other (please specify)   n

14 Please specify the following dates:

Date of initial referral for condition leading to final operation
(eg date on letter of referral):

D D M M Y Y   14

15 Date of first consultation following referral:

D D M M Y Y   15

16 Decision to operate:

D D M M Y Y   16

REFERRAL DETAILS

7 Source of referral to the hospital at which the last operation before death was performed:

a Transfer from another hospital   a
b General Medical Practitioner   b
c General Dental Practitioner   c   7
d Admitted via A&E department   d
e Self-referral by patient (direct to Consultant)   e
f Other (please specify)   f

N.B. If the patient was transferred as an inpatient from another hospital, ie option "a" in Q7, please answer Q8 to Q10 below, otherwise go directly to Q11.

8 Type of referring hospital:

a District General   a
b University/Teaching   b
c Surgical Specialty   c
d Other Acute/Partly Acute   d   8
e Community   e
f Defence Medical Services   f
g Independent   g
h Other (please specify)   h

9 Why was the patient transferred?

10 Did the patient's condition deteriorate during transfer?

Yes
No   10

If **yes**, please specify

URGENT AND EMERGENCY ADMISSIONS ONLY

20   Was there any delay in **REFERRAL OR ADMISSION** on this occasion?

Yes ☐
No ☐   20

If **yes**, please explain.

_____
_____
_____

PREOPERATIVE CARE

21   Was the patient originally admitted under the surgeon whose team undertook the final operation?

Yes ☐
No ☐   21a

If **no**, what was the source of referral to the Consultant Surgeon?

a   A medical specialty

b   Another surgical specialty

c   Other (please specify) _____

☐☐☐   a 21b / b / c

Date and time of transfer to surgical team undertaking final operation.

Date ☐☐☐☐☐☐ 21c   Time ☐☐☐☐ 21d

D D M M Y Y

ELECTIVE ADMISSIONS ONLY

If the patient was admitted on an urgent or emergency basis please move straight to question 20.

17   Date placed on waiting list or entered into admission diary.

☐☐☐☐☐☐ 17a

D D M M Y Y

17b   Was the outcome in this case altered by the time spent on the waiting list?

Yes ☐
No ☐   17b

If **yes**, please explain.

_____
_____

18   Had this patient's admission ever been cancelled on a previous occasion?

Yes ☐
No ☐   18

If **yes**, please explain.

_____
_____

19   Was there a delay in setting a date for surgery?

Yes ☐
No ☐   19

If **yes**, please explain.

_____
_____
_____

Now move to question 21.

22 Specialty of Consultant Surgeon in charge at time of final operation before death.

a   General

b   General with special interest in Paediatric Surgery

c   General with special interest in Urology

d   General with special interest in Vascular Surgery

e   General with special interest in Gastroenterology

f   General with special interest in Endocrinology

g   General with special interest in (please specify) _____

h   Accident and Emergency

i   Cardiac – Paediatric

j   Cardiac – Adult

k   Cardiac – Mixed

l   Thoracic

m   Gynaecology

n   Neurosurgery

o   Ophthalmology

p   Oral/Maxillofacial

q   Orthopaedic

r   Otolaryngology

s   Paediatric

t   Plastic

u   Transplantation

v   Urology

w   Vascular

x   Other (please specify)

a	b	c	d	e	f	g	h	i	j	k	l	m	n	o	p	q	r	s	t	u	v	w	x

22

_____

23 Was care undertaken on a formal shared basis with another specialty (excluding anaesthesia)?

Yes | | | 23
No

If **yes**, please specify.

_____

_____

24 What was the grade of the most senior surgeon **consulted** before the operation?

Please tick the second column if a locum.

         Locum?

a   House Officer

b   Senior House Officer

c   Registrar

d   Senior Registrar

e   Consultant

f   Staff Grade

g   Clinical Assistant

h   Associate Specialist

i   Other (please specify)

		24
a	
b	
c	
d	
e	
f	
g	
h	
i	

_____

25 Please state the working diagnosis by the most senior member of the surgical team;
(PLEASE USE BLOCK CAPITALS)

_____

_____

_____

26 What operation was proposed by the most senior member of the surgical team?
(PLEASE USE BLOCK CAPITALS)

_____

_____

_____

27 What was the immediate indication for the proposed operation? **(PLEASE USE BLOCK CAPITALS)**

_____

_____

PRE-OPERATIVE PREPARATION

ASA class:

☐ 1 ☐ 2 ☐ 3 ☐ 4 ☐ 5

American Society Of Anesthesiology (A.S.A.) Classifications Of Physical Status

Class 1
This patient has no organic, psychological or psychotic disturbance. The pathological process for which operation is to be performed is localised and does not entail a systemic disturbance.

Class 2
Mild to moderate systemic disturbance or distress caused by either the condition to be treated surgically or by other pathophysiological processes.

Class 3
Severe systemic disturbance or disease from whatever cause, even though it may not be possible to define the degree of disability with finality.

Class 4
Severe systemic disorders that are already life-threatening, not always correctable by operation.

Class 5
The moribund patient who has little chance of survival but is submitted to operation in desperation.

29 Coexisting problems (other than main diagnosis) at time of final surgery (please specify the disorder in the space provided). Please put a tick in each appropriate box.

a   None
b   Respiratory _____
c   Cardiac _____
d   Renal _____
e   Haematological _____
f   Gastrointestinal _____
g   Vascular _____
h   Sepsis _____
i   Neurological _____
j   Endocrine (including diabetes mellitus) _____
k   Musculoskeletal _____
m   Psychiatric _____
n   Alcohol-related problems _____
o   Drug addiction _____
p   Genetic abnormality _____
q   Other (please specify) _____

[Boxes a–q, 29]

30 What precautions or therapeutic manoeuvres were undertaken pre-operatively (excluding anaesthetic room management) to improve the patient's pre-operative condition?

Enter a tick in each appropriate box.

a   None
b   Cardiac support drugs or antidysrhythmic agents
c   Gastric aspiration
d   Intravenous fluids
e   Correction of hypovolaemia
f   Urinary catheterisation
g   Blood transfusion
h   Diuretics
i   Anticoagulants
j   Vitamin K
k   Antibiotics (pre- or intraoperative)
m   Bowel preparation (specify method used) _____
n   Chest physiotherapy
o   Oxygen therapy
p   Airway protection (eg in unconscious patients)
q   Tracheal intubation
r   Mechanical ventilation
s   Nutritional support
t   Others (please specify)

[Boxes a–t, 30]

31 Were any measures taken (before, during or after operation) to prevent venous thrombosis?

Yes ☐
No ☐   31a

If **yes**, specify method or combination of methods:

a   Heparin
b   Leg stockings
c   Calf compression
d   Electrical stimulation of calves
e   Warfarin
f   Dextran infusion
g   Heel support
h   Ripple mattress
i   Other (please specify) _____

Before/during   After

[Boxes a–i, 31b]

32 Did the patient's medication (excluding premedication) in any way contribute to the fatal outcome in this case?

Yes ☐
No ☐ 32

If **yes**, please explain:

_____

33 **Previous operations.** If the final operation was the most recent in a sequence please list the other procedures. Please send **all relevant operation notes. (PLEASE USE BLOCK CAPITALS)**

Operation	Date	Specialty and grade of operating surgeon
a		
b		
c		
d		

34 Which grade of surgeon made the **final decision to operate**?

Please tick the second column if a locum.

Locum? 34

a	House Officer	
b	Senior House Officer	
c	Registrar	
d	Staff Grade	
e	Senior Registrar	
f	Clinical Assistant	
g	Associate Specialist	
h	Consultant	
i	Other (please specify)	

35 What was the anticipated risk of **death** related to the proposed operation?

a	Not expected
b	Small but significant risk
c	Definite risk
d	Expected

35

36 If death was **expected**, specify the anticipated benefit of the operation.

_____
_____

OPERATION

37 Classify the final operation (see definitions below and choose the category most appropriate to the case).

a	Emergency
b	Urgent
c	Scheduled
d	Elective

37

Definitions

a **Emergency**
Immediate life-saving operation, resuscitation simultaneous with surgical treatment (eg trauma, ruptured aortic aneurysm). Operation usually within one hour.

b **Urgent**
Operation as soon as possible after resuscitation (eg irreducible hernia, intussusception, oesophageal atresia, intestinal obstruction, major fractures). Operation usually within 24 hours.

c **Scheduled**
An early operation but not immediately life-saving (eg malignancy). Operation usually within 3 weeks.

d **Elective**
Operation at a time to suit both patient and surgeon (eg cholecystectomy, joint replacement).

38 Were there any delays (between admission and surgery) due to factors other than clinical?

Yes ☐
No ☐ 38

If **yes**, please specify:

_____

39   Date of start of final operation before death:

     [ ][ ][ ][ ][ ][ ] 39
     D D M M Y Y

40   Please circle day:

     M T W Th F Sa Sun

   Was this on a

   a Public Holiday?   a [ ] 40
   b Extra-statutory Holiday (NHS)?   b [ ]
   c Neither?   c [ ]

41   Time of start of operation:
   (not including anaesthetic time)   [ ][ ][ ][ ] 41
      (use 24 hour clock)

42   Duration of operation (not including anaesthetic time)

     _____ hrs _____ mins

   Cardiac cases only:

   Ischaemic time: _____ hrs _____ mins

43   What was the grade of the most senior operating surgeon?

   Please tick the second column if a locum.

               Locum?
   a House Officer   a [ ][ ] 43
   b Senior House Officer   b [ ][ ]
   c Registrar   c [ ][ ]
   d Staff Grade   d [ ][ ]
   e Senior Registrar   e [ ][ ]
   f Clinical Assistant   f [ ][ ]
   g Associate Specialist   g [ ][ ]
   h Consultant   h [ ][ ]
   i Other (please specify)   i [ ][ ]

   _____

44   How long had this surgeon spent in this grade in this specialty?

     _____ yrs _____ mths

45   How many similar procedures had **THIS** surgeon performed **in the previous 12 months?**
   (If not known, please enter an estimate)

     _____ procedures

---

46   **If the most senior operator was not a consultant, was a more senior surgeon immediately available, ie in the operating room/suite?**

               Yes [ ] 46
               No [ ]

               Not applicable [ ]
               (Consultant operating)

   If **yes**, please specify grade and location.

     Grade _____

     Location _____

47a   Final operation undertaken:
     (PLEASE USE BLOCK CAPITALS)

     _____

     _____

   N.B. PLEASE ENCLOSE A COPY OF THE OPERATION NOTES.

47b   If the operation was different to that proposed, please explain.

     _____

     _____

48   Diagnosis established at operation:
     (PLEASE USE BLOCK CAPITALS)

     _____

     _____

     _____

49   Were there any unanticipated intra-operative problems?

               Yes [ ] 49
               No [ ]

   If **yes**, please specify.

     _____

     _____

     _____

LOCAL/REGIONAL ANAESTHESIA OR SEDATION

50 Was the procedure performed **SOLELY** under local anaesthetic or sedation **administered by the SURGEON?**

Yes ☐
No ☐ 50

If **yes**, which of the following were recorded during or immediately after the procedure?

a Blood pressure ☐
b Pulse ☐
c ECG ☐
d Pulse oximetry ☐
e Other (please specify) ☐
_____
f None ☐

POSTOPERATIVE CARE

51 Was the patient admitted _immediately_ to an ICU or HDU postoperatively (see definitions above question 2)?

a Intensive Care Unit ☐
b High Dependency Unit ☐ 51
c Neither of the above ☐

51a If **neither**, was the patient admitted to an ICU/HDU after an initial period on a routine postoperative ward?

Yes ☐
No ☐ 51a

After how many days postoperatively? _____ days

If the patient was _not_ admitted to an ICU or HDU, please continue from question 55.

If the patient _was_ admitted to an ICU or HDU please answer questions 52 to 54.

---

52 What were the indications for the admission to ICU/HDU? (This can be a multiple entry).

a Routine for this surgical procedure ☐
b Specialist nursing ☐
c Presence of experienced intensivists ☐
d General monitoring ☐
e Metabolic monitoring ☐ 52
f Ventilation ☐
g Surgical complications ☐
h Anaesthetic complications ☐
i Co-incident medical diseases ☐
j Inadequate nursing on general wards ☐
k Transfer from hospital without facilities ☐
m Other (please specify) ☐
_____

53 Discharge from ICU/HDU was due to:

a Elective transfer to ward ☐
b Pressure on beds ☐
c Death ☐ 53
d Other (please specify) ☐
_____

54 Was the patient subsequently readmitted to an ICU/HDU etc?

Yes ☐
No ☐ 54

If **yes**, please give details.
_____

55 If the patient's condition warranted an admission to an ICU/HDU, were you at any time unable to transfer tł patient into an ICU/HDU _within_ the hospital in which the surgery took place?

Yes ☐
No ☐ 55

If **yes**, why?
_____

56 Please specify the postoperative complications:

a Haemorrhage/postoperative bleeding requiring transfusion
b Upper respiratory obstruction
c Respiratory distress
d Generalised sepsis
e Wound infection
f Wound dehiscence
g Anastomotic failure
h Low cardiac output
i Cardiac arrest
j Hepatic failure
k Renal failure
l Endocrine system failure
m Stroke or other neurological problems
n Persistent coma
o Other organ failure (please specify)
p Problems with analgesia
q DVT and/or pulmonary embolus
r Fat embolus
s Orthopaedic prosthetic complication
t Pressure sores
u Peripheral ischaemia
v Urinary tract infection
w Urinary retention/catheter blockage
x Ureteric injury/fistula
y Nutritional problems
z Other (please specify)

(boxes a–z, 56)

57 Was there a shortage of personnel in this case?

Yes / No 57a

If **yes**, which?

a Consultant surgeons
b Trainee surgeons
c Consultant anaesthetists
d Trainee anaesthetists
e Skilled assistants
f Nurses
g ODAs
h Porters
i Other (please specify)

(boxes a–i, 57b)

58 Date of death.

D D M M Y Y (58)

59 Time of death.

(use 24 hour clock) (59)

60 Place of death

a Theatre
b Recovery room
c Ward
d ICU/HDU
e CCU
f Home
g Another hospital
h Other (please specify)

(boxes a–h, 60)

61 Was cardiopulmonary resuscitation attempted?

Yes / No 61a

If **no**, was this a decision made pre-operatively?

Yes / No 61b

62 What was the immediate **clinical** cause of death? (This need not be a duplication of the death certificate.)
(**PLEASE USE BLOCK CAPITALS**)

BLOCK CAPITALS).

I (a) Disease or condition directly leading to death

_____

_____

(b) Other disease or condition, if any, leading to I(a)

_____

_____

(c) Other disease or condition, if any leading to I(b)

_____

II Other significant conditions CONTRIBUTING TO THE DEATH but not related to the disease or condition causing it

_____

_____

64 Was the death reported to the Coroner?

Yes ☐ No ☐ 64a

If yes, was a postmortem ordered (and performed) under the Coroner's authority?

Yes ☐ No ☐ 64b

If a Coroner's postmortem was performed, please answer questions 66 to 73.

65 Was a hospital postmortem requested?

Yes ☐ No ☐ 65a

If no, why not?

_____

If yes, was a hospital post mortem performed?

Yes ☐ No ☐ 65b

If no, why not?

_____

N.B. If a postmortem was not performed, please move to question 74.

Yes ☐ No ☐ 66

66a If yes, which member of the surgical team attended the postmortem?

a None

b House Officer

c Senior House Officer

d Registrar

e Staff Grade

f Senior Registrar

g Associate Specialist

h Consultant

i Other (please specify) _____

[boxes a b c d e f g h i] 66a

67 If a surgeon did not attend the postmortem, why not?

_____

68 Did the consultant surgeon and his/her team receive a copy of the postmortem report?

Yes ☐ No ☐ 68

69 What was the date of the first written information received giving the results of the postmortem?

[ ][ ] [ ][ ] [ ][ ] 69
D D   M M   Y Y

70 Please list the relevant findings of the postmortem. (PLEASE USE BLOCK CAPITALS)

_____

_____

_____

PLEASE SEND A COPY OF ALL POSTMORTEM REPORTS AND POSTMORTEM REQUEST FORM IF AVAILABLE

AUDIT

71 **Was the pathological information given useful, ie did it contribute additional information to the understanding of the case?**

Yes ☐
No ☐ 71

If **no**, why not?

_____

72 Who performed the post mortem?

a Specialist pathologist ☐
b Consultant pathologist ☐ 72
c Junior pathologist ☐

73 Are you aware of any subspecialty of the pathologist involved?

Yes ☐
No ☐ 73

If **yes**, please specify.

_____
_____

74 Has this death been considered, (or will it be considered) at a local audit/quality control meeting?

Yes ☐
No ☐ 74

75 Did you have any problems in obtaining the patient's notes?

Yes ☐
No ☐ 75

If **yes**, how long did they take to reach you? _____

76 Were all the notes available?

Yes ☐
No ☐ 76a

If **no**, which part was inadequate/unavailable?

a Pre-operative notes ☐ a
b Operative notes ☐ b
c Postoperative notes ☐ c 76b
d Death certificate book ☐ d
e Nursing notes ☐ e
f Other notes (please specify) ☐ f

_____

77 Has the consultant surgeon seen and agreed this form?

Yes ☐
No ☐ 77

78 Date questionnaire completed

☐ ☐ ☐ ☐ ☐ ☐ 78
D D M M Y Y

THANK YOU FOR TAKING THE TIME TO COMPLETE THIS QUESTIONNAIRE

<u>YOU MUST NOT KEEP A COPY OF THIS QUESTIONNAIRE</u>

Please return it in the reply-paid envelope provided to:

NCEPOD
35-43 Lincoln's Inn Fields
LONDON
WC2A 3PN

THIS QUESTIONNAIRE IS THE PROPERTY OF NCEPOD

Appendix E - Pathology proforma

GENERAL FEATURES OF THE PM REPORT

The report is typewritten: Y   N

A Clinical History is provided: Y   N

When present the Clinical History is:-

1 Unacceptably brief, obscure uninformative	2 Poor	3 Satisfactory	4 Good	5 Fully detailed, clear informative

A Summary of Lesions is present: -   Y   N

      When present, this corresponds accurately to the text report   Y   N

An OPCS Cause of Death is present:-   Y   N

      When present, this corresponds accurately to the text report   Y   N

      When present, this follows OPCS formatting rules:-   Y   N

A Clinico-Pathological Correlation is present:-   Y   N

When present, the CPC is:-

1 Unacceptably brief, obscure uninformative inaccurate	2 Poor	3 Satisfactory	4 Good	5 Clear, concise, fully informative, accurate

SPECIFIC FEATURES OF THE PM REPORT

The description of external appearances is:-

1 Unacceptably brief, inadequately detailed, badly organised	2 Poor	3 Satisfactory	4 Good	5 Clear, fully detailed, systematically presented

Scars and Incisions are measured:-   N/A   Y   N

The gross description of the internal organs is:-

1 Unacceptably brief, inadequately detailed, badly organised	2 Poor	3 Satisfactory	4 Good	5 Clear, fully detailed, systematically presented

Organs weighed (paired organs score 1):- 0   1   2   3   4   5   6   7   8   9   >9

The Skull and Brain have been examined: Y   N

Are the serous cavities described?   Y   N

      If an effusion is present, was it measured?   Y   N

Are intra-vascular cannulae recorded?   Y   N

      If yes, is the position of the cannula described?   Y   N

The gross examination, as described, is appropriate to the clinical problem:- Y   N

Samples have been taken for:-

1 Histology	2 Microbiology	3 Toxicology	4 Other	5 None of these investigations

In my judgement, a thorough autopsy in this case would have called for:-

1 Histology   2 Microbiology   3 Toxicology   4 Other   5 None of these investigations

A histological report is included with the PM report: Y   N

When present, the histological report is:-

1 Unacceptably brief, obscure, not relevant to clinical need in this case	2 Poor	3 Satisfactory	4 Good	5 Fully detailed, informative, relevant to clinical need in this case

When absent, does the lack of histology detract significantly from the value of this report?   Y   N

My overall score for this autopsy is:-

1 Unacceptable, laying the pathologist open to serious professional criticism	2 Poor	3 Satisfactory	4 Good	5 Excellent, an exemplary report, meeting the highest standards of practice

CLINICAL RELEVANCE

When the history, ante-mortem clinical diagnosis and cause of death are compared with the postmortem findings, this autopsy demonstrates: - (ring numbers; more than one answer will often apply)

1. A **discrepancy** in the cause of death or in a major diagnosis, which if known, might have affected treatment, outcome or prognosis.

2. A **discrepancy** in the cause of death or in a major diagnosis, which if known, would probably **not** have affected treatment, outcome or prognosis.

3. A **minor** discrepancy.

4. **Confirmation** of essential clinical findings.

5. An interesting **incidental** finding.

6. A failure to explain some important aspect of the clinical problem, despite a **satisfactory** autopsy.

7. A **failure** to explain some important aspect of the clinical problem, as a result of an unsatisfactory autopsy.

8. Some other feature (please give details) ....
   ....

LESSONS TO BE LEARNED

Record any feature of this case which might be quoted in the NCEPOD Report. (Examples of good/bad pathological practice; illustration of value of autopsy; etc.)

....
....
....

Appendix E - Pathology proforma

Appendix F - Participants

Consultant anaesthetists

These consultant anaesthetists returned at least one questionnaire relating to the period 1 April 1993 to 31 March 1994. We are not able to name all of the Consultants who have done so as their names are not known to us.

Abaysinghe M.	Barrett R.F.	Bousfield J.D.	Cameron B.
Abbott T.R.	Barrowcliffe M.P.	Bowen Wright R.M.	Cameron K.S.
Abdel-Salam M.G.	Bashir P.M.	Bowles B.J.M.	Campbell F.N.
Ackers J.W.L.	Baskett P.J.F.	Bowley C.J.	Cantrell W.D.J.
Adams H.	Bassilious M.	Bowman R.A.	Carley R.
Adly Habib N.	Bastiaenen H.L.R.	Boyd J.	Carli F.
Aggarwal K.	Basu S.	Boyd V.	Carmichael J.C.G.
Ahmed M.	Basu T.K.	Boyle A.S.	Carson I.W.
Al Quisi N.K.S.	Bayley P.	Bradshaw E.	Carter A.J.
Albin M.Z.	Bayoumi M.	Bramwell R.G.B.	Carter A.S.
Allen J.G.	Beck G.P.	Braude N.	Carter J.
Allen P.R.	Beeby C.P.	Bray M.	Carter M.I.
Allen S.C.	Beechey A.P.G.	Bray R.J.	Carter R.F.
Allum T.G.	Bell M.D.	Breckenridge J.L.	Casey W.F.
Ammar T.A.A.	Bell P.F.	Brewin M.D.	Cash T.I.
Anandanesan J.	Bellin J.M.	Bricker S.R.W.	Catling J.S.
Anderson I.	Bellman M.	Brighouse D.	Caunt J.A.
Anderson S.K.	Bembridge M.	Brim V.B.	Cave W.P.
Antrobus J.H.L.	Bennett A.	Broadley J.	Chadwick I.S.
Arunasalam K.	Bennett J.A.	Broadway J.W.	Chaffe A.G.
Ashton W.	Berridge J.C.	Brock P.J.	Chambers P.H.
Austin T.R.	Berry M.	Brooker J.	Charlton J.E.
Aveling W.	Besouw J.P. van	Brookes A.M.	Charway C.L.
Avery A.F.	Bhala B.B.	Brookes C.M.	Chater S.N.
Babington P.C.B.	Bhattacharya S.	Brown G.C.S.	Chatrath R.R.
Bailey P.W.	Biggart M.	Brown L.A.	Cheshire M.E.
Bailie R.	Bill K.M.	Brown P.M.	Child C.S.B.
Bainton A.B.	Bird T.M.	Browne B.	Chishti J.M.
Baker G.M.	Bishop D.G.M.	Browne G.A.	Chow A.E.
Baker J.R.	Biswas M.	Bryant M.T.T.	Christian A.S.
Balakrishnan P.H.	Black A.	Buckland R.W.	Christmas D.
Baldock G.J.	Black I.H.C.	Buckley P.M.	Chung N.
Bali I.M.	Bland E.	Buist R.	Church A.B.
Ballance P.G.	Blogg C.E.	Bukht M.D.G.	Church J.J.
Ballard P.K.	Blumgart C.	Burbidge M.	Clark G.P.M.
Bamber P.A.	Blundell M.D.	Burlingham A.N.	Clark J.M.
Banerjee P.	Bond G.F.	Burnley S.	Clarke C.W.M.
Barclay A.J.	Booker P.D.	Burt D.	Clarke R.S.J.
Bardgett D.M.M.	Boralessa H.	Butler J.	Clarke T.N.S.
Barker J.	Bose R.	Calder I.	Clarkson W.B.
Barnes P.K.	Bostock F.	Callender C.	Clayton K.C.
Barr A.M.	Botha R.A.	Cam J.F.	Clements E.A.F.

Clifton P.J.M.
Clunie R.W.D.
Coad N.
Cody M.
Coe A.J.
Coghill J.C.
Cohen D.G.
Cohen M.
Cole A.
Cole J.R.
Coleman A.J.
Coleman S.A.
Collier I.F.
Colville L.J.
Conacher I.
Coniam S.W.
Conn A.G.
Connolly J.D.R.
Conroy P.T.
Conway M.
Conyers A.B.
Cook J.H.
Cook M.H.
Cook P.R.
Cooper C.M.
Cooper J.B.
Cooper P.D.
Copeland P.F.
Coppel D.L.
Corser G.C.
Cory C.E.
Cotter J.
Coultas R.J.
Cowen M.J.
Craddock K.
Craddock S.C.
Crawford D.C.
Creagh-Barry P.
Crew A.D.
Crooke J.W.
Cross R.
Crosse M.M.
Cruickshank R.H.
Cummings G.C.
Cundill J.G.
Cunliffe M.
Curran J.P.
Cutler P.G.
Dallimore J.S.
Daly P.E.
Dann W.L.
Dark C.
David A.C.
Davie J.P.
Davies G.

Davies H.
Davies K.H.
Davies K.J.
Davies M.H.
Davies N.J.H.
Davies P.A.
Davies S.
Davies W.
Davis I.
Davis M.
Day C.D.
Day S.
Daya V.H.
Dempsey B.M.
Denny N.M.
Derrington M.C.
Desborough R.C.
Desgrand D.
Desmond M.J.
Dewar A.K.
Dewar J.A.
Dickson D.
Digger T.J.
Dingle H.R.
Dingwall A.E.
Dixon J.
Dodd P.
Dodds C.
Dodson M.E.
Dormon F.M.
Dowdall J.W.
Dowling R.M.
Drummond R.S.
Dumont S.
Duncan N.H.
Dunnet J.
Dunnett I.A.R.
Dunnill R.P.H.
Dye D.J.
Dyson A.D.
Eames G.M.
Earlam C.
Eatock C.R.
Eccersley P.S.
Edbrooke D.L.
Edmondson L.
Edmondson R.S.
Edwards A.E.
Edwards G.
Edwards H.
Edwards J.M.
Edwards R.B.
Eite E.K.
Elliott P.
Elliott R.H.

Eltoft M.E.
Enever G.R.
Erskine W.A.R.
Erwin D.C.
Eustace R.W.
Evans C.S.
Evans D.
Evans D.H.C.
Evans K.R.L.
Evans M.
Evans R.J.C.
Evans S.F.
Ewart I.A.
Fahy L.T.
Fairbrass M.J.
Fairfield J.E.
Farling P.A.
Farnsworth G.
Farquharson S.
Farrell M.A.
Farrell M.C.
Faulkner D.
Feldman S.A.
Ferguson A.
Ferguson B.J.M.
Ferres C.J.
Firn S.
Fisher G.C.
Fletcher I.R.
Florence A.M.
Flowerdew G.D.
Flynn M.J.
Ford P.
Fordham R.M.M.
Forster S.
Forward R.
Foxell R.M.
Fozard J.R.
Francis D.M.
Francis G.A.
Franklin C.B.
Freeman R.M.
Friend J.
Frimpong S.
Frost A.R.
Fry D.I.
Fryer J.M.
Fryer M.E.
Fuge C.A.
Fulton B.
Furness G.
Furniss P.
Fuzzey G.J.J.
Gademsetty M.K.
Gadgil P.S.

Galizia E.J.
Gallagher L.B.S.
Gallimore A.
Galloway D.W.
Gamlen G.W.
Gandhi D.
Gardner L.G.
Gargesh K.
Garrett C.P.O.
Gaston J.H.
Gautam R.
Gaynor P.A.
Gell I.R.
Gemmell L.W.
Gerrish S.P.
Ghaly R.G.
Ghandour F.M.
Ghosh R.M.
Ghosh S.
Gibson F.M.
Gilbertson A.A.
Gill K.J.
Gill N.
Gill S.S.
Gillespie I.A.
Gillett G.B.
Goat V.A.
Goddard G.F.
Goldberg P.
Goodman N.
Goodwin P.E.
Gorman P.W.
Gothard J.W.W.
Gough M.B.
Goulden P.
Govenden V.
Graham I.F.M.
Graham J.L.
Grainger D.J.
Grant I.C.
Gray H.S.J.
Grayling G.G.
Grebenik C.R.
Green C.P.
Greenbaum R.
Greenwell S.K.
Greenwood B.K.
Greig A.J.
Griffin R.W.
Griffiths J.O.
Groves N.D.
Grummitt R.
Gupta R.K.
Guratsky B.P.
Gwinnutt C.L.

Hadaway E.G.
Haden R.M.
Hall G.
Hall P.J.
Hall R.M.
Hall-Davies G.
Hamer M.S.
Hammond J.E.
Hanna M.
Haque A.K.M.
Hardy I.
Hargrave S.A.
Hargreaves M.
Harley N.F.
Harper K.W.
Harper S.J.
Harris C.
Harris G.
Harris R.W.
Harrison G.R.
Harrison J.F.
Harrison K.M.
Harrison R.A.
Harvey C.R.
Harvey D.C.
Hasbury C.R.
Haslett W.H.K.
Hatts R.
Hawley K.
Hayes B.
Hayward A.
Head B.G.
Heal C.M.
Heath M.L.
Hebblethwaite R.
Hebden M.W.
Hegarty J.E.
Hegde R.T.
Heggie N.M.
Heining M.P.D.
Henderson P.A.L.
Henderson R.
Heneghan C.P.H.
Henly J.G.
Herrick M.J.
Hewlett A.
Hibbert G.R.
Hifzi O.
Higgins D.J.
Higgs B.D.
Hills M.M.
Hilton P.J.
Hinds C.J.
Hinton W.
Hipkin A.H.

Hirsch N.P.
Hobbs A.
Hodgson R.M.H.
Hodkinson J.N.
Holdcroft A.
Holderness M.C.
Holgate S.
Holland D.E.
Hollister G.R.
Holmes W.
Hood G.
Hopkins C.S.
Housam G.D.
Hovell B.C.
Howard E.C.
Howe J.P.
Howell C.J.
Howell C.W.
Howell E.
Howell P.J.
Howell R.S.C.
Howlin S.
Hoyle J.R.
Huddy N.
Hudson R.B.S.
Hughes D.G.
Hughes J.
Hughes-Davies D.I.
Hull C.J.
Hunsley J.E.
Hunt P.C.W.
Hunter J.M.
Hunter S.J.
Hurst J.
Hurwitz D.S.
Huss B.K.D.
Hutchings P.J.G.
Hutchinson A.
Hutchinson H.T.
Hutchinson J.
Hutter C.
Hutton D.S.
Hutton P.
Ievins A.
Imrie M.M.
Ince C.S.
Inglis M.S.
Ingram G.S.
Iskander L.N.
Jack R.D.
Jackson A.P.F.
Jackson A.S.
Jackson I.J.B.
Jackson P.W.
Jagadeesh S.V.

Jago R.H.
Jamali N.
James M.L.
James P.
James R.H.
Jani K.
Jarvis A.P.
Javed E.B.
Jayson D.W.
Jefferies G.
Jeffries G.
Jena N.M.
Jenkins B.J.
Jenkins J.R.
Jephcott G.
Jessop E.
Jessop J.
Jewkes D.A.
Johns G.
Johns R.J.
Johnson C.J.H.
Johnson R.A.
Johnson R.W.
Johnson T.W.
Johnston C.G.
Johnston H.M.L.
Johnston J.R.
Johnston P.L.
Johnstone R.D.
Jones D F
Jones D.F.
Jones G.W.
Jones M.J.T.
Jones N.O.
Jones P.I.E.
Jones R.E.
Jordan M.J.
Jothilingam S.
Justins D.M.
Kai P.
Karalliedde L.D.
Kassi A.G.
Kay P.M.
Kazi G.A.
Keeling P.
Keens S.J.
Kelly D.R.
Kennedy D.J.
Kent A.P.
Kershaw E.J.
Kestin I.
Kethar-Thas S.
Khawaja A.A.
Khiroya C.
King N.W.

King T.A.
Kipling R.M.
Kirby I.J.
Knappett P.A.
Kneeshaw J.
Knibb A.A.
Knickenberg C.J.
Knight C.L.
Kocan M.K.
Koehli N.
Kong K.L.
Konieczko K.
Krapez J.R.
Kulasinghe N.
Kumar B.
Kumar C.M.
Lack J.A.
Laffey D.A.
Lahiri S.K.
Lake A.P.J.
Lalsingh R.
Lamb A.S.T.
Lamb C.J.
Landon K.
Latham B.V.
Latimer R.D.
Latto I.P.
Lauckner M.E.
Laurence A.S.
Laurie P.
Lawes E.G.
Leach A.B.
Lee D.E.
Lee J.
Lees J.F.
Lees S.V.
Leigh J M
Lenz R.J.
Lesser P.J.A.
Lewis D.G.
Lewis I.
Lewis J.R.
Lewis M.A.H.
Lewis P.
Lewis R.N.
Lewis R.P.
Lilburn J.K.
Lindop M.J.
Lindsay W.A.
Ling S.
Linsley A.
Linter S.P.K.
Lintin S.
Loach A.B.
Loader B.W.

Loan W.B.
Locker I.
Lockwood G.
Loh L.
Long T.M.W.
Longan M.A.
Longbottom R.T.
Lord P.W.
Lothian M.
Loughran P.G.
Lowe S.S.
Loyden C.F.
Ludgrove T.
Lumley J.
Lung P.C.
Lutton M.
Luxton M.C.
Lyle D.J.R.
Lynch C.G.M.
Lynch M.
Lyons G.R.
Lyons S.M.
Lytle J.
McAra A.
McAteer I.M.
McAuley D.M.
MacBeath J.T.
McBride R.J.
McCallum D.M.I.
McCaughey W.
McConachie I.W.
McCrory J.W.
MacDonald A.
McGeachie J.F.
McGowan W.A.W.
Mackay I.R.
McKenzie P.J.
McKinlay R.G.C.
McKnight C.K.
Macleod K.G.A.
MacLeod K.R.
McLoughlin K.H.
Macmillan R.R.
McMurray T.J.
McPherson J.J.
McQuillan P.
Madden A.P.
Madej T.H.
Magee P.T.
Maher E.A.
Maher J.J.
Maher O.A.
Maile C.J.D.
Male C.G.
Mallaiah S.

Mann P.E.
Mann R.A.M.
Manus N.J.
Marczak A.
Margary J.J.
Mark J.S.
Markham K.
Marks R.J.
Marsh A.
Marshall A.G.
Marshall C.
Marshall F.P.F.
Martin A.J.
Martin J.L.
Martindale A.
Mason D.G.
Massey N.J.A.
Mather J.S.
Matheson H.A.
Mathews H.M.L.
Mathias I.M.J.
Mathur A.K.
Matthews N.C.
Mawson P.J.
Mazumder J.K.
Meadows D.P.
Mehta M.
Mehta R.M.
Mello W.D. de
Mendel L.
Mendonca L.M.
Messih M.N.A.
Metias V.F.
Michael S.
Michael W.
Michel R.
Milaszkiewicz R.M.
Millar S.W.
Milligan K.A.
Milligan N.S.
Millns J.P.
Mills D.C.
Mills P.
Milne B.R.
Milne I.S.
Milne M.D.
Mimpriss T.J.
Mirakhur R.K.
Misra P.L.
Missen J.C.
Mitchell M.D.
Mitchell R.G.
Moffett J.C.
Moffett S.P.
Monk C.

Monks P.S.
Moon C.
Moore C.A.
Moore J.K.
Moore K.C.
Moore M.R.
Moore P.
Morcos W.E.
Morgan C.
Morgan M.
Morgan R.N.W.
Morris R.
Morrison P.
Morriss G.W.
Moskovits P.E.
Moss E.
Mostafa S.M.
Mourik G. van
Mousdale S.
Mukasa F.J.
Mulvein J.T.
Mundy J.V.B.
Murphy J.
Murray A.
Murray F.P.
Murray J.F.
Mushambi M.
Mwanje D.K.
Myatt J.K.
Myerson K.R.
Myint H.
Nalliah R.
Nandi K.
Naqvi N.H.
Nash P.J.
Naunton A.
Naylor A.F.
Naylor H.C.
Nebhrajani J.
Nelson V.
Nesbitt G.A.
Nethisinghe S.
Newell J.P.
Newman B.
Newman V.J.
Newton D.E.F.
Newton M.
Nicholas M.P.
Nicholl A.D.J.
Nicol A.
Niemiro L.A.K.
Nigam A.K.
Nightingale J.
Nightingale P.
Noble W.A.

Norman J.
Normandale J.P.
Northwood D.
Norton A.C.
Norton P.M.
Nott M.R.
O'Callaghan A.C.
O'Donohoe B.
O'Donovan N.P.
O'Dwyer H.
Ogg T.W.
Okell R.W.
Olver J.
Ordman A.
Ormrod J.
Orr I.A.
Orton J.K.
Osman H.
Owen R.
Packham R.N.
Paes M.L.
Page J.M.
Page R.J.E.
Pais W.A.
Pal P.K.
Palin P.H.
Palmer R.
Park W.G.
Parker C.J.R.
Parry H.
Parsloe M.
Parsons R.S.
Patel A.
Patel D.K.
Patel N.
Pathirana D.
Pattison J.
Paul S.
Pavlou S.
Payne M.
Peacock J.E.
Peebles-Brown A.
Pegg M.S.
Penfold N.
Perkins D.H.
Perks D.
Peters C.G.
Peterson A.C.
Petros A.
Petts H.V.
Phillips D.C.
Phillips K.
Phillips M.L.
Phillips P.D.
Pick M.

Pickford F.J.	Richmond D.J.H.	Severn A.M.	St John-Jones L.
Pinchin R.M.E.	Richmond M.N.	Shah J.L.	Stacey R.K.
Pitt G.M.	Rickford W.J.K.	Shah M.V.	Stainthorp S.F.
Plummer R.B.	Riddle I.F.	Shah R.K.	Stanford B.J.
Pocklington A.G.	Ritchie P.	Shah R.N.N.	Stanley-Jones I.K.
Poobalasingam N.	Ritchie P.A.	Shah Z.P.	Stanton J.M.
Pook J.A.R.	Rittoo D.B.	Sharawi R.	Starkey C.
Poole D.	Robbie D.S.	Sharpe T.D.E.	Steller P.H.
Porter G.E.	Roberts D.R.D.	Shaw E.A.	Stevens J.
Porter J.	Roberts J.C.	Shaw I.	Stevens R.W.
Porterfield A.J.	Roberts P.	Shaw J.	Stevenson J.M.
Potter D.	Roberts W.O.	Shaw T.C.	Stielow E.
Pounder D.	Robertson D.S.	Shaw T.J.I.	Stock J.G.L.
Powell D.R.	Robertson J.A.	Shearar E.	Stockwell M.A.
Powell J.N.	Robinson D.A.	Sheldrake J.	Stoddart J.C.
Pradhan V.S.	Robson G.E.W.	Shenoy M.P.	Stoneham J.R.
Pratt C.I.	Robson J.E.	Short S.	Stray C.M.
Price W.J.	Rodgers R.C.	Shribman A.J.	Streahorn D.
Prince G.D.	Rogers P.	Shutt L.E.	Stubbing J.F.
Pring J.E.	Rouse J.M.	Sides C.A.	Summerfield R.J.
Proctor E.A.	Rowe W.L.	Silk J.M.	Sumner E.
Pryn S.J.P.	Royle P.	Silver J.	Sutherland I.A.
Purcell G.	Rucklidge M.A.	Simpson J.	Sutherland I.C.
Purcell-Jones G.	Ruff S.J.	Simpson M.E.	Sutton D.N.
Purnell R.J.	Rush E.	Simpson P.J.	Swaine C.
Putnam E.A.	Russell M.	Singh J.	Swales B.G.
Puttick N.	Ryall D.M.	Singh K.H.P.	Sweeney B.P.
Pyne A.	Ryan D.A.	Singh R.K.	Sweeney J.E.
Qureshi Z.	Ryan D.W.	Siriwardhana S.A.	Swindells S.
Radford P.	Ryan J.P.	Sivaloganathan G.	Symons G.V.
Raitatha H.H.	Ryder W.	Skinner A.C.	Symons I.
Raithatha H.H.	Ryssen M.E.P. van	Skinner J.B.	Tackley R.M.
Rajasekeran T.	Sale J.P.	Skivington M.A.	Talwatte D.B.B.
Ralph S.	Salmon N.P.	Smales C.	Tamlyn R.S.P.
Ram V.S.	Samaan A.A.	Smethurst P.W.R.	Tannett P.G.
Ramachandran A.	Sanders R.S.	Smith B.A.C.	Tarr T.J.
Ramsay T.M.	Sandhar B.	Smith B.L.	Tatham P.F.
Ramsden W.N.	Savege T.M.	Smith G.	Tattersall M.P.
Rao M.V.S.	Scallan M.J.H.	Smith G.B.	Taylor E.A.S.
Raper J.M.	Schofield N.M.	Smith H.S.	Taylor G.
Raphael G.	Scott J.G.	Smith J.B.	Taylor I.H.
Ravalia A.	Scott P.V.	Smith M.	Taylor M.B.
Ravenscroft P.J.	Seager S.J.	Smith P.	Taylor S.
Rawlinson W.A.L.	Seagger R.A.	Smith P.A.	Telford R.
Ray A.K.	Sealey M.M.	Smith U.G.C.	Terry D.M.S.
Razis P.	Sear J.	Smyth P.R.F.	Teturswamy G.
Redfern N.	Searle A.E.	Sneyd J.R.	Thind G.S.
Redpath A.	Searle J.F.	Snowdon S.L.	Thomas A.N.
Reeder M.	Sekar M.	Soni N.C.	Thomas D A
Rees D.G.	Sellers W.F.S.	Sowden G.R.	Thomas D.A.
Remington S.A.M.	Sellick B.	Spargo P.	Thomas D.G.
Revell S.	Sellwood W.G.	Spencer G.T.	Thomas D.W.
Reynolds A.D.	Selsby D.S.	Spilsbury R.A.	Thomas J.B.
Richards M.J.	Sengupta P.	Sprigge J.S.	Thomas T.A.
Richardson M.E.	Seth A.	Srivastava S.	Thomas V.L.

Thompson J.F.W.
Thompson M.A.
Thompson M.C.
Thomson J.
Thomson K.D.
Thomson W.
Thornberry A.
Thorpe M.H.
Thorpe P.M.
Tipping T.R.
Titoria M.
Tobias M.A.
Tomlinson A.A.
Tomlinson J.H.
Tomlinson M.J.
Trask M.D.
Tring I.C.
Triscott A.P.
Trotter T.
Turner D.J.
Turner M.A.
Turner R.J.N.
Turtle M.J.
Twentyman C.
Twigley A.J.
Twohey L.C.
Tyler C.K.G.
Ulyett I.
Uso D.
Utting H.
Valijan A.
Vanner R.G.
Veitch G.R.
Vella L.M.
Veness A.M.
Verghese C.
Vickers A.P.
Vohra A.
Vyas A.
Wadon C.A.
Wainwright A.C.
Waite K.
Waldron B.A.
Walker A.K.Y.
Walker J.A.
Walker M.A.
Wallbank W.A.
Walmsley A.J.
Walmsley D.A.
Walsh E.
Walsh E.M.
Walters F.
Wanninayake H.M.
Ward M.E.
Ward S.

Ward-McQuaid J.M.C.
Waters H.R.
Waters J.H.
Watkins T.G.
Watson A.N.
Watson D.M.
Watson K.
Watson P.J.Q.
Watt J.M.
Watters C.H.
Watters P.T.
Wauchob T.D.
Webb T.B.
Webster J.L.
Webster N.R.W.
Wedley J.R.
Welchew E.A.
Weldon O.G.W.
Wellar R.
Wenstone R.
West D.
Whelan E.
White D.J.K.
White J.B.
White M.
White P.O.
Whitehead J.
Whitehurst P.
Whittaker D.K.
Whittingham D.B.
Wickremasinghe K.
Wignarajah A.
Wijesurendra I.
Wilkes J.
Wilkinson P.A.
Williams A.B.
Williams A.C.
Williams D.J.M.
Williams E.G.N.
Williams J.G.
Williams K.N.
Williams T.I.R.
Williams W.
Wilson C.M.
Wilson D.B.
Wilson I.G.
Wilson M.
Wilton H.J.
Wiltshire S.J.
Winder J.H.
Wise C.C.
Wise R.P.
Withington P.S.
Wittmann F.W.
Wolff A.

Wood B.M.
Woodall N.M.
Woodham M.
Woods S.D.
Woodsford P.V.
Woollam C.H.M.
Wort M.
Wraight W.J.W.
Wright E.
Wright I.G.
Wright J.H.
Wright M.M.
Wyatt R.
Xifaras G.P.
Yanny W.A.
Yate P.
Young D.
Young P.N.
Youssef M.S.
Zideman D.A.
Zych Z.

Appendix G - Participants

Consultant surgeons and gynaecologists

These consultant surgeons and gynaecologists returned at least one questionnaire relating to the period 1 April 1993 to 31 March 1994

Abbas G.	Angus P.D.	Baker W.N.W.	Bell J.R.
Abberton M.J.	Anthony J.	Bakran A.	Bell P.R.F.
Abdel-Aal K.	Antrobus J.N.	Baldwin D.L.	Belstead J.S.
Abrams P.	Arafa M.	Balfour T.W.	Bendall R.
Abu-Zeid A.S.	Archbold J.A.	Ball A.J.	Bennett J.G.
Ackroyd C.E.	Archer I.A.	Ball C.	Benson E.A.
Ackroyd J.S.	Archer T.J.	Bamford P.N.	Bentley P.G.
Adair H.M.	Argent V.P.	Banerjee D.K.	Bentley R.J.
Adams J.	Arkell D.G.	Banks A.J.	Berry A.R.
Afshar F.	Armitage N.C.	Bannister G.C.	Berry H.E.
Agrawal N.K.	Armitage T.G.	Barber H.M.	Berstock D.A.
Ainscow D.A.P.	Armitstead P.R.	Bardsley D.	Bertfield H.
Albert J.S.	Arnold A.J.	Barker C.P.G.	Best B.G.
Aldam C.H.	Arnold J.M.	Barker J.R.	Betts J.A.
Alderman B.	Ashall G.	Barker K.	Bevan J.R.
Alderson D.	Ashbrooke A.	Barnes A.D.	Beverland D.E.
Aldoori M.I.	Ashby E.C.	Barr H.	Beverly M.C.
Aldridge M.C.	Ashken M.H.	Barr L.	Bevis C.R.A.
Aldridge M.J.	Aston N.	Barrett A.M.	Bhadreshwar D.R.
Alexander-Williams J.	Atkins P.	Barrie W.W.	Bhamra M.S.
Ali A.S.	Atkins R.	Barrington R.L.	Bickerstaff D.R.
Ali S.W.	Atkinson P.M.	Barros D'Sa A.A.B.	Bickerstaff K.I.
Allen D.R.	Atrah S.G.	Barros D'Sa A.A.J.	Bickerton N.J.
Allen N.	Attard R.	Barwell N.J.	Bickerton R.C.
Allen P.R.	Aubrey A.	Batchelor A.G.	Binns M.S.
Allen T.R.	Auchincloss J.M.	Bates C.P.	Bintcliffe I.W.L.
Allen-Mersh T.G.	August A.	Bates T.	Bird D.
Allison J.D.	Aukland A.	Bathard-Smith P.J.	Bird G.G.
Alloub M.	Ausobsky J.R.	Batra H.C.	Bishop M.C.
Allum R.L.	Austwick D.H.	Battersby R.D.E.	Bismil M.S.K.
Allum W.H.	Avill R.	Baum M.	Biswas S.
Almond D.J.	Backhouse C.M.	Bayliss N.C.	Black J.
Alun-Jones T.	Badenoch D.	Beard D.J.	Black J.E.
Alwafi A.A.	Bailey I.C.	Beard J.D.	Black J.H.A.
Amarah S.	Bailey J.S.	Beard R.C.	Black R.J.
Amery A.H.	Bailey M.E.	Beauchamp C.G.	Blackburn C.W.
Anderson D.	Bailey M.J.	Beaugie J.M.	Blackburne J.S.
Anderson R.J.L.	Bailie F.B.	Beaumont A.R.	Blackett R.L.
Andrew D.R.	Bainbridge E.T.	Beck J.M.	Blacklay P.F.
Andrew J.G.	Baird R.N.	Bedford A.F.	Blacklock A.R.E.
Andrews B.G.	Baker A.R.	Beeby D.I.	Blair S.D.
Andrews N.	Baker R.	Beetham M.D.	Blake G.
Angel J.C.	Baker R.H.	Belcher P.R.	Blakemore M.E.

Blakeway C.
Blamey R.W.
Blauth C.
Blaxland J.W.
Blayney J.D.M.
Bliss J.
Bloomfield T.H.
Blunt R.J.
Boardman K.P.
Bodey W.N.
Boggon R.P.
Bollen S.
Bolton J.P.
Bolton-Maggs B.G.
Bourke J.B.
Bowsher W.G.
Boyd I.E.
Boyd N.A.
Boyd P.J.
Bracegirdle J.
Bracey D.J.
Bradley J.
Bradley J.G.
Bradley P.J.
Brain A.J.L.
Braithwaite P.A.
Bramble F.J.
Brame K.G.
Bransom C.J.
Brawn W.J.
Brearley S.
Breeson A.J.
Brigg J.K.
Briggs P.
Briggs T.W.R.
Brignall C.
Bristol J.B.
Britton D.C.
Britton J.M.
Britton J.P.
Brocklehurst G.
Bromage J.D.
Brookes G.B.
Brooks S.
Brooman P.J.
Broome G.
Brotherton B.J.
Brown A.A.
Brown C.
Brown G.J.A.
Brown J.G.
Brown P.M.
Brown R.F.
Browning F.S.C.
Brunskill P.J.

Bryson J.R.
Buckels J.A.C.
Buckler K.G.
Bucknall T.E.
Budd D.W.G.
Bull J.C.
Bulstrode C.J.K.
Bunch G.A.
Bunker T.D.
Burge D.
Burgess P.
Burke M.
Burke P.
Burnand K.G.
Burton V.A.
Butler C.
Butler R.E.
Butler-Manuel A.
Cable H.R.
Cade D.
Cahill C.J.
Cain D.
Calder A.T.
Calderwood J.W.
Callam M.J.
Callum K.G.
Calver R.F.
Calvert C.H.
Calvert P.T.
Cameron A.E.P.
Cameron M.M.
Campalani G.
Campbell A.J.
Campbell C.S.
Campbell D.J.
Campbell J.
Campbell R.
Campbell W.B.
Cannon S.R.
Cape J.
Capps S.
Carden D.G.
Cargill A.O'R
Carleton P.J.
Carpenter R.
Carr A.
Carr R.T.W.
Carroll R.N.P.
Carruthers R.K.
Carvell J.E.
Case B.D.
Case W.G.
Cast I.P.
Castillo A.A.
Caullay J.M.

Cavanagh S.P.
Chadwick C.J.
Chadwick S.
Chamberlain J.
Chan R.N.W.
Chandler G.P.
Chang R.W.S.
Channon G.M.
Chant A.D.B.
Chapman D.F.
Chapman J.
Chapple C.R.
Chare M.J.B.
Charlesworth D.
Charlton C.A.C.
Charnock F.M.L.
Chaturvedi S.
Chester J.
Chilton C.P.
Chisholm E.M.
Chui P.
Citron N.D.
Clague M.B.
Clark A.W.
Clark D.W.
Clark J.
Clarke D.
Clarke J.
Clarke J.M.F.
Clarke N.M.P.
Clarke R.J.
Clarkson P.K.
Clason A.
Clay N.R.
Cleak D.K.
Clegg J.F.
Cleland J.
Clifford R.P.
Coates C.J.
Coats P.M.
Cobb A.G.
Cohen G.L.
Collin J.
Collins R.E.C.
Colmer M.R.
Colton C.L.
Connolly L.P.
Constantine G.
Cooke P.H.
Cooke T.J.C.
Cooke W.M.
Coombes G.B.
Cooper J.
Cooper J.C.
Cooper M.J.

Cooper Wilson M.
Copeland G.P.
Corbett C.R.R.
Corbett W.A.
Cornah M.S.
Corner N.
Cowen M.E.
Cowie A.G.A.
Cowie G.H.
Cowie R.A.
Cowley D.J.
Cox P.J.
Cox R.
Cox S.J.
Craig D.M.
Cranley B.
Crawford D.J.
Crawfurd E.J.P.
Crawshaw C.C.
Craxford A.D.
Creedon R.
Crisp J.C.
Crockard H.A.
Croft R.J.
Crooks M.L.W.
Crosbie J.D.
Cross F.W.
Crowson M.C.
Cruickshank D.J.
Crumplin M.K.H.
Cumming J.A.
Cummins B.H.
Curry R.C.
Curt J.R.N.
Cuschieri R.J.
D'Arcy J.C.
D'Costa E.F.
Da Costa O.ST.J
Dan A.
Daniels R.J.
Dapaah V.E.
Das C.N.
Das G.G.
Das Gupta A.R.
Davidson B.R.
Davies C.J.
Davies H.G.
Davies H.L.
Davies M.
Davies R.A.C.
Davies R.P.
Davies S.J.M.
Davies T.W.
Davis C.
Davis T.R.C.

Davison O.W.
Davison P.M.D.
Dawson P.
De K.R.
De Bolla A.R.
De Castella H.C.
Deacon P.B.
Deakin M.
Deane A.M.
Deane G.
Dehn T.C.B.
Deiraniya A.
Deliss L.J.
Demian A.Z.
Dempster D.W.
Denton J.S.
Derry C.D.
Desai A.
Desai J.B.
Desai K.M.
Desai S.B.
Desmond A.D.
Deverall P.B.
Dhasmana J.P.
Dhebar M.I.
Dhorajiwala J.M.
Diamond T.
Dias J.J.
Dick J.A.
Dickinson I.K.
Dickinson J.C.
Dickinson K.M.
Dickson G.H.
Dillon B.
Dilworth G.R.
Dinley R.R.J.
Dixon J.H.
Doig R.L.
Donaldson D.R.
Donaldson L.A.
Done H.J.
Donell S.T.
Donnelly R.J.
Donovan A.G.
Donovan I.A.
Dooley J.F.
Doran A.
Doran J.
Dormandy J.A.
Dorrell J.H.
Dorricott N.J.
Dossa M.
Douglas D.L.
Dowdell J.W.
Dowell J.K.

Downes R.N.
Drakeley M.J.
Duckworth T.
Dudley N.E.
Duff I.S.
Duffield R.G.M.
Dunn D.C.
Dunn M.
Durdey P.
Durning P.
Durrans D.
Dussek J.E.
Duthie J.S.
Dyson D.P.
Dyson P.H.P.
Eardley I.
Earlam R.J.
Earnshaw J.J.
Eastwood D.M.
Eaton A.C.
Ebbs S.R.
Edgar M.A.
Edge A.J.
Edmondson S.
Edwards A.N.
Edwards J.L.
Edwards J.M.
Edwards M.H.
Edwards P.
Edwardson K.F.
El-Safty M.M.
Elder J.B.
Elder M.G.
Ellenbogen S.
Ellis B.W.
Ellis D.J.
Ellis F.G.
Elsworth C.F.
Emerson D.J.M.
Emery R.J.
England J.P.S.
England P.C.
English T.A.H.
Ennis K.A.
Enoch B.E.
Esah K.M.
Essenhigh D.M.
Etchells D.E.
Evans A.G.
Evans C.M.
Evans G.
Evans G.A.
Evans G.H.E.
Evans J.
Evans M.J.

Evans P.
Evans R.
Everson N.W.
Ewah P.O.
Eyre-Brook I.A.
Faber R.G.
Fabri B.
Fagan A.M.
Fagg P.S.
Fannin T.F.
Farhan M.J.
Farrar D.J.
Farrington G.
Faux J.C.
Fawcett A.N.
Fearn C.B.
Feggetter J.G.W.
Fellows G.J.
Felmingham J.E.
Feneley R.C.L.
Fenn P.
Fentiman I.S.
Fenton O.M.
Fergus J.N.
Ferguson A.M.
Ferguson J.
Fergusson C.M.
Fernandes T.J.
Fernandez G.N.
Ferro M.
Fiddian N.J.
Field E.S.
Fiennes A.
Finch D.R.A.
Firmin R.K.
Fish A.N.J.
Fisher S.E.
Fitzgerald J.A.W.
Flanagan J.P.
Flannigan G.M.
Fleetcroft J.P.
Fletcher M.S.
Flew T.J.
Flood B.M.
Flook D.
Flowerdew A.F.
Floyd A.
Flynn J.T.
Fogg A.J.B.
Fontaine C.J.
Ford D.J.
Fordham M.
Fordyce M.J.F.
Forrest J.F.
Forrest L.

Forrester-Wood C.
Forster I.W.
Forsyth A.T.
Forsythe J.L.R.
Fortes Mayer K.D.
Forty J.
Foss M.V.L.
Fossard D.P.
Foster M.E.
Fothergill D.J.
Fountain S.W.
Fowler C.G.
Fowler J.
Fox J.N.
Fozard J.B.J.
Fozzard C.E.
Francis J.G.
Franklin A.
Franks R.E.
Fraser I.
Frecker P.
Freedlander E.
Freedman L.S.
Freeland A.P.
Friend P.J.
Frohn M.
Fyfe I.S.
Gallagher P.
Gallannaugh C.S.
Galloway J.M.D.
Gammall M.M.
Gardner R.D.
Gartell P.C.
Gartside M.W.
Gatehouse D.
Gazet J.C.
Gear M.W.L.
Geary N.P.J.
Geeranavar S.S.
Gelister J.S.K.
George J.D.
Georgy H.B.
Getty C.J.M.
Ghali N.N.
Gibbens G.L.D.
Gibbin K.P.
Gibbs A.N.
Gibson M.J.
Gibson R.A.
Gie G.A.
Gilbert L.
Gill S.S.
Gilliland E.L.
Gillison E.W.
Gillmer M.D.G.

Gilroy D.
Gingell J.C.
Glasgow M.M.S.
Glass R.E.
Glazer G.
Gleeson M.
Glenville B.E.
Glossop L.P.
Goddard N.J.
Goiti J.J.
Golby M.G.S.
Goldstraw P.
Good C.
Good C.J.
Goode A.W.
Gooding M.R.
Goodman A.J.
Gopalji B.T.
Gore R.
Gough A.L.
Goulbourne I.A.
Gourevitch D.
Gowland-Hopkins N.F.
Grabham A.H.
Grace D.L.
Grace P.
Grace R.H.
Gray D.W.R.
Gray I.C.M.
Gray N.
Gray W.J.
Greatorex R.A.
Green A.D.L.
Green A.R.
Green G.A.
Green J.P.
Greenway B.
Gregg P.J.
Gregson R.M.
Greiss M.E.
Griffin S.M.
Griffith C.D.M.
Griffith G.H.
Griffith M.J.
Griffiths D.A.
Griffiths E.
Griffiths M.
Griffiths M.F.P.
Griffiths N.J.
Griffiths R.W.
Griffiths W.E.G.
Groom A.F.G.
Gross E.
Grotte G.J.
Grover M.L.

Gruwez F.
Guazzo E.P.
Gudgeon D.H.
Guest J.
Guillou P.J.
Gumpert J.R.W.
Gunn A.
Gupta M.
Gurusinghe N.T.
Guvendik L.
Guy A.J.
Guy P.J.
Gwynn B.R.
Habib N.A.
Hackman B.W.
Hagan M.C.
Haggie S.J.
Haines J.F.
Hale J.E.
Hall C.N.
Hall G.
Hall R.
Hall R.I.
Hall R.R.
Hall S.J.
Hallett J.P.
Halliday A.G.
Halliday A.H.
Halliday J.A.
Hamer D.B.
Hamid S.
Hamilton G.
Hamilton J.R.L.
Hamlyn P.L.
Hammad Z.
Hammond R.H.
Hancock B.D.
Hands L.
Hanna L.S.F.
Hannah G.
Hannon M.A.
Hannon R.J.
Haque M.A.
Hardcastle J.D.
Harding-Jones D.
Hardingham M.
Hardwidge C.
Hargreaves A.W.
Harkness W.F.J.
Harley J.M.
Harley K.
Harlow R.A.
Harper W.M.
Harrison B.J.
Harrison D.J.

Harrison G.S.M.
Harrison I.D.
Harrison J.M.
Harrison N.W.
Harrison R.A.
Harrison S.C.W.
Harvey C.F.
Harvey D.R.
Harvey J.S.
Harvey M.H.
Hasan S.S.
Hatem M.H.M.
Hatfield R.
Hawe M.J.G.
Hawley P.R.
Haworth S.M.
Hawthorn I.E.
Hay D.J.
Haynes I.G.
Haynes S.
Hayward R.
Head A.C.
Heal M.R.
Heald R.J.
Heath D.V.
Heather B.P.
Heddle R.M.
Hedges A.R.
Helm R.H.
Henderson A.
Henderson J.J.
Hendry W.F.
Hensher R.
Herschman M.J.
Hetherington J.W.
Heyse-Moore G.H.
Heywood B.F.
Hierons C.D.
Higgins A.F.
Higgins J.R.
Higgins P.M.
Higginson D.W.
Higgs J.M.
Hill J.G.
Hillard T.
Hilton C.J.
Hinchliffe A.
Hindmarsh J.R.
Hinton C.P.
Hirst P.
Hitchcock E.R.
Hoare E.M.
Hobbiss J.H.
Hobbs K.E.F.
Hobsley M.

Hoddinott H.C.
Hodgkinson J.P.
Hodgson S.P.
Hoile R.W.
Holbrook M.C.
Holden M.P.
Holdsworth B.J.
Holdsworth J.D.
Holdsworth P.J.
Hollingdale J.P.
Holmes F.J.
Holmes J.T.
Holms W.
Holroyd J.B.
Holt S.
Hood J.M.
Hook W.E.
Hooker J.G.
Hooper A.A.
Hooper T.
Hope P.G.
Hopkinson B.R.
Hopkinson D.A.W.
Hopton D.S.
Horgan K.
Horner J.
Horwell D.H.
Hosney M.A.
Houghton P.W.J.
Howat J.M.T.
Howcroft A.J.
Howd A.
Howell C.J.
Howell F.R.
Howell G.P.
Hrouda K.S.
Hubbard M.J.S.
Hudd C.
Hudson I.
Hudson J.M.
Hughes M.A.
Hughes R.G.
Hughes S.P.F.
Hulton N.R.
Humphreys W.G.
Humphreys W.V.
Hunt D.M.
Hunter G.
Hunter I.W.E.
Hunter S.G.
Hurlow R.A.
Hurst P.A.
Hussein I.Y.
Hutchins P.M.
Hutchinson I.F.

Hutchison J.D.	Johns D.L.	Kay P.R.	Kulkani R.P.
Hutton P.A.N.	Johnson A.D.	Kaye J.C.	Kumar D.
Hyde I.D.	Johnson A.G.	Keates J.R.W.	Kunzru K.M.N.
Iacovou J.W.	Johnson A.P.	Keenan D.J.M.	Lafferty K.
Imrie A.H.	Johnson C.D.	Keene M.H.	Laine J.B.
Inglis J.A.	Johnson D.A.N.	Kehoe N.J.	Lallemand R.C.
Ingoldby C.J.H.	Johnson F.S.	Keighley M.R.B.	Lamb R.K.
Ingram G.	Johnson G.V.	Kelly J.D.C.	Lambert M.E.
Ingram N.P.	Johnson J.N.	Kelly J.F.	Lambert W.G.
Innes A.	Johnson J.R.	Kelly J.M.	Lamerton A.J.
Innes A.J.	Johnson M.G.	Kelly M.J.	Lamont P.
Ions G.K.	Johnson P.A.	Kemeny A.A.	Lancer J.M.
Irvin T.T.	Johnson P.G.	Kenefick J.S.	Lane I.F.
Irvine B.	Johnson R.W.G.	Kennedy R.H.	Lane R.H.S.
Irving M.H.	Johnson S.R.	Kent S.J.S.	Lang D.
Irwin B.C.	Johnston D.	Kenyon G.S.	Lang-Stevenson A.I.
Irwin S.T.	Johnston G.W.	Keogh A.J.	Lansdown M.
Ismaili N.A.	Johnstone J.M.S.	Keogh B.	Large S.R.
Iyer S.V.	Jones A.S.	Ker N.B.	Larvin M.
Jackowski A.	Jones C.	Kernohan J.G.	Latham P.D.
Jackson A.M.	Jones C.B.	Kerr G.	Lau J.O.
Jackson B.T.	Jones D.	Kerr R.S.C.	Laughton J.M.
Jackson D.B.	Jones D.A.	Kershaw C.J.	Lavelle M.A.
Jackson R.K.	Jones D.G.	Kershaw W.W.	Lawrence D.
Jackson S.	Jones D.H.A.	Kester R.C.	Lawrence W.T.
Jacob G.	Jones D.J.	Keys G.W.	Lawson A.H.
Jacob T.	Jones D.R.	Khan M.A.A.	Lawson R.A.M.
Jacobs L.G.H.	Jones D.R.B.	Khan M.A.R.	Lawson W.R.
Jaganathan R.	Jones E.R.L.	Khan M.I.	Lawton F.G.
Jago R.H.	Jones J.R.	Khan O.	Lawton J.O.
Jakubowski J.	Jones M.	Khemka S.L.	Layer G.T.
James M.I.	Jones M.W.	Khoury G.	Lea R.E.
James S.E.	Jones N.A.G.	Kiely E.	Leach R.D.
James V.C.	Jones P.A.	Kilby D.	Leaper D.J.
Jamison M.H.	Jones R.A.C.	Kinder R.B.	Lear P.A.
Janardhan K.C.	Jones R.N.	King J.B.	Lee B.
Jarrett P.E.M.	Jones S.M.	King T.	Lee J.O.
Jarvis A.C.	Jones W.A.	Kings G.L.M.	Lee P.W.R.
Jayatunga A.P.	Joseph T.	Kingsnorth A.N.	Leese T.
Jefferiss C.D.	Jowett R.L.	Kingston R.D.	Leicester R.J.
Jeffery I.T.A.	Joyce A.	Kipping R.A.	Lemberger R.J.
Jeffery R.M.	Joyce M.	Kirby R.	Lemon G.J.
Jeffreys R.V.	Jurewicz W.A.	Kirby R.M.	Lennard T.W.J.
Jenkins A.J.	Kahn A.H.	Kirby R.S.	Lennox M.S.
Jenkins D.H.R.	Kahn L.	Kirk S.	Lennox W.M.
Jenkins J.D.	Kaisary A.V.	Kissin M.W.	Leonard M.A.C.
Jenkinson L.R.	Kanegaonkar G.S.	Kleanthous L.	Leontsinis T.
Jenner R.E.	Kanse P.	Klimach O.	Lettin A.W.F.
Jennings M.C.	Kapadia C.R.	Klugman D.J.	Levack B.
Jennison K.M.	Kar A.K.	Knight M.J.	Leval M. de
Jepson K.	Karran S.J.	Knight S.	Leveson S.H.
Jeyasingham K.	Kashif F.	Knox R.	Lewi H.J.E.
Johansen K.	Kaufman H.D.	Knudsen C.J.M.	Lewis A.A.M.
John A.C.	Kavanagh T.G.	Koffman G.	Lewis A.C.W.
Johns A.M.	Kay N.R.M.	Kolb C.S.	Lewis B.V.

Appendix G - Participants (surgeons and gynaecologists)

Lewis G.J.	MacKay N.N.S.	Mattock E.J.	Moore K.T.H.
Lewis J.	McKelvey S.T.D.	Maulik T.G.	Moore P.J.
Lewis J.D.	Mackenney R.P.	Maurice-Williams R.S.	Moore-Gillon V.L.
Lewis J.L.	McKibbin A.	Mawhinney H.J.D.	Moorehead R.J.
Lewis P.	Mackie C.R.	Maxted M.J.	Moores W.K.
Lewis S.L.	Mackinnon J.G.	Maxwell R.J.	Morgan M.W.E.
Lien W.M.	Mackintosh G.	Maxwell W.A.	Morgan R.H.
Lightowler C.D.R.	McLardy-Smith P.	May A.R.L.	Morgan W.E.
Linsell J.	McLaren C.A.N.	May P.C.	Morgan W.P.
Lloyd D.M.	McLaren M.I.	May R.E.	Morris B.D.A.
Lloyd R.E.	Maclean A.D.W.	Maybury N.K.	Morris I.R.
Lloyd-Davies E.R.V.	MacLennan I.	Mayer A.D.	Morris M.A.
Lloyd-Davies R.W.	McLoughlin G.A.	Mayers F.N.	Morris P.J.
Lloyd-Jones W.	McManus K.	Mayou B.J.	Morrison J.M.
Lock M.	McMurray A.H.	Meadows T.H.	Mortensen N.
Locke T.J.	McNeal A.D.	Mearns A.J.	Mosley J.G.
Long M.	McNicholas T.A.	Meehan S.E.	Motson R.W.
Lotz J.C.	McPartlin J.F.	Mehdian S.M.	Mowbray M.A.S.
Loughridge W.G.G.	MacPherson D.S.	Meikle D.	Moynagh P.D.
Lovegrove J.	Magee P.G.	Meikle D.D.	Muckle D.S.
Lowdon I.M.R.	Magee S.E.E.	Mellows H.J.	Mudd D.G.
Luck R.J.	Magnussen P.A.	Melville D.M.	Mufti S.T.
Luesley D.M.	Mahaffey P.J.	Mendelow A.D.	Mughal M.M.
Lunn P.G.	Main B.J.	Mendonca D.	Mukerjea S.K.
Lye R.	Mair W.S.J.	Menon T.J.	Muldoon M.J.
Lynch J.M.	Makin C.A.	Menzies-Gow N.	Mullan F.
Lynch M.C.	Makin G.S.	Metcalfe J.W.	Muller P.W.S.
Lynn J.A.	Mal R.K.	Metcalfe-Gibson C.	Mulligan T.O.
Lyttle J.A.	Mander A.M.	Meyer C.H.A.	Munsch C.M.
McAdam A.H.	Manning M.	Meyrick Thomas J.	Murday A.
McAdam W.A.F.	Mansel R.E.	Miles J.B.	Murdoch J.B.
McArthur P.	Mansfield A.O.	Millar R.	Murphy F.
McAuliffe T.B.	Marcus R.T.	Miller A.J.	Murphy P.D.
McCarthy D.O'B	Marczak J.B.	Miller D.H.T.	Murray A.
McCloy R.F.	Markham N.I.	Miller G.A.B.	Murray J.M.
McCoy D.R.	Marks C.G.	Miller G.F.	Murray K.H.
McCoy G.F.	Marriott F.P.S.	Miller I.A.	Muscroft T.J.
McCulloch P.G.	Marsh C.H.	Miller I.M.	Musgrove B.
McCullough C.J.	Marsh H.T.	Miller R.	Musumeci F.
McDermott B.C.	Marshall H.F.	Milligan G.F.	Nadarajan P.
MacDermott S.	Mason J.R.	Milner J.C.	Nadkarni J.B.
McDonald J.	Mason M.C.	Milroy E.J.G.	Nair U.
McDonald P.	Mason R.C.	Milson J.E.	Nairn D.S.
MacDonald R.J.M.	Mason W.P.	Mintowt-Czyz W.J.	Nash A.G.
MacEachern A.G.	Massey C.I.	Misra P.	Nash J.R.
McFarland R.J.	Massey J.A.	Mitchenere P.	Nasmyth D.G.
MacFarlane R.	Matheson D.M.	Modgill V.K.	Naylor H.G.
MacFie J.	Mathews S.J.E.	Moghul M.M.	Neal D.E.
McGeorge A.	Mathias D.B.	Mok D.W.H.	Neal N.C.
McGoldrick J.	Matthews H.R.	Molitor P.J.A.	Negus D.
McGregor A.D.	Matthews J.G.	Mollan R.A.B.	Neil-Dwyer G.
Machin D.G.	Matthews J.G.W.	Monaghan J.M.	Neill R.W.K.
McIntosh G.S.	Matthews M.G.	Monro J.L.	Nelson I.W.
McIntosh I.H.	Matthews P.N.	Montgomery A.C.V.	Nelson M.E.
McIntosh J.W.	Matthewson M.H.	Moore A.	Nevelos A.B.

Appendix G - Participants (surgeons and gynaecologists)

Newman R.J.
Nicholls J.C.
Nicholls R.J.
Nicholson R.A.
Nicholson R.W.
Nicholson S.
Nicolaides A.N.
Niranjan N.
Noble A.D.
Norris S.H.
North A.N.
Northmore-Ball M.D.
Norton E.R.
Notaras M.J.
Notley R.G.
Nouri E.
Nunn D.
Nysenbaum A.M.
O'Doherty D.
O'Driscoll M.
O'Dwyer S.T.
O'Hara J.N.
O'Kane H.O.J.
O'Malley S.
O'Neill J.J.
O'Reilly M.J.G.
O'Reilly P.H.
O'Riordan B.
O'Riordan S.M.
Obeid M.L.
Odling-Smee G.W.
Odom N.J.
Ogilvie C.
Oram D.H.
Ormiston M.
Ornstein M.H.
Orr M.M.
Orr N.W.M.
Osman M.S.A.
Owen A.W.M.
Owen E.R.T.
Owen R.A.
Owen W.J.
Owen-Smith M.S.
Packer N.P.
Paes T.
Page I.J.
Page R.D.
Pai B.Y.
Pain J.A.
Paley W.G.
Palmer J.G.
Palmer J.H.
Panahy C.
Pancharatnam M.

Panesar K.J.S.
Pantelides M.
Parkinson R.
Parr D.C.
Parr N.J.
Parrott N.R.
Parry J.R.W.
Parsons D.C.S.
Parsons D.W.
Parsons K.F.
Parvin S.
Patel A.D.
Patel P.
Paterson I.M.
Paterson M.
Paterson M.E.L.
Pattison C.W.
Pattisson P.H.
Payne S.R.
Peace P.K.
Peach B.G.S.
Pearson H.J.
Pearson J.B.
Pearson R.C.
Peel A.L.G.
Peel K.R.
Peet T.N.D.
Pengelly A.W.
Pepper J.R.
Perkins R.D.
Perry E.P.
Perry P.M.
Peyton J.W.R.
Phadnis S.
Pheils P.J.
Phen H.T.
Phillipps J.J.
Phillips H.
Phillips J.B.
Philp N.H.
Philp T.
Pietroni M.C.
Pigott H.W.S.
Pillai R.
Pinder I.M.
Pinto D.J.
Piper I.H.
Pittam M.R.
Plaha H.S.
Plail R.
Pobereskin L.H.
Pocock T.J.
Pollard J.P.
Pollard R.
Pollet J.

Ponting G.
Pool C.J.F.
Poole D.R.
Porter M.L.
Porter R.J.
Poskitt K.R.
Postlethwaite J.C.
Powell B.
Powell C.S.
Powell M.P.
Powell P.H.
Powis S.J.A.
Powley P.H.
Pownall P.J.
Pozo J.L.
Pozyczka T.A.
Pozzi M.
Preston T.R.
Price A.J.
Price J.J.
Prince H.G.
Pring D.
Pring D.W.
Prinn M.G.
Prior A.L.
Pritchett C.J.
Proud G.
Prout W.G.
Pryor G.A.
Psaila J.V.
Puntis M.C.A.
Pusey R.J.
Pye J.K.
Pyper P.C.
Quayle A.R.
Quayle J.B.
Queen K.B.
Quick C.R.
Quinlan M.P.
Radcliffe G.J.
Radford P.J.
Raftery A.T.
Rahman A.N.
Railton A.
Raimes S.A.
Rainsbury R.M.
Ralphs D.N.L.
Ramsay-Baggs P.
Ramsden G.
Ramsden P.D.
Rance C.H.
Rand C.
Rao G.N.
Rao N.S.
Rao T.G.

Rashid A.
Ratliff D.A.
Ray D.K.
Reasbeck P.G.
Redden J.F.
Reddy P.
Redfern R.M.
Redfern T.R.
Reed M.W.
Rees A.J.S.
Rees B.I.
Rees D.M.
Rees G.M.
Regan M.W.
Regan P.
Reid D.J.
Reid W.
Reilly D.T.
Rennie C.D.
Renton C.J.
Reynolds I.S.R.
Reynolds J.R.
Rhodes A.
Riad H.
Ribbans W.J.
Richards A.B.
Richards D.J.
Richards R.H.
Richardson D.R.
Richardson P.L.
Richardson R.A.
Richmond W.D.
Rickett J.W.
Rigby C.C.
Rigg K.M.
Riley D.
Rintoul R.F.
Ritchie W.A.H.
Roberts A.
Roberts A.H.N.
Roberts G.
Roberts P.N.
Robertson I.J.
Robertson J.F.
Robinson H.I.
Robinson K.P.
Robinson L.
Robinson M.R.G.
Robson M.J.
Rogers H.S.
Rogers J.
Rogers K.
Rolles K.
Rooker G.D.
Rosenberg D.A.

Rosenberg I.L.
Rosenthal A.R.
Ross A.H.M.
Ross B.A.
Ross E.R.S.
Ross H.B.
Ross K.R.
Rossi L.F.A.
Rosson J.W.
Rosswick R.P.
Rostron P.K.M.
Rowlands B.J.
Rowntree M.
Royle G.T.
Rudge S.
Rumble J.A.
Rundle J.S.H.
Rushforth G.F.
Rushman R.W.
Russell C.F.J.
Rutter K.R.P.
Ryall R.J.
Ryan P.G.
Rymer M.J.
Sabanathan S.
Sabin H.I.
Sacks N.P.M.
Sagar S.
Sagor G.R.
Sainsbury J.R.C.
Salaman J.R.
Sales J.E.L.
Salman A.
Salter M.C.P.
Samarji W.N.
Samuel A.W.
Sandeman D.R.
Sanders R.
Sanderson C.J.
Sandhu D.P.S.
Sansom J.R.
Sant Cassia L.J.
Saran D.
Saunders N.R.
Sauven P.
Schiess F.A.
Schofield C.
Schofield J.J.
Schranz P.J.
Schweitzer F.A.W.
Scott A.D.N.
Scott G.
Scott I.H.K.
Scott N.
Scott R.A.P.

Scott T.D.
Scott W.A.
Scurr J.H.
Seal P.V.
Sefton G.K.
Sell P.J.
Sells R.A.
Sellu D.
Sengupta R.P.
Sergeant R.J.
Sewell P.F.T.
Shafighian B.
Shafiq M.
Shah T.
Shaheen M.A.
Shahid M.
Shair A.B.
Shanahan M.D.G.
Shand J.E.G.
Shanker J.Y.
Shaplands D.
Shardlow J.P.
Sharp D.J.
Shaw J.
Shaw L.M.A.
Shaw M.D.M.
Shaw N.C.
Shaw N.M.
Shaw S.J.
Shea J.G.
Shearman C.P.
Shedden R.G.
Sheikh K.M.
Shennan J.M.
Shepherd J.H.
Shepperd J.A.N.
Sheridan W.G.
Sherlock D.J.
Shieff C.L.
Shields R.
Shone G.R.
Shore D.F.
Shorthouse A.J.
Sibly T.F.
Sibson D.E.
Silverman S.H.
Simison A.J.M.
Simpson B.A.
Sims P.F.
Simson J.N.
Singh M.
Singh S.K.
Siva S.
Sivathondan K.
Skidmore F.D.

Skinner P.W.
Slapak M.
Slater E.G.W.
Smallpeice C.J.
Smallwood J.
Smart C.J.
Smellie W.A.B.
Smith A.
Smith D.N.
Smith E.E.J.
Smith G.H.
Smith G.M.
Smith G.M.R.
Smith J.A.R.
Smith J.C.
Smith N.W.
Smith P.H.
Smith P.L.C.
Smith R.B.
Smith S.R.G.
Smith T.W.D.
Sole G.M.
Somerville J.J.F.
Souter R.G.
South L.M.
Southam J.A.
Southgate G.W.
Sparrow O.C.
Speakman M.J.
Speck E.H.
Spence R.A.
Spencer R.F.
Spencer S.R.
Spigelman A.D.
Spivey C.J.
Spivey J.
Spychal R.T.
Squire B.R.
Srinivasan R.
Srinivasan V.
Stacey-Clear A.
Stallard M.C.
Stamatakis J.D.
Staniforth P.
Stanley D.
Stansbie J.M.
Stanton S.L.R.
Stark J.
Stebbings W.S.L.
Steele R.J.C.
Steffen C.
Stephen I.B.M.
Stewart D.J.
Stewart G.J.
Stewart H.D.

Stewart J.
Stewart J.D.M.
Stewart M.
Stewart P.
Stewart R.D.
Stirling W.J.I.
Stockley I.
Stoddard C.J.
Stokes I.M.
Stollard G.E.
Stone C.D.P.
Stone M.
Stoodley B.J.
Stott M.A.
Stotter A.T.
Stower M.J.
Strachan J.R.
Strahan J.
Strang F.A.
Studley J.
Sturzaker H.G.
Subhedar V.Y.
Sue-Ling H.M.
Sullivan M.F.
Sully L.
Suman R.K.
Summers B.N.
Sutcliffe J.
Sutcliffe M.
Sutherst J.
Sutton G.
Sutton R.
Swann M.
Sykes P.A.
Symes J.M.
Symonds E.M.
Szypryt E.P.
Tak Tak S.
Talbot M.
Tam P.K.H.
Tan K.C.
Taor W.
Tarbuck D.T.
Tasker T.P.B.
Taylor A.R.
Taylor B.A.
Taylor D.S.
Taylor G.J.
Taylor K.M.
Taylor L.J.
Taylor P.
Taylor R.M.R.
Taylor R.S.
Taylor S.A.
Taylor T.C.

Appendix G - Participants (surgeons and gynaecologists)

Tayton K.J.J.	Turner D.T.L.	Ward P.J.	Williams B.T.
Teasdale C.	Turner S.M.	Warren-Smith C.D.	Williams C.B.
Temple J.G.	Turnock R.R.	Warwick-Brown N.P.	Williams C.R.
Templeton J.	Tuson K.W.R.	Wastell C.	Williams D.H.
Terry R.M.	Twiston-Davies C.W.	Waterfall N.B.	Williams D.J.
Terry T.R.	Twyman R.	Waterfield A.H.	Williams G.
Thacker C.R.	Tynan M.	Waters J.S.	Williams G.L.
Themen A.E.G.	Ubhi C.	Waterworth M.W.	Williams H.M.
Theodorou N.	Umpleby H.C.	Waterworth T.A.	Williams H.T.
Therkildsen L.K.H.	Urwin G.H.	Watkin G.T.	Williams I.
Thick M.	Usherwood M.M.	Watkins R.M.	Williams M.
Thomas D.G.T.	Valerio D.	Watkinson J.	Williams R.J.
Thomas D.R.	Van Der Avoirt A.	Watson M.E.	Williamson B.
Thomas M.H.	Varma J.S.	Watson R.	Williamson D.
Thomas N.P.	Varma T.R.	Watts M.T.	Williamson E.P.M.
Thomas P.A.	Vasan R.	Way B.G.	Williamson R.C.N.
Thomas R.J.	Vaughan E.D.	Weaver P.C.	Willis R.G.
Thomas T.L.	Vaughan R.	Weaver R.M.	Wilson B.G.
Thomas W.E.G.	Vellacott K.D.	Webb A.J.	Wilson P.C.
Thompson C.E.R.	Venables C.W.	Webb J.B.	Wilson P.E.H.
Thompson J.	Venn G.E.	Webb J.K.	Wilson R.G.
Thompson J.F.	Verinder D.G.R.	Webb P.J.	Wilson R.S.
Thompson M.R.	Vesey S.G.	Webster D.J.T.	Wilson R.Y.
Thompson P.M.	Vethanayagam S.	Webster J.H.H.	Windle R.
Thompson R.L.E.	Vickers R.H.	Wedgwood K.R.	Windsor C.W.O.
Thompson S.K.	Vickery C.M.	Weeden D.	Winslet M.C.
Thomson R.G.	Vinall P.S.	Wellington P.	Winson I.G.
Thomson W.H.F.	Vinnicombe J.	Wells A.	Wise K.S.H.
Thonet R.G.N.	Vishwanath M.S.	Wells F.C.	Wise M.
Thorneloe M.H.	Volivu S.P.	Wellwood J.M.	Wisheart J.D.
Thurston A.V.	Vowden P.	Welsh C.L.	Wojcik A.
Tibrewal S.	Wade P.J.F.	West C.G.H.	Wolfe J.H.N.
Tilakawardane A.L.N.	Wakeman R.	Weston P.M.T.	Wood J.
Tindall S.F.	Waldron J.	Westwood C.A.	Wood S.K.
Tiptaft R.	Walesby R.K.	Wetherell R.G.	Woodhouse C.R.J.
Tivy-Jones P.	Walker A.P.	Wharton M.R.	Woods W.
Todd B.D.	Walker C.J.	Wheeler M.H.	Woodward D.A.K.
Tooley A.H.	Walker D.R.	Whelan P.	Woodyer A.B.
Towler J.M.	Walker K.A.	Whitaker I.A.	Woolfenden K.A.
Townend I.R.	Walker M.A.	White C.M.	Woolfson J.
Townsend P.L.G.	Walker M.G.	Whitehead E.	Wootton J.
Townsend P.T.	Walker R.T.	Whitehead S.M.	Worlock P.H.
Treasure T.	Wallace M.E.	Whittaker M.	Worth P.H.L.
Treble N.J.	Wallace R.J.	Wickremasinghe S.S.	Wray C.C.
Tresadern J.C.	Wallace W.A.	Wilcox F.L.	Wright J.D.
Tricker J.	Wallwork J.	Wilde G.P.	Wright N.L.
Trimmings N.P.	Walsh H.P.J.	Wilkin D.J.W.	Wright P.D.
Tsang V.	Walsh J.K.	Wilkins D.C.	Wyatt A.P.
Tsokadayi C.	Walsh M.E.	Wilkins J.L.	Wyllie G.A.M.
Tuck C.S.	Walsh T.H.	Wilkinson A.J.	Wynn Jones C.H.
Tudor R.G.	Walsh W.K.	Wilkinson G.A.L.	Yacoub M.H.
Tuite J.D.	Walter P.	Wilkinson J.M.	Yates C.
Tulloch C.J.	Walters H.	Wilkinson M.J.S.	Yeates H.A.
Turnbull T.J.	Ward J.P.	Willett K.	Yeo R.
Turner A.	Ward M.W.N.	Williams B.	Yeung C.K.

Appendix G - Participants (surgeons and gynæcologists)

Yogasagarar R.
Yogasundram Y.N.
Youhana A.
Young A.E.
Young C.P.
Young M.H.
Young R.A.L.
Young S.K.
Zahir A.G.
Zaidi A.A.
Zeiderman M.R.

Appendix H - Local Reporters

This list shows the local reporters as of 4 October 1996. We have therefore used the latest regional boundaries, trusts or units.

We recognise that there are many clinical audit and information departments involved in providing data, although we have in many cases named only the consultant clinician nominated as local reporter.

Anglia and Oxford

Addenbrooke's	Dr D. Wight
Churchill John Radcliffe	Dr K. Fleming
Heatherwood & Wexham Park Hospitals	Dr M.H. Ali
Hinchingbrooke	Dr M.D. Harris
The Horton General Hospital	Dr N.J. Mahy
Ipswich Hospital	Mr I.E. Cowles
James Paget Hospital	Mrs C.L. Eagle
Kettering General Hospital	Dr B.E. Gostelow
King's Lynn & Wisbech	Ms J. Rippon
Luton & Dunstable Hospital	Dr D.A.S. Lawrence
Milton Keynes General Hospital	Dr S.S. Jalloh
Norfolk & Norwich Health Care	Dr B.G. McCann
Northampton General Hospital	Dr A.J. Molyneux
Nuffield Orthopaedic Centre	Dr K. Fleming
Papworth Hospital	Dr N. Cary
Peterborough Hospitals	Dr P.M. Dennis
The Radcliffe Infirmary	Dr K. Fleming
Royal Berkshire & Battle Hospital	Dr R. Menai-Williams
South Buckinghamshire	Dr M.J. Turner
Stoke Mandeville Hospital	Dr A.F. Padel
West Suffolk Hospitals	Mrs V. Hamilton

North Thames

Basildon & Thurrock General Hospitals	Dr S.G. Subbuswamy
Central Middlesex	Dr C.A. Amerasinghe

Chase Farm Hospitals	Dr W.H.S. Mohamid
Chelsea & Westminster Healthcare	Mr S.J. Booth
Ealing Hospital	Dr C. Schmulian
East Hertfordshire Health	Dr A. Fattah
Essex Rivers Healthcare	Mrs A. Bridge
Forest Healthcare	Dr K.M. Thomas
Hammersmith & Charing Cross	Dr I. Lindsay (Charing Cross Hospital) Dr G. Stamp (Hammersmith Hospital)
Harefield Hospital	Mr K. Robinson
Havering Hospitals	Dr D.A. Thomas (Harold Wood Hospital) Ms C. Colley (Oldchurch Hospital)
Hillingdon Hospital	Dr F.G. Barker
Homerton Hospital	Ms S. Kimenye
Great Ormond Street Hospital for Children	Professor R.A. Risdon
Mid-Essex Hospital Services	Mr A.H.M. Ross
Moorfields Eye Hospital	Professor P. Luthert
Mount Vernon & Watford Hospitals	Mrs M. Hill (Mount Vernon Hospital) Dr W.K. Blenkinsopp (Watford General Hospital)
The National Hospitals	Mrs J.A. Sullivan
Newham Healthcare	Dr S.I. Baithun
North Herts	Dr D.J. Madders
North Middlesex Hospital	Dr K.J. Jarvis
Northwick Park & St Mark's	Dr S. Boyle
The Princess Alexandra Hospital	Dr R.G.M. Letcher
Redbridge Healthcare	Dr P. Tanner
Royal Brompton	Professor D. Denison
Royal Free Hampstead	Dr J.E. McLaughlin
The Royal Hospitals	Dr D. Lowe (St Bartholomew's Hospital) Dr P.J. Flynn (Royal London Hospital and London Chest Hospital)
The Royal Marsden Hospital	Mr R.J. Shearer
Royal National Orthopaedic Hospital	None
Royal National Throat, Nose & Ear Hospital	None

North Thames continued

St Albans and Hemel Hempstead	Dr A.P. O'Reilly (Hemel Hempstead General Hospital)
	Dr S. Hill (St Albans City Hospital)
St Mary's Hospital	Ms R. Hittinger
Southend Healthcare	Ms L. Bell
UCL Hospitals	Ms A. Glover
Wellhouse	Dr J. El-Jabbour
West Middlesex University Hospital	Dr R.G. Hughes
Whittington Hospital	Dr D. Brown

North West

Aintree Hospitals	Dr W. Taylor (Fazakerley Hospital)
Blackburn, Hyndburn & Ribble Valley	Mr J.C. Tresadern
Blackpool Victoria Hospital	Dr K.S. Vasudev
Bolton Hospitals	Dr S. Wells
Burnley Health Care	Mr D.G.D. Sandilands
Bury Health Care	Dr E. Herd
Chorley & South Ribble	Dr C. Loyden
Countess of Chester Hospital	Mr G. Foster
East Cheshire	Dr A.R. Williams
Furness Hospitals	Dr V.M. Joglekar
Halton General Hospital	Dr M.S. Al-Jafari
Lancaster Acute Hospitals	Dr R.W. Blewitt
Liverpool Cardiothoracic Centre	Mr M. Jackson
Liverpool Women's Hospital NHS Trust	Ms C. Fox
Manchester Central Hospitals	Dr E.W. Benbow
Mid Cheshire Hospitals	Miss H. Moulton
North Manchester Healthcare	Dr I.K. Hartopp (until 1.8.96)
Preston Acute Hospitals	Dr C.M. Nicholson
Rochdale Health Care	Mr S. Murray
Royal Liverpool Children's Hospital	Mrs P.A. McCormack

The Royal Liverpool & Broadgreen University Hospitals	Miss K. Scott
Manchester Children's Hospitals	Dr M. Newbould
Royal Oldham Hospital	Dr I. Seddon
St Helens & Knowsley	Miss C. Gittens
Salford Royal Hospitals	Mr M. McKenna
South Manchester University Hospitals	Dr P.S. Hasleton (Wythenshawe Hospital) Dr J. Coyne (Withington Hospital)
Southport & Formby	Dr S.A.C. Dundas
Stockport Acute Services	Dr P. Meadows
Tameside & Glossop Acute Services	Dr A.S. Day
Trafford Healthcare	Dr B.N.A. Hamid
Walton Centre for Neurology & Neurosurgery	Dr J. Broome
Warrington Acute	Dr M.S. Al-Jafari
West Lancashire	Mr A.D. Johnson
Westmorland Hospitals	Dr R.W. Blewitt
Wigan & Leigh Health Services	Ms S. Tarbuck
Wirral Hospitals	Dr M.B. Gillett
Wrightington Hospital	Mr A.D. Johnson

Northern and Yorkshire

Airedale	Dr R.D. Pyrah
Bishop Auckland Hospitals	Dr D.C.A. Senadhira
Bradford Hospitals	Dr B. Naylor
Calderdale Healthcare	Mr R.J.R. Goodall
Carlisle Hospitals	Dr E.D. Long
Cheviot & Wansbeck	Dr J.A. Henry
City Hospitals Sunderland	Miss K. Ramsey
Darlington Memorial Hospital	Ms C. Evans
Dewsbury Health Care	Dr P. Gudgeon
East Yorkshire Hospitals	Mr G. Britchford
Freeman Group of Hospitals	Dr M.K. Bennett
Gateshead Hospitals	Dr I.M.J. Mathias
Harrogate Health	Miss A.H. Lawson

Northern and Yorkshire continued

Hartlepool & Peterlee Hospitals

Huddersfield

North Durham Acute Hospitals

North East Lincolnshire

North Tees Health

North Tyneside Health Care

Northallerton Health Services

Pinderfields Hospital

Pontefract Hospitals

Royal Hull Hospitals

Royal Victoria Infirmary Group

St James's & Seacroft University Hospitals

Scarborough & N E Yorkshire Healthcare

Scunthorpe & Goole Hospitals

South Tees Acute Hospitals

South Tyneside Health Care

United Leeds Teaching Hospitals

West Cumbria Health Care

York Health Services

Mr C.P.L. Wood

Dr H.H. Ali

Dr D. Wood (Dryburn Hospital)
Dr C.M. Dobson (Shotley Bridge Hospital)

Dr W.M. Peters

Dr J. Hoffman

Dr F. Johri

Dr D.C. Henderson

Dr S. Gill

Dr I.W.C. MacDonald

Dr M.R.F. Reynolds

Miss D. Robson (Royal Victoria Infirmary)
Dr D. Scott (Newcastle General Hospital)
Dr J.D. Hemming (Hexham Hospital)

Mr N.S. Ambrose

Dr A.M. Jackson

Dr C.M. Hunt

Mrs L. Black

Dr K.P. Pollard

Dr C. Abbott

Dr D. Smith

Dr J.M. Hopkinson

South and West

The Royal Bournemouth and Christchurch Hospitals

East Gloucestershire

East Somerset

Frenchay Healthcare

Gloucestershire Royal

North Hampshire Hospitals

Northern Devon Healthcare

Plymouth Hospitals

Ms K. Hatchard

Dr W.J. Brampton

Dr G. Purcell

Dr N.B.N. Ibrahim

Dr B.W. Codling

Dr J.M. Finch

Dr J. Davies

Dr C.B.A. Lyons

Poole Hospital	Dr D.S. Nicholas
Portsmouth Hospitals	Dr N.J.E. Marley
Royal Cornwall Hospitals	Dr R. Pitcher
Royal Devon & Exeter Healthcare	Dr R.H.W. Simpson
Royal United Hospital Bath	Dr P.J. Tidbury
St Mary's Hospital (Isle of Wight)	Mr P. Wellington
Salisbury Health Care	Dr C.A. Scott
South Devon Healthcare	Dr D.W. Day
Southampton University Hospitals	Dr I.E. Moore
Southmead Health Services	Ms G. Davies
Swindon & Marlborough	Mr M.H. Galea
Taunton & Somerset	Mr I. Eyre-Brook
United Bristol Healthcare	Dr E.A. Sheffield
West Dorset General Hospitals	Dr A. Anscombe
Weston Area Health	Dr M.F. Lott
Winchester & Eastleigh Healthcare	Dr R.K. Al-Falib

South Thames

Ashford Hospital	Dr J. Dawson
Brighton Healthcare	Mr M. Renshaw
Bromley Hospitals	Dr M.H. Elmahallawy
Crawley & Horsham	Mr A.J. Campbell
Dartford & Gravesham	Dr A.T.M.F. Rashid
East Surrey Hospital	Ms S. Hatton
Eastbourne Hospitals	Mr T.G. Reilly
Epsom Healthcare	Dr T. Matthews
Frimley Park Hospital	Dr G.F. Goddard
Greenwich Healthcare	Dr Pinto (Greenwich District Hospital) Dr G.G. Menon (Brook General Hospital)
Guy's & St Thomas'	Dr. B. Hartley (Guy's Hospital) Professor S. Lucas (St Thomas' Hospital)
Hastings & Rother	Dr M.E. Boxer
Kent & Canterbury Hospitals	Mr M. Guarino

South Thames continued

Kent & Sussex Weald	Dr G.A. Russell
King's Healthcare	Dr S. Humphreys
Kingston Hospital	Mr R.D. Leach
Lewisham Hospital	Dr C. Keen
Mayday Health Care	Dr S.M. Thomas
The Medway	Mrs J.L. Smith
Mid-Kent Healthcare	Dr V.K. Hochuli
Mid-Sussex	Mr P.H. Walter (Hurstwood Park Hospital) Dr P.A. Berresford (The Princess Royal Hospital)
Queen Mary's Sidcup	Dr E.J.A. Aps
Queen Victoria Hospital	None
Richmond, Twickenham & Roehampton	Mr M. McSweeney
The Royal Surrey County & St Luke's	Dr B.T.B. Manners
The Royal West Sussex	Mr J.N.L. Simson
St George's Healthcare	Dr S. Dilly
St Helier	Dr E.H. Rang
St Peter's Hospital	Mr R.H. Moore
South Kent Hospitals	Dr C.W. Lawson
Thanet Health Care	Mrs B.M. Smith
Worthing & Southlands Hospital	Mrs J. North

Trent

Barnsley District General Hospital	Dr J.M. Frayne
Bassetlaw Hospital	Dr P.A. Parsons
Central Sheffield University Hospitals	Dr C.A. Angel
Chesterfield & North Derbyshire Royal	Dr P.B. Gray
Derby City General Hospital	Ms K. Hillier-Smith
Derbyshire Royal Infirmary	Mr J.R. Nash
The Doncaster Royal & Montagu Hospital	Dr J.A.H. Finbow
The Glenfield Hospital	Miss S. Lee
Grantham and District Hospital	Dr D. Clark

King's Mill Centre for Health Care Services	Ms J. Jenkins
Leicester General Hospital	Dr E.H. Mackay
The Leicester Royal Infirmary	Ms D. Burt
Lincoln & Louth	Dr J.A. Harvey (Lincoln County Hospital) Mr E.O. Amaku (Louth County Hospital)
Northern General Hospital	Dr C.A. Angel
Nottingham City Hospital	Professor D.R. Turner
Pilgrim Health	Dr D.C.S. Durrant
Queen's Medical Centre, Nottingham	Professor D.R. Turner
Rotherham General Hospitals	Mr R.B. Jones
Sheffield Children's Hospital	Dr C.A. Angel
West Lindsey	Dr J.A. Harvey

West Midlands

Alexandra Healthcare	Dr J.C. Macartney
Birmingham Children's Hospital	Dr F. Raafat
Birmingham Heartlands & Solihull	Dr M. Taylor
Birmingham Women's Health Care	None
Burton Hospitals	Dr N. Kasthuri
City Hospitals	Dr. S.M. Abraham
Dudley Group of Hospitals	Dr S. Ghosh Dr O. Stores
The George Eliot Hospital	Dr J. Mercer
Good Hope Hospital	Dr A.M. Light
Hereford Hospitals	Dr F. McGinty
Kidderminster Healthcare	Dr G.H. Eeles
Mid Staffordshire General Hospitals	Dr V. Suarez
North Staffordshire Hospital Centre	Dr T.A. French
The Princess Royal	Dr R.A. Fraser
Robert Jones & Agnes Hunt	Dr P.M. Pfeifer
Royal Orthopaedic Hospital Trust	None
Royal Shrewsbury Hospitals	Dr R.A. Fraser
The Royal Wolverhampton Hospitals	Dr J. Tomlinson

West Midlands continued

Rugby	Dr J.F. Nottingham
Sandwell Healthcare	Dr J. Simon (Sandwell District General Hospital) Dr H.L. Whitwell (Midland Centre for Neurosurgery and Neurology)
South Warwickshire General	Mr M. Gilbert
University Hospital Birmingham	Professor E.L. Jones (Queen Elizabeth Hospital)
Walsall Hospitals	Dr Y.L. Hock
The Walsgrave Hospitals	Dr T. Guha
Worcester Royal Infirmary	Mr A. Singfield

Northern Ireland

Altnagelvin Group of Hospitals	Dr J.N. Hamilton
Armagh & Dungannon	Mr B. Cranley
Belfast City Hospital	Mr S.T. Irwin
Causeway	Dr C. Watters
Craigavon Area Health Group	Mr B. Cranley
Down Lisburn	Dr M. Thompson (Downe Hospital) Dr B. Huss (Lagan Valley Hospital)
Green Park	Dr J.D. Connolly
Mater Hospital	Dr H. Mathews
Newry & Mourne	Mr B. Cranley
Omagh & Fermanagh	Dr W. Holmes (Erne Hospital) Dr F. Robinson (Tyrone County Hospital)
The Royal Group of Hospitals	Ms M. Toner
Ulster, North Down & Ards Hospitals	Dr T. Boyd
United Hospitals Group	Mr I. Garstin Mr P.C. Pyper (Mid-Ulster Hospital) Mr D. Gilroy (Whiteabbey Hospital)

Wales

Bridgend & District	Dr A.M. Rees
Carmarthen & District	Dr R.B. Denholm
Ceredigion & Mid Wales	Mrs C. Smith

East Glamorgan	Dr D. Stock
Glan Clwyd District General Hospital	Dr B. Rogers
Glan Hafren	Dr M.S. Matharu
Glan-y-Mor	Dr S. Williams
Gwynedd Hospitals	Dr M. Hughes
Llandough Hospital	Dr J. Gough
Llanelli/Dinefwr	Dr L.A. Murray
Merthyr/Cynon Valley	Dr R.C. Ryder
Morriston Hospital	Dr S. Williams
Nevill Hall & District	Dr R.J. Kellett
Pembrokeshire	Dr G.R. Melville Jones
Swansea	Dr S. Williams
University Hospital of Wales	Dr A.G. Douglas-Jones Professor B. Knight (Cardiff Royal Infirmary) (until 30.9.96)
Wrexham Maelor Hospital	Dr R.B. Williams

Guernsey / Isle of Man / Jersey

Guernsey	Dr B.P. Gunton-Bunn
Isle of Man	None
Jersey	Dr D. Spencer

Defence Medical Services

All perioperative deaths in Defence Medical Services hospitals are reported to NCEPOD by the Commanding Officer or by a person nominated by the Commanding Officer.

BMI/Columbia Healthcare Hospitals

The Alexandra Hospital	Ms J. Whitby
The Blackheath Hospital	Mrs G. Mann
The Chaucer Hospital	Mr R. Muddiman
The Chiltern Hospital	Ms J. Knight
The Clementine Churchill Hospital	Dr I. Chanarin
Fawkham Manor Hospital	Mrs C. Pagram
Harley Street Clinic	Ms S. Thomas

BMI/Columbia Healthcare Hospitals continued

Highfield Hospital	Mrs C. Bottrill
The Park Hospital	Miss E. Zissler
The Portland Hospital	Miss A. Sayburn
Princess Grace Hospital	Miss M. Hatwell
The Princess Margaret Hospital	Miss J. Jones
Priory Hospital	Dr A.G. Jacobs
The Sloane Hospital	Miss J. Wilson
Thornbury Hospital	Mrs J. Cooper

BUPA

BUPA Alexandra Hospital	Mr P.J. Curtis
BUPA Belvedere Hospital	Mr S.J. Greatorex
BUPA Cambridge Lea Hospital	Miss S. Full
BUPA Chalybeate Hospital	Mrs J. Hartley
BUPA Dunedin Hospital	Mrs H. Mundella
BUPA Flyde Coast Hospital	Mrs K. Beattie
BUPA Gatwick Park Hospital	Mrs D. Wright
BUPA Hartswood Hospital	Ms N. Howes
BUPA Hospital Harpenden	Mrs P. Eaves
BUPA Hospital Bristol	Miss G. Martin
BUPA Hospital Bushey	Mr R. Lye
BUPA Hospital Cardiff	Dr A. Gibbs
BUPA Hospital Clare Park	Miss R. Newbould
BUPA Hospital Elland	Ms M.E. Schofield
BUPA Hospital Hull & East Riding	Mrs J. Fisher
BUPA Hospital Leeds	Mrs G.M. Whorwell
BUPA Hospital Leicester	Mrs C A Jones
BUPA Hospital Little Aston	Mr K. Smith
BUPA Hospital Manchester	Ms A. McArdle
BUPA Hospital Norwich	Ms M. Welch
BUPA Hospital Portsmouth	Ms G. Gibson

BUPA Murrayfield Hospital	Mrs A. Killips
BUPA North Cheshire Hospital	Miss A.L. Alexander
BUPA Parkway Hospital	Mr G. Jones
BUPA Roding Hospital	Ms J.A. Crampton
BUPA South Bank Hospital	Mr B. Gordon
BUPA St Saviour's Hospital	Mr P. Tempest
BUPA Wellesley Hospital	Mrs L. Horner

Nuffield Hospitals

Birmingham Nuffield Hospital	Mrs S. Staton
Bournemouth Nuffield Hospital	Mrs S. Jackson
Chesterfield Nuffield Hospital	Miss P.J. Bunker
Cleveland Nuffield Hospital	Mrs S. Jelley
Cotswold Nuffield Hospital	Mrs J.T. Penn
Duchy Nuffield Hospital	Mrs M. Alsop
East Midlands Nuffield Hospital	Mrs P. Shields
Essex Nuffield Hospital	Mrs B.M. Parker
Exeter Nuffield Hospital	Mrs A. Turnbull
Fitzroy Nuffield Hospital	Mrs R.J. Hackett
Huddersfield Nuffield Hospital	Miss S. Panther
Hull Nuffield Hospital	Miss S.J. Verow
Lancaster & Lakeland Nuffield Hospital	Miss A. Durbin
Mid Yorkshire Nuffield Hospital	Mrs G.A. Duffield
Newcastle Nuffield Hospital	Miss K.C. Macfarlane
North London Nuffield Hospital	Miss J. Ward
North Staffordshire Nuffield Hospital	Mrs A. Woolrich
Nuffield Acland Hospital	Miss C. Gilbert
Nuffield Hospital Leicester	Mrs S. Harriman
Nuffield Hospital Plymouth	Mrs T. Starling
Purey Cust Nuffield Hospital	Mr J. Gdaniec
Shropshire Nuffield Hospital	Mrs S. Crossland
Somerset Nuffield Hospital	Mrs J. Dyer
Sussex Nuffield Hospital	Miss J. Collister

Nuffield Hospitals continued

Thames Valley Nuffield Hospital	Mrs S.E. Clifford
The Grosvenor Nuffield Hospital	Mrs J.L. Whitmore
Tunbridge Wells Nuffield Hospital	Mrs L. Lockwood
Wessex Nuffield Hospital	Mrs C.E. Chandler
Woking Nuffield Hospital	Miss B.E. Harrison
Wolverhampton Nuffield Hospital	Mrs G.M. Nicholls
Wye Valley Nuffield Hospital	Mrs W.P. Mawdesley

St Martin's Hospitals

The Lister Hospital	Miss K. Upton
The London Bridge Hospital	Ms Y. Terry

Other independent hospitals

Benenden Hospital	Mr D. Hibler
The Wellington Hospital	Mr R. Hoff